A LANCASHIRE SQUIRE

To my dear cousin Tony,
with love from
Adèle
x x

April, 2003.

A Lancashire Squire

The Life of
Nicholas Blundell of Crosby,
1669–1737

MARGARET BLUNDELL

with a foreword by

ARTHUR BRYANT

DAY BOOKS
OXFORDSHIRE

ISBN 0953 2213 42

A catalogue record for this book is available from the British Library

This edition first published by Day Books and Mark Blundell,
November 2002

Printed in England by Antony Rowe Ltd, Eastbourne

Day Books, Orchard Piece, Crawborough, Charlbury,
Oxfordshire OX7 3TX
www.day-books.com

CONTENTS

To the memory of my nephew
Nicholas Blundell of Crosby,
who died on September 30th, 1949,
aged twenty-four years

In omnibus requiem quaesivi
(family motto)

FOREWORD

by

ARTHUR BRYANT, C.B.E., LL.D.

MISS BLUNDELL has already done one lasting service to 17th century social history by her charming book, *Cavalier*. She has now done another and equal one for the opening years of the 18th century. Those who labour patiently and accurately transcribing the first-hand materials of the past are the front-line soldiers of the Muse, Clio. And Miss Blundell, after her long researches, rewards us, not with dry-as-dust, but with a picture, intimate and substantial, of a vanished world. As we read we cease to look over her shoulder and find ourselves sitting in the room with her ancestor as he "dined at ye Blew Posts with Cozen Henry Eyre and Mr. Trinder," or had "two Fidlers at night and dansed Country Danses in ye Halle."

REFERENCES

The history of all the Lancashire families mentioned by the Diarist is contained in *The Victoria History of Lancashire*, edited by Farrar and Brownhill.

Many of these families have now become extinct or have merged into others by intermarriage.

A majority of even the humblest of Nicholas Blundell's neighbours are briefly accounted for in *The English Catholic Non-Jurors* of 1715, (ed.) E.E. Estcourt and J.O. Payne. Details concerning the priests, nuns and layfolk met in Flanders are taken from the publications of *The Catholic Record Society* and from *English Catholic Refugees on the Continent*, (ed.) Peter Guilday. The lives of Blundell's more notable contemporary co-religionists are outlined in the *Biographical Dictionary of English Catholics*, Joseph Gillow, and those of all his Jesuit relations and friends in *Records of the English Province of the Society of Jesus*, Vols. V and VI, (ed.) Henry Foley, S.J.

For the background of the England in which the Diarist lived I am indebted to the following authors:

G.M. Trevelyan	*English Social History.*
	England in the Reign of Queen Anne.
Lecky	*History of England in the Eighteenth Century.* Vol. I.
Arthur Bryant	*Postman's Horn.*
Christopher Morris	Editor, 1947, of "The Journeys of Celia Fiennes."
Peet	*Liverpool in the Reign of Queen Anne.*
Christina Hole	*English Home Life.*
	English Custom and Usage.
John Ashton	*Social Life in the Reign of Queen Anne.*
Sir J.A. Picton	*Memorials of Liverpool.*

The publications of the Chetham Society, and of the Historic Society of Lancashire and Cheshire, have yielded information on various matters mentioned in the Diary.

PREFACE TO THE FIRST EDITION

"Blundell's Diary" was published in a much abridged form in 1895; the present volume consists almost entirely of hitherto unpublished matter drawn from the Diary and its author's *Letter Book* and *Disbursement Book*.

Nicholas Blundell was the eldest of the fourteen children of William Blundell of Crosby by his wife Mary, daughter of Rowland Eyre of Hassop in Derbyshire. His grandfather, William Blundell,[1] suffered severely in his person and estates as a recusant and a royalist in the Civil War. Nicholas was born at Crosby Hall in 1669. He was aged thirty-three when, upon the death of his father in 1702, he inherited the estates of Crosby seven miles north and Ditton nine miles south of Liverpool, which had been for centuries in the possession of his family. Nothing is known of his youth except that he was educated at the school maintained by English Jesuits at St. Omer in Flanders, the same school which nearly a century later migrated to England and is now known as Stonyhurst College. In the seventeenth and eighteenth centuries the parents of every pupil educated as a Catholic abroad were still liable to a fine of £100 on re-entering England. Either for this reason or owing to the expense and difficulties of the journey, the boys of the Blundell family never came home for a holiday during their school career, but endured six years of banishment. The solitary letter to Nicholas which has been preserved is from his grandfather, directed to him at St. Omer when he was aged seventeen. (The Cavalier invariably addressed his grandsons as "Nephew" when writing to them.)

To my Grandson Nicholas

"Nephew   London July 7th 1686

I have yours of June 28th which, as to the sense thereof I find to be humble and loving, but I am sorry to perceive that the characters of your letters do still grow worse and worse. I may

[1] Author of the notes edited by Canon Gibson as *A Cavalier's Note Book* and of the Letters edited by Margaret Blundell under the title *Cavalier: The Letters of William Blundell to his Friends, 1620–1698*, both published by Longmans, respectively, in 1880 and 1933.

say the same of your spelling and of your leaving out of words. Your sister Mary is 4 years younger than you and yet she writes a very laudable hand. Now as to your small progress in the school, though your memory may be very bad, you must not also pretend (as you do in your letter to me) an excuse from your want of wit. I think there is no such want, and that, if your memory and genius being defective, your wit being sufficient and your diligence as much as you please, it will be in your own power to come off with credit. To comply with your request to me I have sent to Mr. Beaugrand[1] for your use ten shillings in money, and a book for the Flageolet. I have given your father notice that you tell me your money is spent and I hope, though his charges are very great and his fortune small, he will send you a further supply before the ten shillings is spent. God grant you may deserve his love as he has deserved mine, and so with my blessing and daily prayers for your welfare, I will ever remain

Your truly loving Grandfather."

When Nicholas returned home, upon the completion of his education, he seems to have remained at Crosby, no doubt assisting his father and at the same time learning to manage the estate he was to inherit.

His grandfather's pen again affords a glimpse of him in a letter dated July 4th, 1691, and addressed to another grandson, Richard Butler.[2]

"Nicholas (our young man here) carried the small relics of his long quartan ague to Chorley about 14 weeks agone. He seemed at the first coming thither to be absolutely cleared of it by the change of air, yet now of late it hath seized on him again in some small degree, together with a short hot fever which made him both heartless and weak."

Nicholas will be found suffering from attacks of "quartan ague" at intervals during the whole period covered by the Diary, and the eye trouble which in the end defeated his pen, began while he was still a young man.

[1]Cornelius Beaugrand, a Jesuit lay brother, was assistant Procurator of the English Province. Foley states that he was living in London in 1679. He was probably still there seven years later.

[2]Second son of the fifth Viscount Mountgarret by his first wife Emelia, daughter of William Blundell, the Cavalier.

Apart from his copy of the Warrant[1] under which his father and grandfather were arrested as supposed conspirators, in 1694, he made no contribution to the family archives while his father lived. But his letters, written later and presently to be quoted, show him to have been clearly aware of the most urgent duty of the young heir to an estate in his day: namely, to make a provident marriage under the direction of his father. It seems to have been through no recalcitrancy on his part that this time-honoured programme was not carried out in his case, but because his father was unable to meet the demands of the parents of marriageable daughters in the matter of settlements.

The Diarist's manifold abbreviations have been dispensed with in quotations from his writings in the following chapters, but his lavish use of capital letters and his highly individual spelling have been reproduced. Orthography was an imperfect art in his day, but nevertheless it owned some rules which he completely disregarded; he will be found spelling—or mis-spelling—the same word in different ways in one sentence. He succeeded however in improving the calligraphy which was adversely criticised by his elders while he was at school; in it he has left a completely legible account of himself, his family and their mode of life, his own many occupations and every item of his expenditure during twenty-six years.

His pages contain but scant allusions to public affairs; only the faintest echo from the battlefields upon which the map of Europe was being re-made during the reign of Queen Anne, is to be detected. He does indeed announce news of Marlborough's victories, but makes no reference whatever to the political events and intrigues which so profoundly agitated the country during the Queen's reign, and he does not even mention her death. Historians, aided by the records of important families, have reconstructed the great world of that day for us. Nicholas Blundell depicts the little world of a country squire with a Pepys-like fidelity and a graphic pen.

On the first page of the first volume of the Diary its author wrote its title and set forth its purpose:

"A Diurnall or a Daly Account, wherein I have set down somthing or Other every day that hath happened, from July 27th 1702 till December ye 31st 1712.

[1]*Cavalier.*

I have a fowl drought in some small Books which have something more in some few plaices but in substance ye same. Some of these Following Pages are in Nature of a Table whereby I can find out Severall of ye most remarkable things and allmost anithing set down in this book."

There follow most complicated "Tables of Index" [1] which appear to have afforded great satisfaction to their compiler.

Nicholas copied out the "fowl drought" of his Diary at long intervals, applying himself to the task when sickness or unusually bad weather confined him to the house. Thus on May 8th, 1708, he writes:

"It was a wet slattering day and we had not much sport. I began to transcribe my small Diurnalls into my larg Book of Diurnal.'

Occasionally he adds information to the original text when copying it, as when under date May 8th, 1711, he gives *the result* of his seed-sowing on that day.

"I sowed 655 Graines of Barly in the New Orchard. It grew upon 22 Eares which all came up from one Root and did undoubtedly proceed from one Grain of Barly which grew upon ye burned Ground in ye farthest North-Hey. I sowed these 655 Graines abundantly too thick which was ye reason they came not on, so was frustrated of ye Experiment I intended to make of its incrase by sowing it for some years together."

Nine years after he began his transcription, he reports upon his work:

"July 15th. 1715. I have this day made an end of transcribing my small Diurnalls and have also finished ye Large Indexes at ye beginning of those larger Books, and also ye Small Indexes at ye end as far as I can at present, so that I have at last got even with that tedious piece of Work."

Neither the Small Diurnals nor any records of cash receipts have been preserved.

The *Larger Books* referred to by Nicholas are the three long, narrow, calf-bound manuscript volumes which have survived and which constitute his *Great Diurnall*.

MARGARET BLUNDELL

Note.—All quotations in subsequent chapters are from the *Great Diurnal*, the *Disbursement Book* and the Diarist's *Letter Book*, unless otherwise stated.

[1]Appendix I.

PREFACE TO THE SECOND EDITION

This book was originally published in 1952 under the title *Blundell's Diary and Letter Book 1702–1728*. The self-styled 'editor', Margaret Blundell, was characteristically deprecating about her contribution, and her name did not even appear on the spine of the book. In fact she was no mere editor and her involvement was an essential feature of the book, both in terms of her research and the substantial contributions she made to the text. That is why it was decided for this edition to change the title and give her retrospectively the recognition which is her due.

I do not know if Margaret realised that her book was published exactly 250 years after Nicholas started the Diary, but by a happy chance, the year of publication of this new edition is exactly 50 years after the first, and therefore the tercentenary of the start of the Diary. This provided a good excuse for bringing the book back into print after all these years.

Between 1968 and 1972 there appeared a complete edition of the Diary in three volumes, edited by the redoubtable Frank Tyrer who dedicated a good part of his life to local history, and took a special interest in Little Crosby and the Blundell family. Future local historians and all those with an interest in the subject will be forever in his debt. For a time it seemed the earlier work of Margaret Blundell had been eclipsed. But her book has some advantages over Tyrer. It gives a more rounded portrait of the Squire and his family because of its extracts from his letters and disbursement book as well as from the diary itself. It is also much shorter, and for this reason and also because of her narrative additions, it is more accessible to the general reader.

On the back cover of this book will be seen two illustrations which did not appear in the original edition. One is a drawing of Crosby Hall in 1736, the year before the Diarist's death. Also included is a photograph of the Hall as it is today. The house has been greatly altered in the intervening years. However, it is still possible to recognise the basic features of the front elevation from the old drawing. The old mullioned windows

Left: Frances Blundell, the Diarist's wife.
Facing page: Mally Blundell (*left*) and Fanny Blundell (*right*)

and gabled roofs were 'modernised' in about 1784 by the Diarist's grandson to produce the 'Georgian' appearance which the Hall has today. The stables on the left of the drawing still exist and now form part of Crosby Hall Educational Trust, though the other buildings have since disappeared. The elaborate gardens on the right were added by the Diarist in 1722, and must have been removed at the time of the 1784 modernisation.

It is impossible to do more than speculate about the present location of most of the rooms referred to by the Diarist, e.g, the 'parlour' which his wife and her supporters persuaded him to instal (p.54), but I do believe we can identify (in the Oak Room on the second floor) the 'Streat place for a fat Man' (p.151) in which Nicholas hid in November 1715 during the Jacobite rebellion!

Margaret Blundell, or Madge as she was always called, was born in 1882 in Hightown, near Little Crosby. She was the great (×4) granddaughter of Nicholas Blundell 'the Diarist'. Her father was Francis Blundell, known as 'Tansy', the second

son of Colonel Nicholas Blundell, who was the Squire of Little Crosby for almost all the second half of the 19th century. Her mother was Mary Sweetman, from an Irish family of considerable literary and artistic talent. Tansy died when Madge was only two years old, and her mother thereafter earned her living as a novelist, under the name M.E. Francis. She was very prolific, publishing about 50 novels as well as many stories and plays. In her last years, Madge helped her to write some of her books.

Madge's brother Francis inherited the Crosby Estate in 1909 on the death of his uncle. Madge and her sister Agnes moved with their mother into Crosby Hall with him. Francis served as a cavalry officer in France during the Great War, and Madge was a Voluntary Aid Detachment. Francis married Theresa Ward in 1918, and at this point Madge and Agnes moved with their mother to North Wales. Francis died in 1936 aged only 56 and Madge and Agnes moved back to Crosby again to help his widow and two young children.

During World War Two, Crosby Hall was used as a convalescent home for wounded servicemen, and Madge was the Commandant. She was a qualified nurse. In 1950, Madge and Agnes moved again to make way for their niece Hester, my mother, who married Brian Whitlock. Later they returned to live at St. Mary's Cottage, just next to the Hall. I remember their last years in the 1950s, making their way across the park to daily Mass at St. Mary's Church. Madge died in 1964.

Margaret and Agnes were both writers. They both wrote Catholic pamphlets and short lives of the saints. Agnes also wrote children's books, like *Mr Fuzzy* (the life of a dog) and *They Met Robin Hood*. Madge wrote some romantic novels, in the same vein as her mother, an unpublished biography of her mother, and two works of family history. The first, a life of William Blundell the Cavalier was published in 1933, and I hope to reissue this interesting book in due course. The other, of course, is the present work about Nicholas Blundell the Diarist.

MARK BLUNDELL, July 2002

David Brazendale, a noted local historian, kindly read through the text and made some comments, which are itemised below. I am grateful to him for this and also for his help and support for the new edition.

p.17: "Anne Rothwell's" was located at Four Lane Ends, Little Crosby, not Great Crosby.

p.49: On Indentured Servants there is an excellent article by Hockedy DM in THSLC Vol. 144 1994.

p.54: "Dailes" are defined as flagstones. The word "Dales" or "Deals" was often used to refer to timber and floorboards. In the context, this seems more likely.

p.74: "Willoughby of Pasham" should read "Willoughby of Parham."

p.75: Ellison was curate of Formby not Rector. Formby was a chapelry of St. Mary Walton-on-the-Hill.

p77: Wairing was curate of Crosby as well as Master of the School.

p.104: Christina Holes should read Christina Hole.

p.123: The interest of the Mill having six sails should be noted. Usually credit for the invention of the six-sailed mill is given to John Smeaton, but Nicholas anticipated him by 50 years.

p.127: The words at the bottom of the page "Mr Bouchier's advice evidently coincided with the Diarist's own wish" should probably read "Mr Bouchier evidently pursuaded the Diarist that he should accept the post of Churchwarden."

p.133: "South-East Lancashire" should read "South-West Lancashire."

p.141: The name of Molyneux's steward was Richard Abbot.

p.208: "formerly" should be "formally."

p.262: William Blundell the Cavalier was wounded at the storming of Lancaster, not Lathom House.

CHAPTER I

I

THE NEW SQUIRE

THE Diary opens on the day on which William Blundell, father of the Diarist, was seized by his last illness:

" July 27th, 1702 : My father went after dinner to wate of my Lord Molineux[1] at ye New Stand where he was sodenly taken so very ill that he sent for me to wate of him home and bring ye Coach for him."

As no doctor lived in the neighbourhood a messenger was sent galloping to Preston twenty-three miles away, but " Doctor Farrington[2] was not to be found." The next day Nicholas went himself to Wigan, twenty miles in another direction, whence he brought back Doctor Francis Worthington. But the sick man grew worse and on August 1st Thomas Howard, the butler, rode forty miles to Whitchurch in Shropshire in search of the renowned Doctor Bostock " but he came not." Meanwhile William's nephew, Edmund Butler,[3] "came to Crosby from Durham in his way to Ireland," writes Nicholas; he sent to Wigan for Doctor Thomas Worthington[4] who came late that night."

The doctor's ministrations proved in vain. William died on August 2nd, 1702, at the age of fifty-five. He was buried at Sephton Church three days later.

[1] William, fourth Viscount Molineux, had formed a new park on his estate at Netherton, three miles from Crosby, for sporting purposes.

[2] Dr. Valentine Farington was the younger brother of William Farington of Worden Esq. The career of medicine was frequently followed by the younger sons of country squires.

[3] The future sixth Viscount Mountgarret and elder brother of Richard, mentioned in the Introduction.

[4] Dr. Thomas Worthington, father of Francis, had attended three generations of the Blundell family.

The first page of his son's "Disbursement Book" sets forth details of the funeral expenses. These include large offerings for Masses for the repose of the deceased man's soul, innumerable "sutes of mourning" for members of the family and household, "the Lone of two Mourning Cloakes" at 5s. each, a great deal of food and drink for the entertainment of friends, neighbours and tenants who had gathered to pay their last respects, and "£5 for ye Tax to ye Queene for Buriall of an Esquire." Ten dozen bottles of "Bristoll Beer" cost £2 10s. and the bottles £1; 7s. 6d. was paid for one pound of coffee and £6 15s. for a suit of mourning for the Reverend William Gillibrand,[1] Jesuit priest and cousin to the Blundells, who was chaplain at Crosby.

At the end of the bill Nicholas added the modest sum for burying an old retainer, William Arnold, who died three days after his master.[2] "He had been a faithful and good servant," writes the new Squire, "and brought up from a Chylde in this Hous. He was Groome, Coachman and Butcher.

To his Nurse Keeper	...	...	...		2	6
Coffin	...	...	...	...	6	6
Bread and Bear ...	...	...	...	1 0	0
Church Dues	...	...	...	...	1	2
Doctor and Pothcary	...	...	...		7	6
				4	0	2."

Later Nicholas remembered another item connected with his father's funeral, and scrupulously inscribed it lengthwise in the margin of the page:

"Corne given to ye Poore of ye Parish of Sefton forgot to be mentioned before, it was then very cheap, Vallew in all then given £1.10.6."

The entertainment of friends and relatives, with their horses

---

[1] The Diarist spells his cousin's name indifferently, *Gelibond*, *Gelibrond* or *Gelebrand*.

[2] Buried at Sefton, 6 August.

and attendant grooms, added considerably to the financial out-lay on this sad occasion. Realization of the cost of hospitality thus brought home to him, may have prompted Nicholas to embark upon the accurate record of expenses which he kept from the day of his father's funeral until his own death was approaching. He avers that his ingenious "Index or Table"[1] for every month of each year in his Great Diurnal, informed him at a glance how many members of his family or household had been absent on any day, and how many persons had been fed at his board. The wages of all except two of the men he employed included food and lodging; skilled craftsmen such as carpenters and plasterers were engaged temporarily on the same terms, while both men and women working at such seasonal jobs as sheep-shearing, flax-breaking, spinning, threshing etc., received their "meat."

Nicholas succeeded to an estate encumbered by the debts incurred by his father in the bringing-up of his large family. Eight of William's fourteen children survived infancy, an unusual proportion for that century. The new Squire set himself forthwith to grapple with his financial responsibilities. His mother's jointure and "provisions" for two younger brothers and five sisters had to be found; his great aunt Frances, was still a member of the family and drawing her annuity from the estate. In each generation a majority of the daughters of the house had joined English communities of the religious orders who were forced, by the penal law of their native land, to maintain their convents in France and Flanders. Frances had in her youth resigned her right to the small dowry which would have enabled her either to follow this course had she had a religious vocation, or to marry. Her brother had undertaken to allow her an annuity of £25 a year, but even this little income had, in times of stress, been placed at the service of the family as generously as her personal good offices. At the close of the Civil War William Blundell the Cavalier had been a maimed and hunted fugitive. It was his sister "Francke" who then stood by his young wife when she resisted the Justices' de-mand that she should educate her children in the religion of the

[1] Appendix I.

State, when she had to bury her children's bread to save it from the bands of marauding soldiers, and when she bought an ox and a horse to plough up the portion of her husband's sequestered estate allotted to her, in order to provide that bread. Later Francke had fought the battle for the recognition by the fourth Lord Mountgarret of the children of his heir Richard Butler, who had married the Cavalier's eldest daughter Emelia against his father's will. After the Cavalier lost his wife, his sister cared for him in his old age. In one of his last letters he wrote of her: " She hath indeed been one of the best spokes in the wheel on which our fortunes have turned."[1]

Great Aunt Frances was not a person who could be ignored by the new inheritor of the Crosby estate.

Each succeeding heir had increased his fortune by marriage. No other way was open to him to provide for the large family which he expected to have in his turn. Nicholas's great-grandfather had had thirteen children, his grandfather twelve and his own father fourteen. His duty, as he saw it, was to do as his forbears had done, make a provident marriage, and in due course became a parent of many. His father had offered him as a desirable prize to parents who were in a position to endow their daughters well. Indeed William had proposed to pay off his own debts with the fortune of his son's bride, an arrangement usually considered eminently satisfactory by all the parties concerned. For the heir could then hope to succeed to an unencumbered estate, his bride's jointure would be more secure, and the respective parents satisfied with their bargain. Evidently William Blundell could not give a sufficiently high price with his son, for his calculations and negotiations alike proved abortive.

" My Father," writes Nicholas in a letter on the subject of his debts, " was disappointed in his Hopes of receiving a good Fortune with a Wife who was proposed for me, but however nothing came of it."

He makes no comment on the name, age or appearance of the bride proposed on this occasion; possibly even so dutiful a son may have resisted the completion of the arrangement on one of

[1] *Cavalier.*

these accounts. Although he bore no ill-will to his "dearest Father" for thus seeking to clear his future inheritance of debt, the prospect of marriage must have acquired a distinctly more interesting aspect now that he could negotiate for himself. A week after the funeral he was agreeably occupied with the idea, but not prepared to be hurried. He had received a letter addressed to his father and found it to contain particulars of the fortune of a young lady whose name he does not reveal in his reply.

"To Mr. Joseph Hawley at Martin Sands

"I give you many thanks for the Care you have taken, but at this Juncture I cannot as yet think of marrying, much less resolve where to Pitch. Many Ladyes have been proposed with fifteen Hundred Pounds, and if formerly that Poursion was considered fitt for me, I may now deserve better, my Father having left me in very good Cercumstances."

But when Nicholas found himself called upon to pay a tax of thirteen shillings "for being a Squire and a Batchler for ½ Yeare," his mother and great-aunt may have pointed the moral. For he spent some time "perusing ye Pedigree of this Family"; he also no doubt studied *Two heads for a Treaty of Marriage* compiled by his grandfather when seeking a bride for his son William, and entered by him in his *Blew Book.* One was entitled *Some Heads for a Treaty of Marriage with a person inferior,* and the other *Heads for a Treaty of Marriage with a person above our degree.* In both a third of the Crosby lands were to be settled on William junior and his heirs male, but the conditions differed. The bride of inferior social status was required to bring £500 in cash to the bargain. If she was unable to do this, but her portion was worth £500 or more, the young couple were to be allowed £10 per annum for every £100 of the bride's fortune "for maintenance during his father's lyf, and so if her husband dye that shall be her joynture for so much." No settlement of land was to be made in her favour. If the bride owned land worth £40 per annum or more and would "make an estate of all her lands and rents to be disposed of by her husband's father," the said father would increase the allowance for jointure and maintenance to the full yearly value of her lands and rents.

"A person above our degree" was to be invited to bring twelve hundred or a thousand pounds into the settlement, but might also expect a bigger jointure and more generous fortunes for the younger children of the marriage. In either case power was to be reserved to produce a jointure for a second wife.

"I desyre not any powers to make a joynture for a second wife," wrote the Cavalier of himself, "but I think it very reasonable that som powers be left to my son."

Nicholas was thus primed with what he might justly consider to have been his ancestor's guidance as to the bargain to be concluded when he decided "where to pitch" in his search for a bride. He betook himself to Scarisbrick Hall, about twelve miles from Crosby, to take counsel of his cousin, contemporary, and life-long friend Robert Scarisbrick. The result of this consultation is set forth under date March 3rd 1703 :

"I writ to my Lady Webb[1] and sent Walter Thelwall with it the next day to Haythorp."

It was as easy as that. There was no registered post to which such an important letter could be confided, but a servant could be ordered to carry it from Lancashire to Oxford, a journey which he seems to have accomplished without any difficulty. He was back in ten days, having presumably spent four days on the road both going and returning, as his master subsequently did, and having rested his horse for two days at his destination. It was not an economical method of securing the delivery of a letter and its answer, for Thelwell's expenses amounted to £1 7s. 4d.

The result of the correspondence was encouraging but Lady Webb desired to know more before allowing any nearer approach to her granddaughter Frances Langdale[2], who was in her care and had expectations from her. Nicholas does not

---

[1] Widow of Sir John Webb of Odstock and Canford, second baronet, and daughter of John Blomer of Heythrop Castle, Oxfordshire.

[2] Daughter of Marmaduke, third Baron Langdale.

relate how he came to "pitch upon" this young lady. There is no record of his ever having left his native county after his return from school in Flanders, so it may almost certainly be concluded that he had never seen her. From the fact that he now immediately wrote to Mr. Philmot, among others, suggests that the Jesuit priest of that name had been an intermediary in the negotiations. Nicholas always alludes to priests as "Mr—" except in the case of close friends when he calls them "Pat.—" (Pater). Father Philip Philmot S.J. was at the time in Staffordshire, and Lady Langdale, mother of Frances, was a Miss Draycott of Painsley in that county before her marriage.

Lady Webb evidently requested more precise and possibly more generous terms, for the day after Walter Thelwall's return from Heythrop, Nicholas "writ letters all day to Lord Molyneux, Lord Langdale, Mr. Philmot etc." These letters were "sent to ye Post at Leverpoole" by Henry Bilsbury the groom. Four days later another letter was dispatched to Lady Webb, this time also by the ordinary post from Liverpool. The only other post town then serving the neighbourhood was Ormskirk, ten miles from Crosby.

The next entry in the Diary shows that the negotiations were progressing.

"March 28th. I writ to Lord Langdale, enclosed to Cozen Eyre ye Lawyer, and sent it to ye Poste by Pat. Gelibrand."

On April 4th a reply was received from Lord Langdale, but it would seem that intervention on the part of Great Aunt Frances brought the affair to a head.

"April 6th. Aunt Frances had account from Mrs. Bloare by Orders of Lady Webb that I might wate of Mrs. Frances Langdale as soon as I pleased."

Now all was preparation for the journey. The first thing to be considered was suitable attire for the wooer. Doubtless his mother and great aunt deliberated on this point. His country broad cloth would never do, yet he must not spend too much for he was not yet accepted. A black cloth coat was decided upon and the day after the receipt of Mrs. Bloare's letter, the

Reverend William Gillibrand repaired to Liverpool to buy the material which, with lining and buttons, cost £4 9s. 9d. It then had to be sent twenty miles in another direction to Burdkin, the tailor at Wigan, to be made up. Great must have been the family indignation three days later when Richard Jump the Ploughman, who had been sent to Wigan to fetch the coat, brought back only the uncut cloth. Burdkin had been faithless to his word. The master now took the material himself to Edward Porter in Liverpool, who made up the coat in one day. A " painted Caine " was also acquired for 4s., a pair of slippers for the same price, and a pair of pistols for £1 10s. Thomas Howard, the butler, had borrowed pistols for his master but these were " rather larg and so extraordinary fine " that Nicholas decided to buy a pair for himself rather than be responsible for them.

The wooer rode in some state on this exhilarating journey, accompanied by his chaplain and three menservants. The first day they dined at Warrington and lodged at Holmes Chapel, eight miles south of Knutsford. On the second day they dined at Stone and lodged at Aldridge, on the third day they baited at Birmingham and Droitwich and lodged at Worcester. This last was a long ride and it is not surprising to learn that Nicholas's mare, Bonny, was so lame the next day that she had to be left in the care of a farrier. A fresh horse was hired at a charge of 9s. and the party proceeded by Winchcombe in Gloucestershire to Northleach, a détour not explained in the Diary. Possibly it was due to road conditions. The last stage of their journey was thirty miles; on the previous four stages they seem to have ridden an average of fifty miles daily.

" April 17th. I came from North Leach to Haythorpe and found the famoly all there and my Lord Langdale."

Nicholas is unromantically silent about his first meeting with his bride-to-be. She was only seventeen and was evidently a high-spirited girl, judging by the degree to which she presently asserted herself in her new home. Her portrait at Crosby represents a slight, graceful woman with delicate features but a decidedly discontented expression. She was an heiress in her own right, her maternal grandfather Philip Draycott having bequeathed £1000 and her great uncle John Blomer £500 to her. Lord Langdale agreed to pay £500 into the bridegroom's hands providing the wedding took place within two months; Lady Webb covenanted to hand over John Blomer's £500 within ten days of the wedding; payment in each case was to be made at the house of Richard Pierson, goldsmith, the Sign of the Acorn, Fleet Street, London.

The story of the businesslike courtship is fully told in the Diary.

"April 19th. I discoursed Lord Langdale in his Chamber and Lady Webb in ye Dining Room. I made my first Addresse to Mrs Frances Langdale."

On the 21st., after "discoursing Lady Webb in ye Garden," he "discoursed Mrs Frances Langdale in ye Kitchen Garden," and the next day "Lady Webb read the Heads of Agreement of Marriage between Mrs Frances Langdale and Mee, N. Blundell in presence of Lord Langdale and Sir John Webb."

All was satisfactory, Mr. Trinder the lawyer was summoned from London to draw up "Artickleys of Marriage," and the happy suitor at last writes triumphantly on April 28th:

"I presented my Diamond Ring to Mistress Frances Langdale."

His head was not turned however; he did not forget to record that he had sent Thomas Howard to Worcester to fetch Grey-Bonny, and that Howard had returned with the mare the same day. The farrier's charge was heavy—£1 15s. 6d. for treatment and keep of the animal for ten days. But Nicholas was not anxious about his disbursements now. A thousand pounds was almost within his grasp, with the promise of a second thousand. His first reaction was to order an extremely expensive article for himself. He sent to London for a "Campaign Perry-Wig" at the price of £10, and the additional cost of "Coach hier by ye Buyer of ye Wigg 2s., a Trunk for ye Wigg 7s. and Carriage of ye Wigg from London 3s." Perhaps Mistress Frances expressed a wish that her future husband should turn himself out more stylishly. They were allowed to walk together, accompanied by the Chaplain, before the accepted suitor withdrew to the house of Lady Webb's neighbour Sir John Curzon[1] of Waterperry near Oxford. From here he made his preparations to go to London for the dual purpose of fitting out himself and his servants adequately, and making sure that his Cousin, Lawyer Eyre, attended sharply to his interests in the matter of marriage settlements.

"May 4th. I sent George Howard, Sir John Curzon's servant, to take a place in the Coach for me to London.

May 5th. I writ to Mrs Frances Langdale from Waterperry and sent it by Oxford Post.

May 6th. I took Coach to Wheatley near Waterperry, dined at Wickham and came to London in company of Mr John Curzon, Mr Bayley Doctor of Divinity belonging to Oxford and some others."

He paid 10s. for his seat inside the coach and 5s. for the accommodation of his servant in the rumble.

On his arrival in London the North country squire evidently discovered his hat not to be in keeping with his wig, for he at once spent 2s. 6d. on silver lace to embellish it and 2s. for "sewing on ye lace and trimming up my hat."

The week in London must have been a most cheerful experience for one whose prospects were now so rosy. Business and pleasure were suitably interspersed.

"May 7th. I dined with Cozen Henry Eyre, Mr Lewson etc., in Fuller's Rant. I saw The Silent Woman acted.

May 8th. I made my first visit to Mr Trinder with Cozen Henry Eyre.

May 9th. I dined at Thomas Arnolds. I made my first visit to Mrs Norris,[2] my cousin. She is I think sister to Cousin Henry Eyre. I supped at the King's Head in Vere Street with Cousin John and Francis Eyre, two Mr Dormers[3] etc.

[1] He was succeeded by his son Francis, who died s.p. in 1750 when the title became extinct. Burke's *Extinct Baronetage*.

[2] Henry Norris married Teresa Eyre, of Hassop.

[3] Charles and John, sons of Charles, fifth Baron Dormer, who succeeded to their father's estates in turn. Charles was a priest and did not assume the title.

May 10th. I writ letters all ye Forenoone in my Chamber. I
saw Ye Jew of Venice acted at Lincoln's Inn.
May 11th. I walked to Westminster and saw ye Tombs. I
went at night to Wills Coffy Hous where I heard Mr Lawson
talk of calculating Nativityes."

He paid 2s. 3d. for "seeing ye Tower etc." and 3s. for his
place in the theatre. Then he had much business with the mercer
and tailor for there was to be no economy in outlay on his wedding finery. He bought 5½ yards of "Blew Cloath" at 18s. per
yard, 16 yards of durance for lining at 1s. 3d., 3¾ oz. of silver
thread for button holes at 6s. per oz., 3½ dozen silver buttons at
7s. 6d. per dozen, and 5 dozen silver "brest buttons" at 2s.
There were additions of "bayes for ye Sides of ye Coate,"
"Shammy Pockets" and "Puffs for ye Britches." The tailor
was paid £1 15s. "for making this my Wedding Sute"; a pair
of scarlet stockings costing 10s. completed the bridegroom's
festive garb. Purchases did not stop there for Nicholas intended
to carry off his bride in a style befitting her rank and his own
"good cercumstances." He ordered two suits of livery consisting of grey cloth coats lined with blue serge, blue waistcoats and
shoulder knots of the same material, plenty of silver lace and
white metal buttons for adornment, and blue stockings. These
outfits for the two grooms, including the tailor's work, cost
£9 3s. 5d.

Nicholas was not forgetful of presents for his bride but these
need not be too expensive : he bought half a dozen "gilt Coffy
Spoones" for 18s., a "fals Diamond Necklase" for £1 1s. 6d.
and "a fals Diamond Ring" for 14s. He gave £1 5s. for his
"Weding Ring."

"May 12th. I dined at ye Blew Posts in Devereux Court with
Cozen Henry Eyre and Mr Trinder and examined things relait-
ing to my Marriage."

The next day Nicholas and his servant returned by coach to
Waterperry. There, before seeking his lady-love again, he took
advantage of his host's invitation to view the sights of Oxford,
"the Theater, Library, Chapel, Laboratory etc." He does not

specify which chapel. On May 15th he and Father Gillibrand, who had remained at Waterperry while his cousin was in London, returned to Heythrop together.

"May 16th. I walked in ye Kitchen Garden with Lady Webb senior and gave her an Account of my London Journey.
May 17th. I walked with Mistress Frances Langdale to Fairford. Morris Dansers came to Heythrop.
May 20th. The Lords and Ladies of May came to Heythrop. I presented my gilt Coffy Spoones.
May 21st. Young Lady Webb[1] lent Mrs Frances Langdale a Booke of Heraldry to seek for my Lord Langdale's Coat of Armes."

Visits were made to Sir John Webb's neighbours; lawyers came and went; Henry Bilsborough's measurements were sent to the London tailor, for he was to drive the newly-wedded pair attired in one of the grey and blue livery suits; there was dancing to the pipe and tabor; Father Gillibrand transcribed the marriage articles twice, but before these were finally engrossed a respectfully conducted tussle with his Lordship took place.

"May 30th. Much intercession made to my Lord Langdale to make him sign a single Draft to me for the Payment of the two thousands Pounds."

Nicholas had successfully upheld his claim to be worth more "than a dowry of £1500 with his bride," but Lord Langdale with equal firmness declined to pay down £2000 at once.

The lines of the Marriage Settlement finally ran thus:

"Whereas a Marriage is intended between Nicholas Blundell and Frances Langdale, there shall be paid to the said Nicholas for the fortune of the said Frances sums amounting to £2000."

The whole dowry was not to be placed in the bridegroom's hands immediately; moreover a jointure of £200 a year was secured to Frances in the event of her being left a widow, and "ye Lady Dowager Webb" made a further contribution to her

[1] Hon. Barbara Belasyse, wife of Sir John Webb, third baronet, and daughter of John, Lord Belasyse, Baron of Worlaby.

granddaughter's future fortune by settling £100 a year upon her after her own death.

All now went merrily towards the culmination of the happy affair. Henry Bilsborough was sent back to Crosby to fetch the chariot which was to carry the bride and bridegroom home. What a stir his arrival there must have made! What excitement must have attended his setting forth again, with seven horses and accompanied by two more servants!

Nicholas meantime returned to London. He made the journey on horseback, spending a night at Oxford on the way. It was a more extravagant mode of travel than that provided by a seat in the coach but more convenient since he had the use of his horses in London. The cost of keeping the two mounts there for twelve nights was £1 17s. 11d., fourpence more than he paid for "meat and drink" for himself and his servant during the same time.

"For washing Linnen at London 1s. 4d." was another carefully recorded item of expense. Naturally Nicholas dined with friends more often than in his lodging.

"June 10th. I dined with Lady Curzon, tryed on my Weding Sute there and at other Plaices."

The bridegroom was back at Heythrop on June 14th.

"June 15th. Lord Langdale, Lady Webb, Sir John Webb etc. heard the Marriage Deeds read, all we at Haythorpe concerned therein subscribed them before four Witnesses."

The wedding of recusants had to be celebrated quietly since the officiating priest was liable to imprisonment for life and was at the mercy of any informer who, upon his conviction, might claim the reward of £100. Nicholas himself was only told when his wedding was to take place on the eve of the appointed day.

"June 16th. Lady Dowager Webb acquainted me the Marriage was to be the day following. Lady Dowager Webb signed the Deed for Payment of £100 per annum to Mistress Frances Langdale."

After the protracted negotiations and preparations, the entry in the Diary on June 17th reads very tamely.

"I was married to Lord Langdale's Daughter by Mr Slaughter, a Clergyman."[1]

The Disbursement Book yields a few more details on a page thus endorsed:

"An account of what I spent and waired from April 13th. 1703, when I began my Journey to Heythrop, till July 2nd when I brought my Wife to Crosby." The first item follows:

"Spent on Coz. William Gelibrand, myself, three Servants and five Horses from Crosby to Heythrop we lay out four Nights and spent in all £4 4s 11d."

All the expenses of the wonderful six weeks are then set forth and finally those of the wedding day:

"June 17th. Given my Wife in gold and silver when I married

	£	s	d
her	£8	2	6
Given Mr. Slawter	1	1	6
To Musick at my Wedding		10	0
To ye Ringers at Heythorpe		5	0
Given ye Parson of Haythorpe for dues		10	9
For Service done me by ye Collecter of ye tax for Wedding		10	9
Tax to the Queen for my Marriage ...	£5	2	6 "

It may certainly be assumed that the bride was beautifully clothed, for the Disbursement Book reveals her to have possessed a feminine love of dress. Once she was married she depended upon her husband for everything, literally down to her "pinns," and, the farm accounts excepted, no other items occupy so much space as "Wives' Clothes."

More visits were now exchanged among the neighbours, more field sports were enjoyed in the interval before the chariot arrived, and during the subsequent three days required to rest the horses and repair vehicle and harness. These suffered wear

---

[1] It was then the custom to designate a secular priest as "a clergyman" to distinguish him from a member of one of the religious orders.

on the journey across five counties along the deeply rutted roads of the day. The horses had to be newly shod too, and the servants' linen washed. " A Gunn " was bought " at Bermidgham," and Mrs. Blundell's box arrived from London.

Finally the party consisting of the newly-wedded couple, their chaplain, six servants and eleven horses, set out for Crosby on June 28th. Nicholas distributed generous largesse to Lady Webb's many servants as they left.

" Vales at Heythrop," he wrote in the Disbursement Book " to ye HousKeeper one dubble Pistole, to the Butler one Pistole[1] and ½ Guinney, Chamber Maid one Pistole and ½ Guinney, Cook one Broad Peece,[2] Groome one Guinney, under Cook, Under Butler and under Chamber Maid each half a Guinney, my Wives Chamber Maid 10s, under Gardiner 5s, Dary Maid 5s, in all £9-10-9d."

A whole quarter's wages to all whom he employed at home, both indoors and out, only amounted to £12. 2s., but he could afford to be generous on this occasion for part of his wife's dowry was already " lying at London " for his use.

The homeward route in the chariot was somewhat different from that followed on horseback on the outward journey. The travellers lodged the first night at Towcester, the second at Birmingham, the third at Stafford and the fourth at Coalbrook.

" July 2nd. I came from Cole Brook, baited at Warrington, was met by Doctor Lathom[3] and treated by him in ye Rode. I brought my Wife home to Crosby."

---

[1] A Pistole was worth about 16s. This is the only occasion on which Nicholas alludes to the old coinage. Throughout the Disbursement Book and the rest of the Diary, he writes of money in terms of pounds, shillings and pence.

[2] 20s. piece.

[3] Among the documents from Crosby Hall now at the Lancashire County Record Office, Preston, is a Licence to practise Surgery and to keep a Boarding School granted respectively to Richard Latham and Judith, his wife, in 1686, they being recusants. Dr. Latham died at Aintree in 1713. Blundell helped him to draw up his will and was one of his executors.

CHAPTER II

I

HUSBAND AND WIFE

WHILE Nicholas was away great preparations were made at Crosby for the reception of the bride. Money had been left in the hands of Walter Thelwall, the steward, to meet the expenses of house and farm in the master's absence. In his accounts the cost of a number of things which must have been ordered by Mrs. Blundell or Mistress Frances is set forth between such items as :

	£	s.	d.
" Spent at ye Beas[1] Fare		4	10
" Hay, 5 Loads	4	15	0 "

Nine pewter dishes weighing 40½ lb. were bought at 10d. per lb., and one superior dish at 11d.; five dozen plates cost £3. 15s., two pair of brass candlesticks 6s. 6d., a looking-glass 8s. Some of these goods were ordered from London :

" Carrying 114 lbs. wight from London to Leverpoole at 1½d. per pound 14s. 3d."

Heavy boxes were transported at this low charge by the ponderous carrier waggons which slowly crawled from the metropolis to provincial towns.

Smaller purchases suggest that the ladies thought the rooms required tidying up and that the kitchen lacked some necessaries. "Rubing and sweeping Brushes, Curtin Rings, Latches, Catches and Hinges for within the Hous and for the Garden doors, a new Jack, Puleys for ye Jack, Saucepans, pewter Solvers, Basons etc.," are among the items enumerated.

Probably Nicholas had ordered the wine beforehand.

" Wine, whit and red, most of it at 28s. per doz	£13	14	0
Bottles at 2s. 2d. per dozen		13	0 "

[1] Beast.

At the foot of the long column in the Disbursement Book Nicholas wrote:

"Thus far reach the Accounts of W.T." and himself added these final incidental expenses:

	£	s.	d.
"To Musitions at my Hombringing ...	1	6	0
"To Mr. Hurst's Servant for bringing a Present		2	6
"To Coz. Scarisbrick's Servant for bringing a Present		2	6"

So there was music, and doubtless feasting when the tired occupants of the chariot reached their journey's end; we are not told how many bottles of red and white wine were opened.

During the ensuing days neighbours called "to give me joy" writes Nicholas, while his various cousins "waited upon" his bride. Indeed the couple immediately inaugurated the life of intense sociability which they were to pursue together for thirty-three years. Nicholas usually concluded a busy morning devoted to estate management and his own farming, by dining at home in the early afternoon. After dinner he sallied forth to horse-races, or coursing-matches or to the bowling-green, or to attend to such matters as Courts Leet and the regulating of water-courses. When the business and sport of the day were over, he repaired to "The Wool Pack" or "The Angel," both inns in Liverpool, or perhaps merely to "Anne Rothwell's" in Great Crosby. He invariably concludes the account of his day by stating with whom he shared his potations—his lawyer, his tailor, a timber-merchant, tenants and yeomen from his own estates of Little Crosby and Ditton, or some of his innumerable cousins and friends.

Affairs were arranged by "discoursing" between the interested parties up to the actual point of signing a legal document in the office of Mr. Plumbe, the lawyer.[1] Often a tenant,

[1] Mr. Plumbe build a house for himself in Wavertree, near Liverpool, and later bought some of the Moore property in Liverpool. In 1718 he bought the Aughton estate from Richard Hesketh. His grandson, Thomas, married the daughter and heiress of John Tempest, of Tong, near Bradford. John Plumbe, son of Thomas, added the name and arms of Tempest to his own. Picton, vol. ii, p. 19.

unable to write, could only make his mark over his name inscribed by Mr. Plumbe's clerk. But whether business was between Nicholas and my Lord Molyneux or the village blacksmith, when it was settled all, including Mr. Plumbe and his clerk, went to an inn and there drank together.

"March 1st. Two came from Ditton to discourse me about my timber at Ditton.

March 4th. I went after dinner to Liverpool and sold 156 Oak Trees at Ditton to Robert Letherland, Robert Barrow and James Gregory for £46 10s.

May 27th. I went to Wigan and there discoursed with Sir Roger Bradshaw[1] concerning £100 owing by him to Mr Christopher Bradshaw."[2]

News was received and disseminated by movement among the neighbours.

"Aug. 13th. Mr Howett[3] dined here, he brought news of a great victory got by Lord Marlborough and of three generals taken. I went with my wife to meet Coz. Scarisbrick, Mrs. Hesketh of Rufford[4] etc. at Lathom Spaw. We dansed with young Mr Hesket of Aughton,[5] Mrs Entwistley,[6] Mis Ann Bold[7] etc."

The waters of Lathom Spaw were much esteemed as health-giving in the seventeenth century. William Blundell the Cavalier wrote that he had greatly benefited by them, but in his grandson's time Wigan was more favoured as a health resort,

[1] Sir Roger Bradshaigh of Haigh was a descendant of Roger Bradshaigh whose sister Jane married Nicholas Blundell, great grandfather of the Diarist. The manor and estates of Haigh descended through the female line to the Earls of Crawford and Balcarres.

[2] Christopher Bradshaigh was brother of Sir Roger, the first baronet.

[3] Thomas Howet Esq. of Ormskirk.

[4] Wife of Thomas Hesketh Esq., of Rufford Hall, Ormskirk, who was ancestor of the present Lord Hesketh of Easton Neston, Towcester.

[5] Alexander, son of Richard Hesketh.

[6] Probably widow of John Entwistle of Ormskirk, J.P.

[7] Sister of Richard Bold of Bold, Esq. Her will, in which she is described as of Ormskirk, was proved in January. 1706.

although it may be the last town in Lancashire to be thought of in such a connection today.

Two days after taking part in the gathering at Lathom, Nicholas and Frances set out on quite a different expedition, namely a pilgrimage to Holywell in Flintshire—the Holy Well of St. Winefride. This shrine[1] has been the resort of pilgrims in an unbroken stream since the seventh century. Nicholas constantly records visits made there not only by himself and his wife, but by his servants and workfolk.

On this occasion Mrs Blundell's maid, Mary St. Legar, accompanied her mistress; she would be mounted behind Thomas Howard, while Mrs. Blundell rode on a pillion behind her husband, and Henry Bilsborough no doubt brought up the rear leading a pack-horse.

They dined at Liverpool, then crossed the Mersey by ferry at Runcorn, and rode on to Chester where they stayed the night at the Golden Lion. They met friends there and entertained them in the evening at their hostelry. The next day they rode by twenty miles of green lanes, through marshy land, to Holywell and put up at the Cross Keys. The third day of the pilgrimage was occupied by devotions at the Well and bathing in its waters. On the fourth day they began their homeward journey.

Sometimes pilgrims from Crosby took the more direct route over Wirral, making the perilous crossing of the Dee Sands with a guide when the tide was out. Shortly before his wife's confinement Nicholas did so in company with his cousin Thomas Gillibrand.

" Spent at Holywell staying two nights,
        myself, man, and two horses   ...   ...   18s. 7d.

But he could not resist the détour by Chester on the homeward way.

" Coming home from Holl. through Ches." he adds 3s. 7d.

Six weeks after Nicholas had brought his bride to Crosby he wrote :

" My Wife took ye Charge of house-keeping upon her."

His great aunt and his mother, who had severally kept house

1 See *Trans. Hist. Soc. Lanc. and Ches.*, Vol. 99.

for long years at Crosby, may have been critical of the young wife's methods, and she may have kept too strict a hand upon the domestic staff than they had been wont to do. The Diary offers no certain information on these points, but it reveals by implication complete disagreement between the older ladies in the house and its new mistress. Her own maid Mary St. Legar was the first of many to give warning, but she did not actually depart for another six months. Meanwhile she was most obliging, even when afflicted with toothache.

"Oct. 28th. St. Legar let me blood. St. Legar and Marg. Winstanley went to get their teeth drawn. I walked with my wife to the seaside."

As the story of her life unfolds, Frances is found constantly at loggerheads with her maids and the succession of housekeepers engaged by her husband when he found her to be unpractical.

Every now and then Nicholas bestowed a pound, or perhaps even a guinea, upon his wife, and he paid for everything she needed, but she had no fixed allowance until they had been married for fifteen years. She must have been handed over to him with a well-stocked wardrobe as he did not contribute anything towards it for several months, during which time the sole item of expense he incurred directly on her account was fourpence for patches. But by January, 1704, the record of small sums " given my Wife " becomes less frequent while the lists of articles bought " for my Wife " lengthens as the months go by :

	s.	d.
Thus " Shoes for my Wife 5 pare	13	9
Gloves for my Wife	1	2
Cotten, Needles, Ferret etc for my wife	4	8
In part for my Wives Boddis	10	0 "

This was when the first child was expected and the bodice had to be let out.

The penal law of William III only allowed a recusant to have a life interest in his estate. If he had no heir his home and property would pass to the Crown on his death. It must then have been with especial satisfaction that Nicholas wrote in his diary on January 23rd, 1704:

" My wife sent for Doctor Fabius,[1] he said she was with child."

Frances was evidently fretful and hard to please for one servant after another gave notice to leave, and soon her mother-in-law and Mistress Frances were affected by the general unrest.

" April 12th. 1704. Mary St. Legar went hence to Liverpool. She said she would not return to Crosby.
April 13th. My Mother declared to my Wife she would not stay here.
April 14th. My Mother was busy packing up.
April 15th. My Mother and her maid bade adue to Crosby. They went to lodge at Ince. I went with them in the charriot.
April 16th. My Aunt went to lodge at Ince. My Wife went to Leverpoole to fetch Mary St. Legar back but without Suckcess.
April 17th. I went with my Wife to Ince to see my Mother."

This last entry suggests that Nicholas had persuaded his wife to patch up her differences with his mother. Squabbles between their respective maids seem to have had something to do with the family disagreement.

" Mary Winstanley brought word my Mother expected Mary Barton would be turned away ere she would come."

Young Mrs. Blundell however would not part with Mary Barton whom she had engaged as "under-maid." Nicholas seems to have placated the elder lady by assuring her that the girl should be dismissed as soon as he could act without fear of upsetting the expectant mother, a promise which he subsequently

---

[1] Doctor Fabius, an apothecary, is chiefly noted in the records of Liverpool as a Baptist who gathered a small congregation in his own house at Everton in 1700. His real name was Bean, but he was known by the latin word for that vegetable. When he died in 1718 he was buried in a graveyard in Everton Road provided by his family for Baptists. Thomas H. Bickerton, *Medical History of Liverpool*, 1936. Picton, Vol. II.

kept and upon which Mrs. Blundell senior consented to return to his home.

"April 22nd. I fetched my Mother back to Crosby in my Coach from Ince."

In the very rare entries in his Diary which record, or to be more accurate, imply disagreement between Nicholas and his wife, he alludes to Frances as " she," instead of beginning with the usual " My Wife and I." Thus when the poor woman, half through her pregnancy, was evidently maddened by toothache, he states succintly :

"July 18th. She gladly would have rode to Leverpoole to get her Tooth drawn but I prevented her."

Evidently no riding was to be allowed until the important child was safely brought into the world. Only on November 3rd, is it stated :

" Mr Gildus came to draw a Tooth for my Wife." And on the 6th of the same month : " I sent Rich Cartwright for Mr Gildus to draw a second Tooth for my Wife but he would not come."

Was Frances critical of Mr. Gildus's methods, or did her husband hint that the charge of 1s. for the job was too high? The Diary does not enlarge upon the matter. On another occasion the day's entry consists solely of the following lines :

" She quarreled with me about her not taking Phisick and my not coming to see and Pity her."

But Nicholas was not an inconsiderate husband. When his wife was not well we find him writing a letter for her on the feminine matter of clothes. For young Mrs. Blundell continued to procure her finery from London as she had done when she lived in Oxfordshire, an extravagance which we may suspect was roundly condemned by Great Aunt Frances.

The lady to whom the letter is directed seems to have been the housekeeper left in charge of the second Lord Langdale's town house. Well-born women often undertook such posts.

" To Mrs Berry at the Hous of ye late Lord Langdale in King Street near St. James's Park London. January the 13th, 1704 :

" My wife has Received her Mantew and Pettycoat, tis much

to her liking, especially considering the Price, but tis too straight in the Shoulders and she could have wished it had not been so grave a Colour. I have sent the Paper to Mrs Houghton[1] as desired and by the Receipt here enclosed you may see I have paid the £3 According to Order, yet one Exception I have against your bill which is that you have not set anything down for Portage of letters or Porteridge, but this is a fault may for once be pardoned but for the Future please do put down all your Expenses, tis enough that you have the Troble for which my wife returnes you Hearty Thanks, she is now above halfe gone with Chylde, and is yet extremely sick, otherwise she would have writ Herself to wish you much joy

Your humble servant

Nicholas Blundell."

On July 7th Nicholas confided to his diary :

" I opened a box of Babby Cloths which was sent to my Wife by my Lady Webb."

Some trouble in the air over this matter is reflected in the next letter written by the husband for the wife three weeks later. It was addressed to Mrs. Bloare who seems to have been companion to Lady Webb :

" Fryday's Post brought dear Mrs Bloore's Letter. I am Sorry to find by it ye good Lady Webb should think my Wife would be so ungrateful as not to owne with Gratitude so Noble a Present which I am sure she did and to the Best of my Remembrance it was upon ye 14th., and sooner she could not, being ye Box was directed to Crosby near Wigan which made it be longer 'ere it came to Hand and consequently longer 'ere my Wife could owne the Receipt or give her Ladyship her Hearty Thanks which to have forgot would have been a Peece of Ingratitude never to be Pardened."

Nicholas had meanwhile accomplished some intimate shopping at Chester himself. He bought a cradle for 15s. and " set it up in ye Store House "; other purchases at the same time were :

---

[1] Probably the wife of Richard Houghton, a prominent Liverpool merchant and a friend of the Diarist.

	s.	d.
" A quilt	5	0
" A Chylde's Linnen Basket	2	6
" Muslin and Holland for Babby Clothes £1 14	11½	
" Flannel, 7 yds at 1s. 10d.	12	0 "

It was easier to smooth over the little misunderstanding with
Lady Webb than to adjust the disagreements between the
womenfolk at home. At a moment when peace obviously did
not reign in his home, Nicholas writes without comment:

" Coz. John Gillibrand[1] read to me ye Play called The Taming
of the Shrew."

A few days before the birth of the longed-for child, Great-
Aunt Frances went off to live with another great nephew,
Colonel Edmund Butler at Ormskirk. Edmund Butler and his
younger brother Richard had been brought up at Crosby[2] under
the especial care of Mistress Frances until they were old enough
to be sent to school at St. Omer. Edmund retained the strongest
affection for her; although he was now married and had children
of his own, he received her and provided a home for her until
her death several years later.

Mrs. Aspinwall, the midwife, was installed at Crosby in good
time. Indeed there had previously been a false alarm and Mrs.
Fletcher, another midwife, had been sent for in haste, but her
services having proved unnecessary she was paid 5s. and dismissed again.

On September 20th Nicholas writes:

" My Wife began to feel ye Paines of Labor," adding
undramatically: " I brake Flax."

The baby was not born for another two days but its father
was not concerned about the delay. He spent the intervening
day " discoursing " his tenants about watercourses.

" Sept. 22nd. My Wife was delivered of her first Chylde called
Mary."

[1] Cousin and great friend of the Diarist. He purchased a moiety of
the Manor of Chorley and lived at Astley Hall. *Victoria History.*
[2] *Cavalier.*

The arrival of a daughter was doubtless a disappointment, but the parents may have consoled themselves with the reflection that it was usual to have a great many daughters in the family. Some pleasurable excitement is allowed to glimmer in the Diary of the next few days, and the Disbursement Book reveals considerable outlay in an unusual quantity of food that week.

"Sept. 23rd. I sent Rich. Cartwright to Ormskirk to acquaint them of the Berth of my Doughter and to invite to the Christoning.

Sept. 24th. We prayed on ye Stayres. I sent to Croxteth[1] and many Letters to ye Post."

Prayers seem to have been offered " on the stairs " when the congregation was too large to be accommodated in the private oratory. Presumably the priest officiated on the landing, and the worshippers gathered on the stairs and in the hall below. No doubt a number of tenants and villagers joined on this occasion in giving thanks for the birth of the Squire's first child, for the Diary amply illustrates how intimately neighbours of all degree shared their joys and sorrows in that friendly countryside.

"Sept. 28th. My eldest Chylde was christoned Mary, Coz. Scarisbrick Godfather, Sister Middleton[2] Godmother. I first acquainted my wife with my Intention to part with Mary Barton."

Next "many Crosby Wives came to see my Wife," writes Nicholas. It was a festive time but not an untroubled one. For the elder Mrs. Blundell was determined to leave Crosby, in spite of her son's promptness in dismissing the mischief-maker.

Mary Barton was given three months notice and in due course the Squire bestirred himself to obtain another place for her.

---

[1] The seat of William, fourth Viscount Molyneux. The eighth Viscount was created first Earl of Sefton in 1771.

[2] Mrs. Blundell's sister, wife of Peter Middleton of Stockeld, Yorks.

"To Mr Oldfield,[1] at Sumnerford near Brugnall Green, Cheshire by ye Warrington Bag

Dec. 10th. 1704.

"Honoured Sir

Thô I have not the Honour to be Acquainted with you, yet I Presume to send these few Lines being your Stuard told me you were in want of a Chamber Maid. I am now Parting with mine. She is a Catholic and a brisk mettled Workwoman, gets up Linnen both fine and corse very well, rubs well and is a neat Cleanly Lass. I shall be glad to have your Speedy answer whether you will have her or noe, as if you will, pleas to let Her know what her Work must be and what Waiges. I think she will expect something above 40s. If I can be Provided at Christmass she will then be at liberty.

Sir
Your most obedient Servant
Nicholas Blundell."

Mary Barton's wages at Crosby were 7s. 6d. per quarter. She and Mr. Oldfield probably came to terms for she left Crosby on January 5th, 1705, but long before her departure Mrs. Blundell senior had resolutely turned her back upon the home of her married life.

"Oct. 18th. My Mother bade Adue to Crosby and went to table at Ormskirk with Colonel Butler. Lord Langdale and I went with her."

It looks as though Lord Langdale too had tried in vain to pour oil on the troubled waters; evidently Mrs. Butler was easier to get on with than his daughter.

Mrs. Aspinwall departed after having cared for her patient for eighteen days. She received seven guineas, a high fee considering general values at the time, but skill was recognised and paid for. "She delivered my Wife," writes Nicholas; there was no commotion, no sending for the doctor when the confinement was prolonged. Mrs. Aspinwall knew her job as far as it was understood in her day, and she accomplished it.

The baby was placed with a wet nurse when a month old.

[1] George Oldfield of Somerford.

The Diary records that " Mally was wained" and her first tooth appeared when she was not quite ten months old. She was sent off at that early age to Doctor Fabius to be treated for some infantile indisposition. After a few days in his care she was next confided to Ellen Harrison, the wife of a tenant, to be "dry-nursed" for three months. Thereafter she was installed in her own nursery at Crosby to be the joy of her father's heart, despite the fact that she was his heiress-presumptive instead of an heir.

II

Nicholas and his wife had hitherto occupied a bedroom called "Ye Garden Chamber." One John Mawdesley made a cupboard in it to Mrs. Blundell's[1] requirements, and Aldridge, a joiner, had set up "a blew bed" in it to order. This however proved "not at all to content," and the joiner's wife was called into consultation as one who could understand a lady's taste.

"Mrs. Aldridge came after Dinner and brought a Joyner with her to mend the Falts in my new Bed. She supped here. I sent a Man and Hors with her to Leverpoole."

But the apartment was still not to Mrs. Blundell's liking and, very soon after his mother's departure, Nicholas states with finality :

"My Wife and I removed our Lodging into my Mother's Chamber."

Peace now reigned. Various maids indeed "left their service," but they were immediately replaced by others, almost invariably drawn from the tenants' families.

Nicholas was continually accomplishing little tasks to please his wife.

"I fited up a Tent for my Wife to work a Pettycoat in as I think . . . I hunted for Sope and found a great Deale . . . I set up the China upon my Wife's Chest of Drawers . . . I carried her Dutch table to Gray[2] and got it Mended."

[1] The Diarist's wife will henceforth be designated Mrs. Blundell.

[1] William Gray is mentioned among leaseholders of Little Crosby in Catholic Non-Jurors.

In August, 1705, there occurs one of those entries in the Diary which mark a difference of opinion between the couple :

" She first proposed seting¹ of the Hous and going to live in Ireland."

Mrs. Blundell may have thought that, as living was cheaper in Ireland, she might hope for more money to spend on clothes and amusements if she could persuade her husband to take her there. The idea is never alluded to again. From the Diarist's own unconscious portrait of himself in his candid pages it may surely be concluded that the suggestion was rebuffed very firmly indeed. The Squire's home county was his world; his interests and duties in life were centred in his estates and all his neighbours, rich and poor; how could he have been expected to transplant himself to Ireland? It can hardly be supposed that his wife really hoped to win her cause, but she must have tried hard since Nicholas specified that she *first* made the suggestion on the occasion in question. Perhaps it was as a measure of compensation that he consented to plan a journey into Yorkshire and a series of visits to her relations in that county during the following summer.

Meanwhile his mother's proceedings continued to cause some perturbation in the family.

" Sept. 22nd, 1705. My Mother told me of her desyre to take a Long journey."

Not even to his own journal could he confide the fact that Mrs. Blundell senior proposed to visit her daughters in their convent schools in Flanders. He had nothing to fear from his own neighbours who must have known that the girls were being educated " beyond ye seas " as their phrase went, in defiance of the law. But no recusant was safe from the designs of a profit-seeking informer or from unexpected search of his house and papers. Lord Mountgarret, still an outlaw, was staying at Crosby and had recently received a warning letter from Mistress Frances at Ormskirk " advising him to keep in private."

Nicholas tried to persuade his mother to pay a long visit to Crosby during the following spring before she left the country.

¹ Seting, i.e. letting.

She sent him her silver salver by his messenger, together with an intimation that she would come, but he had to seek her out himself before she would finally make up her mind.

" April 14th, 1706. My Wife went upon Hors back to Scarisbrick. She dined there. I dined at Colonel Butler's and invited my Mother to Come soon to lodg here.

April 15th. I fetched Home a Cartload of my Things from my Mother.

April 17th. I fetched My Mother in my Coach from Ormskirk (when she came quit away from thence) to stay here some time."

The " some time " resolved itself into less than a week, during which all the ladies of the surrounding Manors called to bid the widow farewell.

" April 21st. My Mother bid adue to Crosby. Most of the Neighbours " (the Diarist always designated the villagers thus) " came to take Leave of Her. I went in my Coach to Warrington with my Mother. My Wife came with us. She rid part of the way. We lodged at Warrington."

After this parting all was preparation for the journey to Yorkshire in spite of the fact that Mrs. Blundell was expecting the arrival of her second child in less than three months. It does not appear to have occurred to either parent that the journey should be postponed on that account, great as was the father's longing for an heir. During his own boyhood and youth his mother had always either been expecting a birth or occupied with the care of an infant. Such was the normal condition of a young married woman and alteration of plans on her account was out of the question.

Orders were now sent to London for broadcloth, buttons great and small, " shammy " for pockets, silk for lining, all these for the Squire's new suit. For his wife came muslin, ribbons and wiring for heads, silver trimming " a gause hankarchaff and a fann "; her two best mantuas and petticoats were considered good enough after they had been dyed at the modest price (in comparison to that of new clothes) of 26s., and re-made. Walter Thelwall's new coat cost more than his quarter's wages, while Henry Sumner, who had been promoted in status from that of ploughman to "coachman etc." was to be resplendent in a new livery with livery stockings and a silver-trimmed hat.

"May 27th. Nick Johnson came to make Henry Sumner's Livery.

May 29th. My Wife's Cloaths and Mine came Home from London.

June 4th. Jane Harrison and I were very busy most of the Afternoone packing up for our Yorkshire Journey.

June 5th. I weighed my Luggage, or most of it that I desygned to take with us into Yorkshire."

On June 6th, having confided their small daughter to the care of their friends and neighbours the Wolfalls of Moor Hall, they set off in their coach-and-six, with one maid and three men servants.

"June 6th. My wife and I began our Journey into Yorkshire. We called at Colonel Butler's in Ormskirk. We made a small Stay at the Anchor in Eccleston. I left the Coach and rid to Rushton[1] Moor where I found Coz. Thomas Gillibrand.[2] We lodged at the Blew Bell in Walley.

June 7th. From Walley we went to Gisbourne thence to the Lamb at Skipton where we lodged.

June 8th. From Skipton we went towards Blober House[3] and were overturned a little short of Hazelwood,[4] where we were assisted as I take it by one Mr. Knip, thence we came to Harrogate and so to Stockeld."

The mishap described was of such ordinary occurrence owing to the state of the roads, that the Diarist probably considered the party lucky not to have suffered the like repeatedly. He makes no comment on his wife's reaction to it, nor the fact that it might have threatened the safety of the hoped-for heir.

"June 9th. My Brother Middleton shewed me his Fishponde and my Sister shewed me outhousing.

[1] Rishton.
[2] Son of John Gillibrand and his wife Alice Westby.
[3] Blubberhouses.
[4] The seat of Sir Walter Vavasour, cousin to Mrs. Blundell.

June 11th. My wife and I went with my Sister in her Coach to Ribston, Sir Henry Goodricks[1] Fine Hous. Mr Witham, formerly of ye Bass suped at Stockild.

June 13th. My Brother and Sister took my Wife and me in their Coach to Haslewood Sir Walter Vavasours, where we dined with Sir Walter and his Lady.

June 14th. Coz. Michael Ann,[2] his Wife, Mr Marmaduke Ann and Mrs Carlton dined at Stockhild.

June 17th. My Sister Middleton took my Wife and me in her Coach to Bramman,[1] Cozen Michael Anns, where we dined with Sir Walter Vavasour, his Lady, two Mr Chorltons etc. . . .[4]

June 18th. My Brother Middleton took Coz Mick Ann and me in his coach to see the Dropping Well at Knaresborough. Thence we went to Harrogate where I tasted both the sweet and Stinking spaw waters. I saw there Morrison the Rhyming Musition. He played very well."

Morrison had been stone blind from his youth but his boyhood's exploits in climbing fruit trees and walls, poaching and stealing in spite of his handicap, had made him a far-famed character. Now at the age of seventy-six he had long pursued his tranquil calling of fiddling to the many visitors to Knaresborough's petrifying well. He lived to be 102.[3]

The travellers went on to Holme, Lord Langdale's country seat, on June 19th, after bestowing "vales" on the staff at Stockeld to the value of £1. 13s. 6d. The entertainment provided by Lord Langdale seems to have been adapted mainly to the tastes of male guests. There was a bowling-match at which Nicholas lost 4s. 6d., a buck hunt, and dinner-parties both at

[1] Sir Henry Goodricke, seventh baronet, in 1833 bequeathed the Ribston estates to Sir Francis Holyoake, first baronet, of Morton Bagot, Warwickshire, who assumed the surname Holyoake-Goodricke.

[2] Michael Ann of Frickley and Burgwallis was married to Jane, daughter of Marmaduke, second Lord Langdale.

[3] Bramham.

[4] Probably William and Edward, sons of Edward Charlton of Hesleyside, Northumberland.

[5] Baring Gould. *Yorkshire Oddities.*

Holme and in the neighbourhood for men only, probably because they were followed by drinking-bouts which could be more freely indulged in without the presence of the ladies. When three neighbours called upon Lord Langdale, Nicholas writes :

"We drank hard in the Summer Hous."

The coach with its occupants next rumbled on to the city of York and put up at the Black Swan. The following day was devoted to shopping.

	s.	d.
"A Hat	10	6
Toyes for my Sister Middleton's Children	3	0
Ezop's Fables for my Niece Middleton ...	3	6
Sizars for my Wife...	1	0
Some small Things for my Wives Apparrall as Lases, Head Wyers, etc.	11	6
York Gingerbread	3	0
Part of a Sute of Babby Cloaths ... £1	6	0 "

The coach was left at York and only Mrs. Blundell's maid, Mary Winstanley, and one mounted servant accompanied their master and mistress on their next journey. They went by stage coach from York to Durham, lodging one night at Darlington on the way. The return fares for three places in the coach amounted to £6, while meals and tips on the road cost £1. 11s. 3½d., making this section of their travels expensive compared with the outlay when using their own coach.

At Durham they were the guests of the Diarist's "Uncle and Aunt Gerard"[1] who entertained them for a week. One evening was especially hilarious.

"We dansed at Mr Wood his School and afterwards we drank together and went with our Musick about ye Streets."

Can Mrs. Blundell have been a member of such an indecorous party?

In more sober humour they saw the sights of Durham.

[1] Mrs. Gerard was Bridget, youngest daughter of the Cavalier. Her husband, a member of the family of Gerard of Garswood, was a doctor.

"My Uncle and Aunt Gerard went with my Wife and me to see ye Castle. We walked in ye Cathedral and heard them sing. We saw a Puppy[1] Play."

On the return journey "there was myself and five Women in ye Coach," states Nicholas.

They again stayed two nights at Holme but on this occasion the Diarist has nothing more exciting to report than that he took part in a great bowling match, and "gathered gooseberries in ye garden with Mrs Errington."[2]

The next visit was to the Anns of Burgwallis with whom they stayed for a fortnight; here the usual neighbourly entertaining took place in their honour.

"July 29th. My wife and I began our journey homeward from Burgwallis. We came through Wakefield and baited at the Red Lion in Yelland,[3] a very good inn. Thence we came over Blackstone Edge to Rochdale where we lodged at the George.

July 30th. At Wigan I discoursed Mr Graddall concerning the Commissioners who were sitting upon the estate of Mr Dicconson of Wrightington."

William Dicconson, the owner of Wrightington, was governor to James II's son at the court of St. Germain and was treasurer to his queen. He had been outlawed and his confiscated estates were granted to the bishop of London.[4]. Part of his property was however settled upon his younger brother Roger, who remained in the family home. During this year (1706) the attempted invasion of Scotland by French forces in support of the Stuarts caused intense excitement in the country, and the estates of many known Jacobites were seized by the government. Roger Dicconson successfully resisted the confiscation of his property at this time.

"July 30th. We came from Wiggane.

July 31st. I put part of my Cloathes and other Things in their

[1] Puppet.
[2] Several branches of the Errington family are mentioned in *Non-Jurors*.
[3] Elland.
[4] Gillow, Vol. II.

D

proper Plaices again after my return home. I led home some Turfs with Boone Carts."

Thus Nicholas applied himself forthwith to his usual avocations after his excursion into "ye World." He was harassed by financial difficulties which he could only hope to overcome through successful farming and sound estate management. His disappointment must have been great when a second daughter was born to him.

"Sept. 24th. My Wife felt ye Paines of Labour coming upon her. Captain Robert Fazackerley[1] and I went a-coursing. . . Being it rained we went into John Oughtons. I discoursed him about a Chees which he had found on ye Marsh.

Sept. 25th. My Doughter Frances was born between three and four of ye Clock in ye Afternoone. Captain Fazackerley went hence.

Sept. 29th. My Doughter Frances was christoned. Collonel Butler stood Godfather for my Brother Langdale and Mrs Mills stood for my Lady Gerard.

Oct. 25th. Fanny was taken hence to nurs."

---

[1] The Fazackerley family owned country estates in Fazackerley, Walton and Spellow, all now incorporated into Liverpool. By the will of Robert Fazackerley, dated 1730, the properties passed through the female line to John Hawarden of Liverpool and eventually to Henry Gillibrand of Chorley who took the name Hawarden-Fazackerley. His daughter and heiress married Jocelyn Tate Westby of Mowbreck. She and her husband dropped the name Hawarden and became Fazackerley-Westby. *Victoria History.*

Chapter III

FAMILY AFFAIRS

I

1702-1705

DURING the first few years of his life as head of the family Nicholas had much ado to satisfy the claims of his younger brothers and sisters under their father's will, to pay his father's debts and to provide the annuities due to his aunts. In one of his letters to his brother Richard he candidly announces:

" Although I received £1000 with my Wife, that and a great deal more is already gon in paying off som of my Debts."

It was highly convenient to him when his youngest brother Joseph and his two youngest sisters Winifride and Frances all developed vocations to the religious life. His three older sisters were already nuns in Flanders.

Of Joseph he wrote: " My brother Joseph is gon up ye Hill," by which his correspondent understood that Joseph, having completed his studies at St. Omer, had entered the Jesuit seminary at Watten, situated on a hill two miles from the college.

It is difficult to assess the relative value of money between the Diarist's day and our own. The high cost of clothes indicates the scanty purchasing power of the " poursions" which William Blundell had been able to provide for his daughters. In 1710 Nicholas paid 28s. for silk " for a mantew for Mally" aged six, while the annual wages of his housemaid were £2. Home grown food was cheap, groceries were very dear. Coffee cost from 6s. to 6s. 8d. and sugar 4½d. per lb. when the price of a cow was only £3.

Perhaps the salaries of the professional classes afford the most consistent reflection of the gradual rise in the cost of living.

As an instance the stipend of the headmaster of the Liverpool Free School may be cited. In 1704 it was £40. 13s. 6d. per annum, out of which sum, he had to provide £10 for the school usher. In 1759 the annual salary for the same post was £105.

Nicholas had promised his mother that he would make up his sisters' dowries to £200 if their share of the £1200, left by their father for his younger children, did not amount to so much (including the accrued interest) by the time they were grown up.

"This much both you and I know," he wrote to his mother after she had left Crosby for Flanders, where Winifride and Frances were still at school, "that £200 will not marry either of them to so much as one of Mr Houghton's Prentises. But . . . as to their coming into ye World, I can assure you they will be as wellcome both to my Wife and me as these hard Tymes and our sercumstances will permit, thô I am of Opinion that their Education at Saumur has given them a better Idea of ye World than it deserves."

As the elder brother dutifully penned this somewhat chilly invitation to his sisters to make their home at Crosby if they wished, he must have hoped devoutly (in every sense of the word) that the girls would not accept it, in view of his wife's somewhat quarrelsome disposition. Winifride was irresolute for many months, and he reiterated his invitation in a later letter to his mother, adding: "My Wife, for a further Assurance of her hearty Wellcom, intends herself to write to you."

Eventually the mother and both daughters entered convents, while Joseph duly became a Jesuit and returned to England to labour among the Catholics at first in Yorkshire and subsequently in Derbyshire. Nicholas paid away the whole of his wife's fortune in settling his family affairs and his debts, but it did not stretch to the full amount required to cover all his liabilities.

"Though I have received my Wives whole Poursion, viz £2000 and also Interest for it to wit £50," he wrote later to his mother, "yet upon my word I owe above £400, so judge whether I am in so good Sercumstances as to Send all you have writ for with as much Expedition as you could wish. However dear

Mother I assure you nothing shall be Wanting on my syde as far as I am able, to make both Yourself and my Sisters easy, and when I can get more Money I promis you faithfully to return it with all expedition."

His mother and the Superiors of the various convents in France and Flanders where his relatives pursued their religious calling, wrote with great insistence for the money due to them. Nicholas conscientiously paid all to the last farthing, knowing the hardships under which these exiled Communities kept together. They were forbidden by ecclesiastical authority to ask for alms in the foreign towns which gave them shelter, while their co-religionists at home had much difficulty in transmitting money to them.

In a letter to Mr. Cole, who acted for the English Poor Clares at Rouen, Nicholas complains that money is hard to get in the country " thô there is no sign of want of it in ye Town," (meaning London). Tenants, he explained, were unable to sell their cattle, consequently they could not be " straned" for rent. "Nothing sells in the Country" he writes. It is difficult for us to visualise our country as an exporter of surplus grain, but such she then was, in times of peace. At this date however her commerce with the outside world was dislocated by the war with France, and a glut of cattle and corn had accumulated in the purely agricultural district of south-west Lancashire where inland communications were hampered by lack of bridges over the Mersey.

The difficulty of transmitting money was also great in the days before cheque books, and banking accounts. Matters were often arranged at the cattle fairs. This was possibly the case with regard to the bill for £14 " of which," wrote Nicholas to Mr. Cole, " £12 is for one year's annuity for my Aunt Margaret Blundell[1] and the remaining 40s. you may be pleased to keep until further orders." The fact that it was sent from Kendal by a man who could not sign his name, suggests that a farmer or cattle dealer had been charged by Nicholas with the money.

[1] Daughter of William Blundell the Cavalier. She was a Poor Clare nun at Rouen.

"Kendal.Aug.28th.1705

"Sir,

Twenty-eight days after the date hereof pray pay to Henry Wilson or order £14, ye like value received here, and place it to account as per advice from

His Mark

Joseph   IF   Fisher

To Mr Thomas Woolhead at the Bank of England London
Pay contents to Mr Richard Houghton or order its mine

Henry Wilson

Pay contents to Nicholas Blundell Esq. or order for value received

Richard Houghton

Pay contents unto Mr Jo. Cole or order Its mine.

Nicholas Blundell."

Occasionally money received for rents, or from a sale of cattle or timber, was sent up to London in specie, the cost being set down in the Disbursement Book as though the transport of a considerable sum in coin from Lancashire to London by carrier called for no special precautions. Thus:

"Carrying £30 to London by ye carrier 6s. 9d."

When the demands of his relatives abroad were exceptionally pressing Nicholas was sometimes able to borrow or, as he expressed it, to "hier" money at a high rate of interest, to meet the immediate need. He thought his mother was dissatisfied at her daughters' receiving only 5% interest on the money left to them by their father when they finally received their portions.

"You may perhaps say," he wrote, "that severall put money out at 6 per cent. To that I answer that after my father's death I found those who were desirous to let me have money at £5 per cent with which I paid off all the debts that I had at 6 per cent. And you know 5 per cent is the general rate among Catholics and even the Government now only gives 4 per cent and have money brought in plentifully at that Rate."

In the course of this long letter it transpires that the sum of £126 which had been paid into Henry Eyre's hands in London, should have been forwarded to Mrs. Blundell senior a con-

siderable time before she made her plaint to her son. Nicholas
wrote in forthright indignation to his cousin, concluding by
expressing his ruffled feelings over a minor matter :

"I sent you up a Pot of Hairs in February and gave you
Advice once or twice about it. I thought it would be Worth
your Acceptance but as yet you have never mentioned Word of
it eather good or bad. If I had thought you would not have
Accepted so small a Present I could have found Others that
would have taken it in good Part."

When Mrs. Blundell senior had seen her younger daughters
happily settled in their convents, and their dowries paid up,
she herself joined the English Benedictine community at Ghent
where her elder daughter Margaret was Abbess.

"I heartily wish your health may permit you to perform the
task you have taken in hand," wrote her son to her, "being you
have now left ye World I shall not give you the Distraction of
to many Trifles relating to our Neighbours as formerly I did.
However it may not be Unacceptable to you to hear that Cousin
Stanley[1] of Hooton has a Son born, but when myne will come I
know not for my wife is not yet with Chyld."

In letters to his mother the Diarist frequently mentions his
brother Richard who had been apprenticed by their father to
Mr. Houghton, merchant of Liverpool. When the Diary opens
Richard is already established as his employer's "factor" in
Virginia.

Nicholas had taken thought for his younger brother as soon
as he was in a position to benefit him.

"August 28th. 1702. I writ to my Cozen Standley[2] at Preston to
get my brother Rich. made a Member of ye Guild."

At that time membership of the Preston Guild still carried
practical as well as social advantages. These only ceased when
the Municipal Corporation Act of 1835 rendered the Guild

[1] Sir William Stanley of Hooton, third baronet, married Catherine,
daughter of Rowland Eyre of Hassop.
[2] Edward Stanley Esq. of Preston died there in 1755, aged 103. He
was cousin to Thomas Stanley of Bickerstaffe, who was ancestor of the
eleventh Earl of Derby.

obsolete after it had presided over the life of the ancient town for upwards of 600 years.

The career of Merchant Adventurer was one of the few open to recusants, and much favoured by parents for their younger sons, especially when these were allowed to do some business on their own account. William Blundell, and his ever helpful Aunt Frances, had advanced money for the purchase of merchandise which Richard was to sell for his own profit in Virginia.

Nicholas wrote in his Diary on September 19th of the same year : " I received Letters from my brother Richard in Virginia."

Unfortunately these letters, in common with the others received by the Diarist, were not preserved, although he kept meticulous copies of his answers. By these it is plain that Richard had written to ask for merchandise to be consigned to him pesonally, by the same ship which brought his employer's goods.

Nicholas replied without delay.

" To my Brother Richard Blundell in Virginia, sent by the *Elizabeth*. Captain Moone.

I sent my dearest brother a very long letter in June by the *Lamb*, with account of all newes I could pick up for you but now, though I have (as formerly I did) set down many things that happened to acquaint you with, and let you see I am not forgetful of you, yet this I fear will wholy be taken up with business, not having any spare time, especily if Mr. Houghton be as forward as he says, for I received yours the 19th. ultimo, and Mr. Houghton told me he hoped to saile within fourteen days. So that now I am going roundly about to dispatch your affaires with all expedition I can, which truly falls out at a very inconvenient time, I having very much business on may hands, which I do assure you shall be laid aside to serve you. . ."

The Diary reveals the elder brother's exertions on behalf of the younger. On September 22nd indeed he only found time to note that he had " sold codlings at 6d. per cent and other apples at 2s. per Buss " (bushel), but subsequent entries are concerned with his search for suitable merchandise for the colony.

A vast network of roads, railways, canal wharves and warehouses, and building estates now covers the once placid area through which Nicholas passed when he went "roundly about" his brother's business. He rode along the shore to Liverpool, (then an inconsiderable town although on the eve of its great expansion), and on by field and moor to Prescot and thence to his own demesne of Ditton.

Here he stayed for the night with his principal tenant, and, having bestowed sixpence upon the farmer's daughter, he continued on his way the next morning to Warrington. This was an especially busy town owing to its position on the right bank of the Mersey, for it was served by one of the very few bridges which spanned the river. It was also on the main coach road which connected the north-west of England with the rest of the country. Nicholas gave some unspecified orders to one Mr. Harrop, then went again to the small town of Prescot, already famous for its pottery. There "I bought fine Muggs of Mr Cubben," he writes, "thence I came to Leverpoole where I discoursed Mr Houghton, Merchant, and so came Home."

The next day an order was given to the Great Crosby shop-keepers, John Steward and his wife "Ailes" (Alice), who carried on a general trade in goods purchased by them in person at the Chester Fairs.

Finally Nicholas gave his brother an account of all the goods he had been able hastily to gather together.

"If I have not answered expectation in providing this cargoe exactly to your orders, or made any mistake in the accounts of the goods I send, I hope you will ascribe it to the Haste I have been in and not to want of my endeavours ... I send you two Hatts of different Rates, the Prices set out on each Hatt. One thin Wigg the lightest I could find, for now Bobbs are made so extreamely full that it is very hard to light upon a thin one, especially of a light Colour. Being you writ for knives, I send you one with a marble Shaft and also a plush Saddle, and Cravatt with gold Fringe which I suppose you may sell to Advantage, being they look fine and are really good; though I have set them of a price in the list of Particulars, yet sell them as you please, for being you are bound out from trading for others I will not expect any Advantage by my things but make the best of them to your Profitt. Two pair black Stockings, one fine and short, other Rollers and coarser, the price the same. Two muslin Cravatts rowed at the ends as they are now worne. Six payre of Gloves, the best Mr Moorecroft gives you. Liverpool and all Chester fair would not afford such Kaps as you desired, nor could Mr Moorecroft find six fit to send to you, so has only bought you Four. I have sent you I think good Sope. My father has disposed of his Dictinary, so that I have none to spare, nor could I light on a second-hand one either at Warrington or Liverpool, so I have bought you a new one. You will scarce beleeve if I tell you I could not buy a Dozen Pound of Powder at Liverpool, but 'tis true I assure you. Captain Fleetwood has had Great Doing at Marton Meer,[1] which notable Exploits have destroyed a World of Powder and made it very dear. I have procured you 4 lbs. There is none of the largest size of Shott in town. So I have sent 100 of the second Sourt. Three Barrs of Lead weighing 20 lbs.; one Payre large Lether Baggs and Straps. I have sent all the Inke Mr Moss could spare; I know you like his best so would not buy elsewhere; an old Trunk of my own but have set a new lock to it; lace paper and Ribanding is to be bought at Chester Fair by Harrop of Warrington. Knives, Razors, Hones and Tobacco Tongs to be bought at Chester by John Stuard ... If I send any Clocks to you it must be by the next Vessel for now I have not time to procure them before this is bound out. I have agreed for a good Watch but have not yet received it. I have sent you three dozen of strong October[2] in your own Bottles; one Hogshead of Muggs, one Caske of Prescott Ware ... being told they are like to be a good Commodity. Your Merchants are not willing to let you

---

[1] By an Act of Parliament of 1692 Thomas Fleetwood of North Meols had received authority for a period not exceeding three lives and twenty-one years, to carry out the draining of Martin Mere, a great waste of water covering about 3,632 acres in south Lancashire. His use of the gunpowder was no doubt connected with this undertaking which failed. The work was eventually executed by Thomas Eccleston of Scarisbrick in 1781. Matthew Gregson's *Lancashire*.

[2] Ale brewed in that month.

have a Prentice, and as for procuring you a Servant I do assure you I have taken all care imaginable and have done what lies in my power but cannot get a man or boy . . . My Mother has sent you a worked Comb-Case, a Cravatt with one Row of gold through each End, an Apron and Nightrail which she presents you with for your own Traffic. Thanks for the concern you are in about Plants for my use. Whensoever they come they are welcome, but most especially so if you come along with them."

Eighteenth century fops were wont to produce combs from smart cases and comb their flowing wigs in public, hence Mrs. Blundell probably thought that her present to her son would command a price even in the remote colonies.

The Disbursement Book sets forth the cost of some of the wares stowed in the hold of the *Elizabeth* for the voyage in question, or subsequently dispatched at intervals:

	£	s.	d.
"Bristoll Beer 10 Dozen at 5d. per dozen ...	2	10	0
For one Bobb Wigg and dressing up two long Wiggs	1	17	3
For a second hand Silver Watch	3	0	6
One Pad Saddle of Lether with Sterrop and Sterrop Lethers	1	1	6
Ball Sope, 20 Dozen	1	0	0
Castle Sope, 12 Pound		4	6
Gloves at 15s. per Dozen Pare	1	6	4
A Hatt and looping up an Old One ...		8	4
Cours Muslin for two Cravatts		5	0"

When months had passed without bringing any word from Richard, Nicholas wrote to him on January 26th, 1703.

"There is a Ship dear Brother lately come from Maryland But she brings no Letter from you which makes me not a little concerned for Feare of your Death, though still I am willing to hope for ye Best. I think Mr Houghton will pay me for your Tobacco also for your last Years Service which I shall lay out for you when I have your Orders. In the Mean tyme it will be for repaying myself what I have already expended on your Account . . . Mr Houghton says Butter and Chees will be a good

Commodity and so I think to send you som. I perceive by Mr Houghton that you are lykely enought to continew in Virginia, which if you doe I shall be glad to know how Accounts stood betweene my Father and you when you went hence, that I may know what part of your Poursion you have had, and so know what is still remayning, for I promis to pay you all when I am able and in ye mean Tyme I will assist you and hope you will find in me a Father as well as a Brother."

At the present time inhabitants of south-west Lancashire must smile wryly at the notion that their county once exported butter to the New World!

Nicholas personally attended to the packing of some of the goods.

"I was busy all ye Afternoone packing up goods in ye Hall to be sent to my brother Richard in Virgina."

A footnote to the last-quoted letter states that a "List of Parcels went with this Letter."

Nicholas cautiously wrote at the same time to the ship's captain :

"To Captain Brown, Master of the *Loyalty,* Jan. 26th, 1703. ... If my Brother be not living I desyre you will dispose of all his Goods to the best Advantage, as well what you find in Virginia as those you take along with you; unless it be his Books and such like Things which will be of little Worth, and those you may please to bring back at your Returne. Though I have given you the truble of this I hope you will find my brother living, however for feare of ye worst I thought it Prudence to take some sourt of Care though at the same time I am not willing to think he is dead."

The Diary shows us Nicholas sending off the goods to the port and bustling backwards and forwards to Liverpool "discoursing" now Mr. Houghton, now Father Richard Latham, a Jesuit Missionary who was going out to Maryland in the *Loyalty*. Nicholas, knowing what was useful in the American Colonies, helped the priest to equip himself.

The next letter to Virginia is dated September 2nd, 1704.

"To my Brother Richard,

"In answer dear Brother to your two of April ye 24th and June ye 19th (which four Letters came all to Hand about ye middle of last Month), take as followeth: ... I have set two or three hands on work to make your Cloggs, being in Haste to get them redy, so fear they will not be so well suited to different Sizes as if they had been made all by the same hand ... I shall mark each pair A. B. C. etc. and give you Account of ye Price of each pair as they are rated to me; they will be all of old Lether, for to have made them of new they would have been halfe the price of new shoes and have done no more service. As for your giving yourself much Troble to procure Curiosities for me, 'tis what I do not desyre to have done to the Prejudice of your Health or purse, but Lord Molineux doth still desyre that you Procure him a Mock-Bird ... I do not expect what you had for your Newfoundland Voyage would be part of your Poursion, my Father having received great part of ye Product, but as to your Freight to Virginia, I hope you will not be against that being in part of Poursion, you having had the whole Management and profitt of it yourself, and even part of that Virginia Freight was purchased with £20 of my Aunt's money which, since my Father's death, I have already paid her upon your Account by a note under my hand ... I sent you about 200 newspapers, I think it was either by ye *Elizabeth* or ye *Great Elizabeth.* It was a second Parcel of news ... Mr Houghton sent by the *Elizabeth* some Butter but she is taken[1] ... As to your Marriage, none at this distance can tell what to say, unless they knew what the Widdow's Plantations are worth, you are on ye Spott so hope you will consider well on it and be sure of Something considerable before you enter into Matrimony, which if you do before I see you, I wish you with all my Heart the best of Wives and that you may live to your Hearts Content, and though you are ye younger Brother I do not despayre of seeing you live in as great plenty as ye Elder. It was no small affliction to hear your health

[1] By the French. Much correspondence between Thomas Johnson and Richard Norris concerning the voyages of this vessel is included in *The Norris Papers.* She seems to have escaped on the occasion mentioned in this letter, but was captured in 1707 and taken to St. Malo.

continues so bad. I hope when you are out of Mr Houghton's Service and less business upon your Hands, with the Assistance of Crosby air, you will recover your Health perfectly. If not pray assure yourself you shall find Crosby your home and me your loving brother . . . I question not but on your arrival several of our Liverpool merchants will be willing to join in Partnership with you, and none more so than myself if I had wherewith, and probably I shall venture to take up a little Money upon that Account if it will turn to your Advantage and my own. It is extreamely hard to Procure you any Servants . . . If the Overseers could send away their Poore 'twere a good thing if not Abused, but it seems to me unwarrantable, so shall not Propose it."

As time went on the proceedings of the young factor in Virginia caused his mother and elder brother much trouble and anxiety. His employers had dispatched a second cargo to him at his request, but thereafter a deadlock ensued because Richard had sent no accounts. His dilatoriness seems to have had two causes in addition to carelessness on his part: he was in very bad health, and he had married a Mrs. Tawny, described by Nicholas as a rich widow, who had carried him off to her own home at Battle Town in Maryland. Apparently neither of them took much further interest in business, but Richard had again written to ask his brother to send him a servant.

"To my brother Rich. Blundell in Battle Town Potuxon River, Maryland.
Dec. 16th. 1704 I think I gave it to Mulberin's Mate.
. . . Mr Houghton refused to accept your Bill of £55 11s. 3d. because you neyther gave your Accounts to Mr Worthington, nor has stated them to your Merchants, so that they do not know what effects you have in your Hands, what Debts contracted in Virginia and Maryland, or what Cargo you have sent by the *Elizabeth* . . . Till these Things are rectifyed you cannot expect your Bills to be answered by him so that the whole Charge must be upon me to procure money to save your Credit which I am labouring now to get, and am resolved to hire the whole sum for your use, not having £3 of my own towards it. I must ask you

to draw *no more bills* upon me for I assure you I have not the wherewith to answer . . . Dearest brother do not take it amiss at me I pray that I am not able to assist you, for 'tis not for want of good will but of a good Purs answerable to the desire I have to serve you . . . I cannot conceive it possible for me to get you a Prentice with money, though I have some Hopes if you were here, to help you to one, but none will be willing to hyre his son as a Merchant Prentice to me (to assign him over to you) who cannot perform covenants, so think that to be impracticable. As for a Boy to wait on you, there are enough would be willing to send their Chylde along with you that are not willing to send him to you. Besides som (as I think) would be willing to go Along with you as Servants and yet care not to be sent to you. I cannot advise you to come over considering the Charges, so leave it wholly to yourself, you know the business better than I. But till taxes grow less, of which there is not the least sign, or my Circumstances much improved, I do greatly fear I shall be deprived of the power to assist you as I would, or even of joining stock with you."

Nicholas duly "hired" the money to meet the bill which Mr Houghton had refused to honour.

"Jan. 1st. 1705. I payed to Mr Houghton, Merchant, at Liverpool £55 11 3 upon account of a bill drawn by my brother Richard."

But no account-books arrived and the next letter is couched in sterner tone.

"I find Mr Houghton he thinks it convenient you should come to England, and in my Opinion it would be to your Reputation to adjust things verbally rather than in writing."

Meanwhile Nicholas had succeeded in persuading the son of one of his tenants to emigrate as apprentice to Richard, the difficulty of "performing the covenant" having been got over through the good offices of the Mayor of Liverpool.

"Sept. 13th, 1704. I bound John Blundell Apprentice for Virginia before Mr Mair of Liverpool.

Sept. 15th. I went to Leverpool and put John Blundell on

bord ye *Lorrel* for Virginia. I paid £5 to Captain Tarlton for his Passage.

Sept. 16th. I went on Bord ye *Lorrel* with Captain Tarlton to see John Blundell who I was sending to Virginia to my Brother Richard."

John Blundell cannot have arrived in Maryland in time to see the master to whom he was consigned, for Richard died on November 30th, 1704. The news did not reach Crosby for nearly a year, but immediately upon receipt of it Nicholas, greatly concerned both as to his brother's good name and the fate of the poor young apprentice, wrote a long letter to the widow. After expressing his grief at the loss of his brother he continued :

". . . since it hath pleased Almighty God to bless you with a son by him, I hope you will be so kind not to Settle anything from him which ought to be his Right. You are now both Father and Mother to him and if it be your fortune to marry again, I hope you will not be unkind to your Son whose father would have been I am sure most tender and kind to you and yours . . . I should be glad to hear how you like John Blundell. I hope you will be kind to him, my Bargan was that he should not be sold, so hope you will keep him, and in your Next let me hear how he carryeth himself. He is Son to one of my Tennants and he went over purely out of Love to my brother and me . . . I should be glad to hear oft from you and you may frequently expect to hear from one who am Your ever loving Brother."

Among the records of the Corporation of Liverpool there is a *List of Emigrants to America from Liverpool between the Years* 1697-1707. In this it is stated that John Blundell was twenty years of age and was bound to serve for seven years. During the period covered by the indenture, servants could be sold by one master to another. Thus a cruel uncertainty as to their fate shadowed unprotected young folk adventuring into the New World, even when consigned to an employer who was known to them. However, the son of a Lancashire farmer would have been of the type most likely to profit by the grant of fifty acres of land made to each white indentured servant in

Maryland when he had attained his freedom.[1] Meanwhile Mrs. Richard Blundell was probably glad to retain the services of a young Englishman, and there is reason to think that John Blundell lived to found a family in the New World, although no records to that effect exist at Crosby.

The widow failed to send her husband's accounts to his employers, her little son died when a few months old, and Nicholas finally entered the sum of " £83 14s. paid for goods for my brother Richard" in his own Disbursement Book, adding " for particulars see my book of Debts."

The Book of Debts is not among the Diarist's voluminous manuscripts, neither are there any receipts to show to what extent, if any, he profited by his investment of £500 in Mr. Houghton's business. It was a very large sum for a landowner to divert from his land in those days.

---

[1] For an authoritative account of indentured servants in the American Colonies see *Colonists in Bondage*, by Abbot Emerson Smith, The University of North Carolina Press. Thomas Johnson writes to Richard Norris on December 10th, 1706, "I hope the *Elizabeth* sailed in Convoy. God send them a good voyage. They have now about 50 servants on board."

E

CHAPTER IV

DAILY LIFE

1706-1714

I

MRS. BLUNDELL'S first concern upon her return from Yorkshire, was to provide her little daughter, now nearly two years old, with an outfit considered suitable for her age. Material and whalebone were bought for stays for the poor child, stuff for a coat, "flaxon for shifts, callicow for frocks," shoes and stockings; the cost of all, including 2s. 11d. for tailor's work on coat and stays, amounted to £1 10s. 9½d., a stiff sum when compared, for instance, with the steward's wages of 30s. for a quarter of a year, or the charges totalling £1 3s. 11d. for a party of five staying two nights at inns on the journey to Stockeld.

The second little girl's infant career followed the same pattern as her sister's.

Both Diary and Disbursement Book reflect the father's constant preoccupation with his children, especially with the elder. Mally was his companion whenever possible from the age of three. Indeed she was not yet three when he first took her out with him to visit her baby sister at her nurse's house in Great Crosby, one mile from Little Crosby.

" May 14th, 1707. I went to see Fanny and Parson Wairing. I took Mally with me.

May 29th. I went after Dinner to Leverpool with my Wife. We bought materials for a Coat for Mally.

June 14th. My Wife and I came . . . home. We found William Holme ye Taylor making a Coat for Mally.

July 10th. I rid with Mally on Henry Bullen's Cart to ye Turf

Moss, thence she and I went to Bryan Bryonsons,[1] thence to Thomas Blanchards and so home.

July 16th. I sent John Bannister[2] to Mrs Bootle[3] for some Phisick for Mally.

July 21st. Mally was sick.

Aug. 10th. My Wife and I went to Great Crosby to see Fanny, she having now one tooth."

There is nothing in the Diary to suggest that the two little girls were subjected to the harsh discipline which was the usual lot of young folk of their time. On the contrary, Mally and Fanny would surely have recalled blissfully happy nursery days if they had been able to publish their earliest recollections, according to the present fashion among many of our own contemporaries.

Mally was taken by her parents in their coach to dine at the houses of relatives and friends at a very early age, the dinner hour being at about two o'clock. Children learned early to walk far. Mally accompanied her parents on foot to visit their neighbours the Molyneuxes of Alt Grange, three miles from Little Crosby, when she was four years old. She walked the six miles " except some few roods as she was carried."

In nearly every house they visited there were nurseries full of the children or grandchildren of their host and hostess. Mally, having been duly exhibited to members of the older generation, no doubt romped with those of the younger.

While Fanny was with her nurse in Great Crosby, her parents constantly visited her there, sometimes accompanied by the friends who had dined with them. There was great coming and going when the year-old child fell ill.

" I think she is ill of an Ague," wrote her father.

According to him both children suffered from ague, but possibly the rigor preceding an undiagnosed illness may sometimes have been mistaken for the prevalent complaint.

[1] Bryanson and Blanchard were tenant farmers.
[2] The gardener.
[3] "A woman named Mrs. Bootle of Peele, Cheshire, seems to have acquired considerable skill in such matters." *Bickerton's Medical History of Liverpool.*

"My doughter Mally has very often the Ague Fitts," wrote Nicholas again to his mother when the child was three years old, "but otherwais she is a very Healthful lively Chyld, very nimble of her Feet, but extreamely backward on her Tong. Franke comes on bravely."

As soon as the little girls were old enough to enjoy the pastimes of the countryside they were sent to any festivity within reach. Thus in 1711, when they were aged respectively seven and five :

"June 29th. My Children and Mayds went to Formby Fair.
Oct. 14th. My Children went to Great Crosby Goose Feast. They lodged in Great Crosby."

At the Goose Feast all the neighbours entertained each other with special Goose Feast fare which presumably included Michaelmas goose. The Feast however was connected with an ancient club, and not with the actual sale of geese; no doubt all the usual amusements of a fair were provided during the two days of merry-making, and the two children were allowed to lodge in Great Crosby in order that they might witness the fun in the evening.

"Nov. 1st. My children went in ye Coach to Formby Allowtide.
Nov. 12th. My Wife and Children went to Leverpool Fair."

The coach was seldom used in winter owing to the almost impassable state of the roads. Only a very indulgent father would have ordered it out in November to take the nursery party to its entertainment. And what entertainment those country gatherings offered both to children and their elders! If Mally and Fanny did not themselves scamper round and in and out between roaring bonfires, it is safe to conclude that they watched the maids who accompanied them indulge in this frolic, pursued by swains trying to catch and kiss them. They will have urged on the Little Crosby lads to hit hard in a boxing bout, or to fetch down a prize from the top of a greased pole; they will have screamed shrill encouragement to the boys and girls from their own village when couples were competing in a dancing contest of endurance. Morris dancers and mummers will have claimed their attention; and if they did not yet understand the finer points of bull-baiting or cock fighting, they must have watched the fortunes of a Little Crosby dog or of a game-cock whose owner was known to them, with burning interest. As children of their century they will have been unconscious of the cruelty involved in these popular sports.

Then all manner of things were to be bought at the fair booths, including unfamiliar sweetmeats, and fruit not easily come by, such as oranges; meanwhile their elders did much useful shopping.

" Bought at Chester Fayre	s.	d.
" Muslin, Ribbon, Gloves etc.		
for my Wife	11	11½
Shoes, two Pare for Mally	1	8
Iron Skewers for ye Kitchen		10
Powder 6 lbs 1s., Starch half a hundred 9s.	10	0
Corks three groce 4. 6d.		
Sugar Horns 3s. 6d.	5	0
Flower Roots and Whip Cording ...		8
Pack Cloth for ye Goods	1	2 "

Items of sums spent at fairs almost invariably included "Toyes for ye Children," which usually cost 3d. Even one generation ago treasures for small folk could be bought for a penny.

When Mally and Fanny were taken on a visit to their Uncle and Aunt Middleton at Stockeld, their father spent one shilling on toys for them and the generous sum of seven shillings on "toyes for Nephew Middleton."

Upon her return from the round of visits in Yorkshire, Mrs. Blundell seems to have been dissatisfied with the accommodation in her own home and to have demanded a second parlour, possibly because the many ladies who visited her enjoyed " a dish of coffy," while the men of all degree who were continually calling upon her husband liked a great deal of very much stronger drink. Nicholas had engaged workmen to convert the buttery into a dairy, but his wife enlisted outside support for her own plan.

"Aug. 19th. Edward Hawksey, Mason, and Philip Syer his partner, came to prepare the Buttery for a Dary.

Aug. 30th. Mr Wofold came home with me from Moor Hall. Colonel Butler came hither. Their Business was to persuade me to make the Buttery into a Parlour and not the Dary. I intend to follow their Advise."

Divers craftsmen now came to offer their services.

"Rich. Sefton and Jos. Cartwright came to saw joysts for my Parlour. Rich. Robinson ye Joyner came to see what Work I had for him to doe in my Parlour. . . Ned Spencer ye Hous-Wright came to see what Work I had for him in my Parlour. . . Two of Ned Spencers men came to work here, Rich. Robinson ordered ye sawyers what to do. He and Ned Spencer looked over ye Dailes[1] and examined them. We considered all Ways to make ye Parlour to ye best Advantage."

The highest pay of a shilling a day was earned by the head joiner, his underlings receiving eightpence and fivepence accord-ing to the proficiency they had attained. The sawyers who cut up the squire's own trees into planks were paid eightpence, the carpenters who fashioned the planks for use, sixpence per day, masons tenpence and eightpence according to skill, slaters eight-pence, daubers and plasterers sixpence.

Work in the parlour was begun in August, 1706, and was not completely finished until Christmas Eve but directly it was possible to make use of it the family moved in.

"Dec. 11th. We dined in ye Parlor it being ye first time it was used as a Parlor. We had two Fidlers at Night and dansed Country Danses in ye Halle."

The total cost was £58 5s. 6d., this sum including "Dyet and Lodging to Workmen of all Sourts above 600 dayes at 4d. per day."

The next seven years were passed by the family at Crosby in a life of great tranquillity, yet it was very far from being one of stagnation. The next chapter will tell of that neighbourly intercourse throughout the countryside by which a perpetual flow of news and interchange of sympathies and interests was kept up.

While farming and estate management formed the Squire's

---

[1] Flagstones.

main occupation, gardening and forestry were also major interests. Wherever he went he bought, begged, or exchanged cuttings, roots, seeds, and bulbs. He transplanted wild flowers that pleased him into his " garden knot." The nurseryman's profession as we know it was in its earliest infancy, and his wares were proportionately dear. Nicholas gave a shilling each for " tulop" and fourpence each for narcissus bulbs. He sent to Chester and to London, and even to his missionary friend in Maryland for seeds. On one occasion, when he had been ill, he writes :

" Thomas Whithead, Gardiner in Chester, came to see me whilst I was in bed."

It was in December. Probably Thomas Whitehead had not the assistance of glass houses in preparing for his spring work for these were still only within reach of the rich, so he had time in winter to ride far in search of orders. He seems to have secured only a cautiously small order at Crosby for March delivery. In that month Nicholas recorded: " Henry Bushell brought me three Layers of Geliflowers from Thomas Whithead of Chester."

Entries such as the following occur throughout all three volumes of the Diary :

" I took up my Best Tulop Roots. . . I set about 132 Walnuts in Part of my Bed in ye long Garden. . . . I began to make an Asparagus bed. . . . I helped to flatten the raised bed for my Flower Sets. . . . I began to remove some of my Flower Sets in my knot and set them in Earth prepaired for them. I helped to set some Tulop Roots as were dresed with Ink after different manners and some as were ordered otherwayes in hopes to change their colour but to no good effect."

John Bannister, the only gardener regularly employed during the years under review, could not possibly have got through all the work described, had he not been actively assisted as well as supervised by his employer, who pruned and planted, dug and sowed with his own hands.

" We planted an Avenew of Firrs. I helped John Bannister to remove some 24 Cowslops into a more Regular order in ye Knot . . . Lawrence Gilbertson planted some Spanish Ash in the left hand from ye Park Gate to ye Hous. . . . I pricked out severall of my young Firrs that were sowed about this time twelvemonth. I think they were Scotch Firrs. Bannister and I etc. sowed Broom Seeds in ye Sandhills."

Presumably the trees described as Spanish Ashes were in reality Spanish *chestnuts*. Many old trees of that species still flourish on the ground designated in the above quotation. Wild broom grows sparsely in the sandhills along the coast bordering the Little Crosby Estate, but is not found elsewhere in the neighbourhood. Nicholas tried to control the inroads of smothering sea sand by sowing these seeds and thousands of haws and elderberries. Although the erosion which has since done so much damage had not yet begun, sand blown inland by gales, harmed crops then, as now. The planting of starr grass is also mentioned by Nicholas, and was carried on perseveringly by succeeding generations of his descendants.

Landowners were everywhere establishing private plantations to supplement the nation's dwindling supply of timber, and Nicholas was not behindhand in so congenial an undertaking. Young trees being unobtainable in the numbers required, he indefatigably sowed acorns, holly berries, fir seeds, and haws on a large scale, and transplanted young willows and ash saplings into suitable places.

" I sowed Acorns in ye Stock Roots with four Hands. . . .
I planted and layed cutings of Withen[1] in ye Stock Roots. . . .
I planted and layed cutings of Poplars in ye Stock Roots. . . . I sowed Hollin[2] Berries in ye Cow Orchard." These are but a few quotations from scores that could be cited.

The Diarist's great grandson, who established the belt of woodland which now bounds the park at Crosby Hall on all sides, must have found much material to his hand as a result of the long-term planning of his ancestor. His son claimed that every known variety of holly found a place in his park and gardens. Many kinds still abound at Crosby, hollies with crimson, scarlet, yellow and orange berries, hollies with ordinary

[1] Willow.
[2] Holly.

prickles, extra prickles, and without prickles, hollies with the familiar foliage, variegated foliage, and with dark smooth leaves.

The Disbursement Book shows that haws were obtained in enormous numbers at a halfpenny a bushel; while eightpence was paid for the same weight of "heps" or hips. The wild rose briars were used to form protective thickets against wind and sand for more valuable seedling trees.

II

1706-1714

MRS. BLUNDELL does not appear to have taken any special interest in the garden apart from its contributions to her housekeeping, but she was her husband's constant companion when he was not employed in strenuous occupations. Together they made and received visits, went to the theatre[1] in Liverpool and made purchases there of Mr. Hurst the draper, and Mr. Ledbetter the grocer; together they strolled across their land in the evening.

"My wife rid behind me to Ditton ... My Wife and I went to see ye Ditchers in the New Laine and to see Bryanson plant Ashes in ye West Laine. . . . My Wife and I walked to Great Crosby, thence we went to Ned Hattons,[2] and from thence we rid Home. . . . My Wife being out of Order, I sat by her part of ye Afternoone. . . . My Wife writ in ye Pantry, I writ letters in my Closet, Bannister writ in ye Gallery. . . .My Wife went with me to Bryan Bryansons and stayed there till I came back from ye Sand Hills, then we came Home together. . . . My Wife, I and ye Children went out to take ye Aire in ye Coach. . . . I walked with my Wife to ye Hay-Makers in the Cow Hey. . . .

[1] The Cockpit Yard Theatre was situated in a yard behind a house in Moore Street. The street was built at the end of the 17th century. Broadbent, *Annals of the Liverpool Stage.*

[2] A Copyholder of Great Crosby. *Catholic Non-Jurors.*

I showed my Plantations to my Wife. . . . My Wife and I walked after supper to see the Mares and Colts."

Nicholas was an ardent bee-keeper as well as gardener. He knew nothing of the present-day apiarist's scientific methods, but the "hunny" which his bees nevertheless produced in great quantities was of far more importance to household economy than it is today. It was less used in the kitchen than it had formerly been since sugar from the colonies could now be had for 4d. a pound, but it was a principle ingredient in mead which was still a universal drink in Lancashire.

"I helped to cut Apple tree Boughs to set Bee Hives on."

A pleasing picture is evoked of his "mugg hives" perched among the apple trees : "a border of rew was planted in ye Stone Garden opposite to ye Bees." His first straw hive was introduced some years later.

In August (1707) when, according to the old adage, a swarm is worthless, he took one from "the back of ye Garner." There are bees in the back wall of the old barn to this day. It is impossible to reach the honey, but swarms have been captured from the stock occasionally within the past few generations. Nicholas ingenuously hoped to woo the bees from this impregnable fortress.

"I hung a Hive at ye Granary to intice ye Bees into it but it took not effect."

He was only partially successful in preserving his bees through the winter.

"I made a Mixture to feed my Bees, one halfe was Sugar, one quarter Treacley and one quarter ye Scumings of Sweet Meats but it did not keep them all Alive."

The Diarist, unlike his grandfather the Cavalier, is not often to be found reading but "I read a Spirituall Booke in my Closet," is an entry which occurs every now and then. When his great-aunt Frances was a guest at Crosby, he and his wife both read to her "from a Spirituall Booke." Perhaps they found the old lady somewhat captious and difficult to entertain. Once he writes :

"My Wife and I read most of ye Afternoone in the Sun's Trap in ye Garden, and in the Hous."

When he describes himself as unusually "ill of my eyes" he sometimes adds: "My Wife read to me."

On a few occasions he bought books at sales, as after the death of his neighbour Mr. Molyneux[1] of the Grange.

"I dined at the Grange. Was present at ye valewing of Bookes. I bought some."

The titles are unspecified in the Disbursement Book where they are accounted for as

	s.	d.
"Books bought at ye Grange	6	10"

Another item is:

	s.	d.
"Books of Husbandry and Gardening ...	5	8"

Only on one occasion during the years under review does he name a book:

"Aug. 10th. 1708. I finished reading the Tome of ye History of ye Church of Japan."

When "it snewed," or on the very rare occasions on which he was otherwise housebound, he industriously copied the entries in his "Small Diurnall" into his "Great Diurnall," went through his farm accounts with his bailiff, inscribed these and all other items of expenditure in his Disbursement Book, and brought the Tables of his "Great Diurnall" up to date. He found many other occupations too, when inclination or circumstances kept him within doors, for not the smallest matter requiring adjustment in the house escaped his attention.

"I redied my Closet and fixed som pictures etc. in ye Gallery. John Bannister and I layed up som Things in ye Lofts. . . . I meanded a Looking-Glass in ye Nursery. I put up som Pegs in ye Pantry to hang Hatts on and nailed up three Black-and-White Pictures under ye Lintel. . . . I glewed my Wives Wheele, ye Coffy Mill etc. . . . I made up som Necklases for my Wife and Children. . . . I smoaked som Chests upon Account of ye Moth. . . . I dressed the Larrum Pendulum in our Chamber. . . . I put up ye white window Curtins in ye Blew Chamber and

---

[1] His was a junior branch of the widespread Molyneux family.

Chapel. . . . I clensed a good many Needles that were ill-rusted. . . . I dressed ye Parlor Chimney with Flowers. . . . I began to burn Ashes in the Dining Roome, both to aire ye Roome and for the Ashes. . . . I roasted my steeped Wheat to make Coffy but it did not doe well. . . . I mended a great many Bad Pens. . . . I mended a smoothing iron. . . . I placed my Wives Chinea on her Screwtore."[1]

The Squire was in fact what is now described as a "handy man." A more important affair than the minor tasks mentioned, was the making of ale and mead. Coffee costing from 6s. 8d. to 7s. 6d. per pound could only be drunk sparingly, although "Coffy Dishes and Cups" were bought at 6d. a piece and later 3s. were invested in "Six Coffy Potts of Prescott Wair."

The coffee was often ordered from London at the same time as some article of attire for his wife.

"Coffy at 6/8 per lb....	...	...	...	£2	0	0
Carriage of Coffy and Scarf from London					2	3
Box and Porteridge	...	...	...		3	0 "

It must have been with considerable indignation that Nicholas wrote on one occasion: "I picked stones out of about 3 lbs of Coffy as came from London."

The purchase of brandy and "red and whit wine" was made fairly frequently but as these drinks had to be paid for in hard cash they constituted luxuries, while home-brewed ale and mead were consumed in large quantities.

In 1709, 6s. 6d. a gallon was paid for Sack and 3s. 8d. a gallon for brandy; five years later the price of brandy had risen to 13s. The activities of smugglers caused much variation in the price of imported alcoholic drinks, the country gentlemen being ever ready to buy in the cheaper market when opportunity offered. Later in this narrative we shall find that the Diarist did not lag behind his neighbours in taking advantage of such agreeable transactions.

Birch wine was appreciated by the ladies. One day the only words committed to the Diary are these:
"She drunk too much Birch Wine."

[1] Escritoire.

Nicholas usually sent his own home-grown barley to be malted in Liverpool. In June, 1706, he paid 9s. for the making of forty-eight bushels of malt and almost treble that amount in "Duty to ye Queene," namely £1 6s. 9½d. By 1714 the tax was slightly less, being £1 3s. 9d. for fifty-eight bushels which cost 11s. to make.

Women were employed "to brue" the ale but when it came to "tunning" and bottling it, Nicholas and his butler were very busy.

"April 29th. 1707. I racked off one Hoggs Head of October which I think was brued in 1703.

May 2nd. I bottled off about 11 Dozen of October Beer.

May 12th. I helped Mary Molyneux to bottle some strong Aile and cork up som Bottles of Meath."

Mary Molineux is styled *chambermaid* in the Wages list.

"Sept. 7th. 1708. I helped to make two Sourts of Meath, a stronger and a smaller Sourt.

Dec. 16th. I was present most of ye tyme whilst they were tunning and gave orders how some of it should be mixt, viz old aile and new small beer.

June 15th. 1709. I bottled off a little very ordinary Birch wine. I helped my Wife to make 32 quarts of Mead."

Such entries as the above abound, and there are many receipts in the Recipe Book for making both "Meath" and "Small Meath."

III

1706-1714

Mrs. Blundell seems to have busied herself in the stillroom as much as her bad health, complicated by the barbarous medical treatment of the date, would permit. The Diary announces on one occasion that she "made good Provision of Gingerbread," on another that she bought a quantity of "bullons" (bullaces or small plums) presumably for jam-making. She acquired damsons at the mysterious rate of 6d. for 120.

"Betty Bolton of ye Carr Side came to help my Wife to preserve Damsons."

It is matter for astonishment that the poor woman was able to lead so active a life in view of the frequency with which she was "let blud." This operation was sometimes performed by one of the maid servants, but most often by the butler, Richard Cartwright. After he left the Squire's service, Marmaduke Maltus, always alluded to in the Diary as "Duke," an innkeeper of Great Crosby who trained horses for Lord Molyneux, was summoned for the purpose. His fee of 2s. was however evidently considered too high and an arrangement was made with Richard Cartwright, now a butcher in the neighbourhood, to bleed the lady of the Manor for 1s. each time.

"April 21st. 1710. Rich. Cartwright came in the evening to let my Wife Blud but being it was too late, he is to come some Morning.

April 23rd. Rich. Cartwright let my wife Blud in ye Foot. She fainted, having parted with 20 ozs of Blud as is supposed."

On a later date Rich. Cartwright was only paid 6d. for his services. Possibly the amount of blood produced by the poor lady on that occasion was not considered sufficient to warrant a more generous fee.

Mrs. Blundell is reported at different times to have been "extreamely sick," or "to have like to have dyed of a pain in her head and throat," or "to have a pain in her back as she could not sit or stand upright" or to be "very ill of the gravel" or to have "a bad fitt of the stone."

These frequent indispositions may have aggravated a naturally perverse temper, judging by her endless difficulties with her household. But she never lay in bed more than a day at the most. Two days after she has been reported as at death's door, she is up and off on a shopping expedition to Liverpool or to "wate of a Neighbour." She made a pilgrimage to Holywell very shortly after she had been laid low for half a day by a very bad attack of "ye gravel." She drove as far as Liverpool but, her husband writes, "it was her Intention to walk the rest of ye Way."

After crossing the Mersey by ferry she would have had to traverse the Wirral on foot and make the hazardous passage of the river Dee and its treacherous sands so vividly described by

Celia Fiennes.[1] The journey ended with the long hill from the shores of the Dee to Holywell—it was a pilgrimage indeed.

Many doctors were consulted by Mrs. Blundell in the course of her life. In July, 1708, she, with her maid, stayed for some weeks in Dr. Worthington's house at Wigan, for treatment and to drink "ye Hilton Spaw Waters."

"July 20th. I went to Wigan to see my Wife, she being at Dr. Worthington's. I dined there but my Wife was walked out to make a visit. When she came back I came from thence."

Some days later he wrote the only letter to his wife of which he preserved a copy:

"My dear
    Considering how ill you are of ye Gravell I wonder you should be so very imprudent as to come Home, especially seeing your Doctor was quite against it, 'tis by him we must be ruled as to your Health. You may be assured I would much rather have you at Home, but being 'tis for your good we must both of us submit. I hope you have by this Time found Benefit by drinking of ye Waters but am afraid so much Raine as there has been of late may have made ye Spaw not to be of the Strength as at another Time, so feare it has not had so good Effect as I could wish. But if you and the Doctor think it Proper for you to come Home I here send Horses for you, so leave it freely to your own choyce to come home or stay at Doctor's, but to do what is best for your Health which is what is much desyred by
                                        Your ever loving Husband
                                            Nicholas Blundell."

Mrs. Blundell had evidently had enough of weak "Spaw Waters" and decided to come home whatever Dr. Worthington might say. After spending two nights with her friends the Pooles at Birchley,[2] she returned to Crosby on July 31st.

The following year an expensive excursion into Shropshire

---

[1] *The Journeys of Celia Fiennes.* Edited by Christopher Morris. The Crescent Press, 1947, p. 182.

[2] William Poole of Birchley was the younger brother of Sir James Poole of Poole, Cheshire, first Baronet.

was made in order that the renowned Doctor Bostock might be consulted.

"August 18th. 1709. My wife and I began our Journey towards Whitchurch. We came too late for Ye Botes at Liverp— so we went over at Runk Horn after which we lost our Way and went to Windy Weston where we got a Guide that brought us to Frodsham.

Aug. 19th. We went from John Webster's, ye Signe of ye Bears Paw at Frodsom, to Whitchurch ye Signe of ye Red Lyon where we dined and discoursed Dr. Bostock about my Wives paine in her Back. From Whitchurch we went to Chester where we lodged at Mr. Taylor's, ye Signe of ye Golden Lyon.

Aug. 20th. We saw several of ye Paletines in the Wool Hall etc. We dined at Chester and thence went to ye Rock Hous but the Bote was gon, so we got a Smoak made, but no Bote coming to us, we went to the Wood-Side where Mr. Darcy Chantrell[1] came to us and got a Bote for us, and so we came home."

The unfortunate patient with a pain in her back must have been sorely tried by the journey on horseback of about forty miles each way. It was all very costly, between the Doctor's high fee of £1 1s. 6d., the bill of 15s. for physic, and the travelling charges amounting to £1 4s. 11d. Nicholas took care to consult Dr. Bostock about the children and to bring home some physic for them which was duly administered. On another occasion he states that he drank half of his wife's medicine. As there is no record of his having any of the aches and pains from which she suffered, he may have taken medicine that she had refused to finish, in order that it should not be wasted.

One result of the excursion to Whitchurch was that Nicholas enthusiastically applied himself to what he describes as "my Paletine Work" during the following winter. He made his own "Drought" for the picture of a church and actually completed his piece of craftmanship in "299 Sticks in different Peeces of Wood." He was very proud of it, showed it to all comers, and transferred it from room to room until satisfied that it was placed to the best advantage.

[1] Of Noctorum, Cheshire. He had bought this estate from William Blundell, father of the Diarist.

"Dec. 6th. 1709. I hung my Paletine Church in ye Hall."

Mrs. Blundell seems upon the whole to have had more faith in the ministrations of various "wise women" than in the skill of doctors. Mrs. Bootle, described as "of the Peel"[1] was much consulted, but when she failed to cure "a soar leg" Nicholas summoned Betty Bolton[2] on his own account. Probably the patient suffered from varicose veins, for at a later date she again had "a soar place on her legg" and again had recourse to Betty Bolton who this time stayed in the house.

"My Wife went to bed after Dinner, she being very ill of her legg and Head. . . . Betty Bolton was sent for to look after my Wives Legg. . . . My Wife took physic by advice of Betty Bolton. . . . I gave Betty Bolton a good Book of Physick and Cherugery. . . . Betty Bolton went hence, she having much-what cured my Wives Legg. She has been here almost constantly for a fortnight last past."

The "Chirugieness", as she is sometimes importantly styled, was paid quite a large fee for those days.

"Betty Bolton, for Physick and dressing my
Wives Legg   ...   . £1   0   0"

V

1706-1714

The two little girls continued to "come on bravely" in spite of the violent treatment meted to them for childish ailments. They suffered from a skin eruption in 1709.

"June 1st. I put Mally into ye Seller well for some Outbreaks she had.

Aug. 3rd. I went part of the way towards ye Sea with my

[1] The designation was no doubt used to distinguish her from the wife of his neighbour, the yeoman Robert Bootle of Thornton. Peele, Cheshire, where Mrs. Bootle lived, is now known as Morton-cum-Peele.

[2] A widow living in Liverpool. *Bickerton.*

F

children but turned back. My wife and Dorothy Blundell[1] went with them. They were put in ye Sea for some outbreaks.

Aug. 4th. I bathed my children in ye Sea, it being the first time I was with them and the second time they was bathed in ye Sea.

Aug. 5th. I went with my Children to ye Sea. William Ainsworth bathed them."

The fact that the services of the bailiff were enlisted suggests that Mally and Fanny were carried willy nilly into deep water, and were not permitted the dalliance among seaweed, little crabs and pink shells, which was to delight later generations.

As salt water did not prove effective in banishing the children's spots, recourse was had to the treatment tried two generations earlier on the Cavalier's grandson Edmund Butler[2] when, as a child he lived at Crosby. "An issue" was cut in Mally's arm, and four days later "Mary Pilkington cut a second issue in Mally's arm."

Presumably Mary Pilkington was a "wise woman" especially skilful with children.

"The issue" was supposed to allow the evil humours to escape. Before medical science came into its own, blood poisoning must surely have been one of the many causes which took such heavy toll of child life. If Mally had been given her choice, however, she would probably have preferred to suffer the infliction of a third issue than the next remedy tried.

"March 29th, 1710. Doctor Francis Worthington pulled up some of the Hairs of Mally's Head."

This drastic measure was considered to have proved beneficial and a few months later Nicholas, economically dispensing with a doctor's services, carried out the treatment on his second daughter himself.

"Nov. 18th. I pulled up by ye Roots som of ye Hairs of Fanny's Head."

When the Squire was ill himself he accepted divers ministrations.

"Jan. 3rd. 1710. I lay in bed till towards evening, being ill of my eyes.

[1] The nursery maid.
[2] Cavalier.

Jan. 5th. I lay in bed till after dinner. Mr. Aldred[1] put oyled paper over ye window. Thomas Marrow shaved behind my ears and layed blistering plaster on."

Thomas Marrow was a tailor.

" Jan. 9th. Doctor Smithson came to see me and let me blood.
Jan. 16th. I was ill in my Head great part of ye Afternoone.
Jan. 17th. Mr. Aldred shaved my head and put on three plaisters which he brought from Dr Smithson."

Whether the plasters were successful, or whether wrath on the Squire's part on hearing that one of his men had " robed " him banished his pains, is not known, but January 18th found him downstairs and taking active measures to bring the thief to justice.

During this year Nicholas made a great effort to achieve the cure of the eye-trouble from which he suffered all his life. He purchased " Spectacles by way of Preservation," but these did not turn out to be very useful. It is surprising that his eyesight lasted as long as it did in view of the pills, potions, salves and drops which he successively tried upon them. His Recipe Book contains twenty-nine prescriptions for " Sore Eyes," or " Rheum in the Eyes " or " Burning in the Eyes," among them one recommending dried and powdered eyebright to be taken " with food and drink for it hath been proved to be most excellent for all impediments of the sight." Both Diary and Disbursement Book record the gathering and drying of quantities of this weed.

" June 24th. Dr Cawood ye Occulist from Dublin came to look at my Eyes. He lodged here.

June 30th. Dr. Cawood took me in hand to cuar my eyes. He made an Issue in each Eare.

June 28th. I went with Dr Cawood to Leverpool to assist him in geting acquaintance and to procure a Chamber for him where his Pasients may come to him. We drunk at the Post Office with Dr Smithson, Dr Person etc. . . .

July 20th. I began by orders of Dr Cawood to take drops, eyebright tea, and to put Clary Seeds in my Eyes."

---

[1] Rev. Robert Aldred, S.J., chaplain in succession to Rev. W. Gillibrand.

The oculist evidently did not find quarters to suit him in Liverpool for he remained six weeks at Crosby, seeing patients there as well as treating the Squire, and taking part at leisure in various fishing and other sporting expeditions. He returned to Ireland after some delay at the start of his journey.

"Sept. 7th. Dr Cawood gave me his full Instructions in Writing what I was to doe for ye Benefitt of my Eyes when he was gon for Ireland.

Sept. 8th. I gave Doctor Cawood my Gratification for his Advise and Attendance and for things for my Eyes.

Sept. 9th. Doctor Cawood went hence with Intention to have gone for Ireland, but the wind being cross, he came back."

It was customary to hail a ship bound for Ireland from the Crosby shore, as when Edmund Butler left Crosby in 1702: "We halled" (hailed) "ye *Mary* with a Hand Karchaff but she answered not." Presumably a small boat could be hired to row a chance passenger out to the deeper channel, or sometimes the traveller rode out:

"Mr Wairing told us his Son was in danger to lose his Passage for Ireland, ye Ship being gon and he was fourced to ride after her on Shore and so get on Borde if he could."

"Sept. 11th. Dr Cawood went towards ye Sea Side in Hopes to have met ye Ship which he designes to goe in for Ireland but he mist of Her.

Sept. 19th. Dr Cawood took shiping at Leverpoole for Ireland."

Nicholas omitted to record the amount of his "gratification" to the eminent man when he inscribed his accounts at the end of that month, so intent was he upon setting down the cost of every brick and nail then being used in an alteration to part of his house.

It is truly astonishing to discover that the oculist's treatment was at least partially successful, for there is no further mention of eye-trouble for some years. The patient was careful to make continued use of eyebright, not only as a beverage:

"March 19th. 1711. I cut a good Deale of Eyebright for me to smoak."

Dr. Cawood stayed at Crosby again in the summer of 1712

and treated local patients from there, but of himself the Diarist merely writes:
"I took a Doce of Phisick by Advice of Dr Cawood for an Outbreak at ye Syde of my nose."

He may have been counselled to avoid reading for a time after the treatment, for on several occasions his wife read to him " in a spirituall book," and during leisure winter hours he attempted, with his indefatigable industry, to make a rug.
"Dec. 16th. 1711. I cut Woosted for painting."

From the Disbursement Book.

					s.	d.
"For my Rugg Work						
Jan. 9th. Read lead	...	...	...	...	1	0¼
Hair Sive	...	...	...	...		6
Woosted	...	...	...	...	1	11
Pensalls	...	...	...	...		6
Linceed Oyle ...	...	...	...		4½
A Cabinet	...	...	...	...	6	0
Pictures	...	...	...	...		3

There was an interval of outdoor activities and then:
"Jan. 25th. I powdered some Whit Lead and red lead in order for my painting or Rugg Work.
Jan. 29th. I sifted my woosted coulors as were cut for my Rugg Work and divided them into 42 different Sourts.
March 13th. I began to draw out some Pictures with my Pensall for my Rugg Work and to try to finish one of them with cut Woosted but it did not doe right."

After a yet longer interval the next effort is recorded:
"Aug. 31st. I began to work at my Rug-work-Paint thô I once had an unsuccessfull tryall at it before."

That is the last we hear of the rug. As there is no triumphant announcement of its completion it is safe to conclude that it was never finished.

The education of Mally and Fanny was not hurried. Mally's first letter was dispatched when she was only five, but it was dictated to her proud father.
"I writ a letter to my Sister Middleton from my doughter Mary. It was of her own Endighting."

Mally "began to goe to Catherine Fazackerley to learn to sow," at the age of seven. Her preceptress received one shilling per quarter. A few months later: "Mally reads pretty redily in ye Spealing Book so we have left it off and she has now Begun to read." This last quotation from the Diary does more credit to the pupil than to her parent who gave the reading and writing lessons himself. Only on her eighth birthday did Mally "begin to joyn in writing."

Dancing lessons for both children were next inaugurated. Mr. Evans the "dansing master" received 2s. 6d. per month for each pupil. He kept his own horse and seems usually to have stayed the night at the house where he was giving the lesson. After he had been in the neighbourhood a few months he died suddenly in Liverpool, and a little later a Mrs. Richardson taught the children dancing. Mally and Fanny were not oppressed by much book-work. Sometimes they went with their father to see the glorious bonfires made by "ye burners of fleas" when the rough growth on the surface of the turf fields or "mosses," as they are still called in Lancashire, was skinned off and burned to improve the pasture. When turf was being cut and carted under the Squire's supervision, he took his little girls for rides in the farm-carts. As they grew older the two children went further afield to any gathering they could reach, was it a race-meeting at Ormskirk, Wakes at West Derby or a "bawle" in Liverpool which Mally attended when ten years old, staying the night with a Mrs. Maginnis who was later her school-mistress. It has been seen that at an early age Mally was a dauntless pedestrian. With companions from Little Crosby she walked to the village of West Derby,[1] a distance of about nine miles, stayed the night in the house of a yeoman friend of her father's, enjoyed all the Wakes[2] had to offer that evening and the next day, and returned on foot on the third day. She was then not quite eight years old.

Mally's first experience of witnessing a funeral had a very natural result a few days later:

[1] Now a division of Liverpool.
[2] For diversions at country Wakes see Appendix II.

" My children buried one of their Babbies with a great deal
of Formallity. They had a Garland of flowers carried before it,
and at least twenty of their playfellows and others that they
invited were at the Buriall."

It rather looks as if the Squire himself had been invited to the
doll's funeral.

These halycon days were interrupted by illness in accordance
with the usual fate of young mortals. In the summer of 1710
Mally had smallpox. There was a very high annual mortality
from this disease and her parents promptly took all the precautions known to them. These did not include sending for a
doctor but the child was evidently isolated, for a nurse was summoned from a neighbouring village, and Fanny escaped the
infection. Mally rejoined the family in a fortnight. The history
of the illness is set forth in the diary, mixed up with other
information.

" Sept. 22nd. Mally was extreamely ill all day thô she began
yesterday to be out of order.

Sept. 24th. Mally began to be pretty much brock out of ye
Smallpox.

Sept. 29th. Coz. Scarisbrick sent to see " (i.e. enquire for)
" Mally. She was blind of ye Smallpox. I went to Leverpoole
and paid off Pothecary Burrow's bill. I drunk with him and
Jo. Simpson at ye Wool Pack.

Ost. 1st. Mally began to see, the smallpox beginning to abate.

Oct. 3rd. I redied my closet and put severall things in their
Plases as should not be in my Closet.

Oct. 7th. I helped to put up six posts in ye Bleaching Yard to
hang linnen upon. Mary Davy went hence. She had been some
time here tending Mally of ye Smallpox.

Oct. 8th. Mally came down into ye parlor, it being ye first time
since she was ill.

Oct. 23rd. Mally took a purge, it being ye first time since she
was ill."

Perhaps in the absence of science, instinct warned against the
use of the violent medicines of these days while a patient was
weakened by fever. The illness did not call for much outlay
in cash. Two shillings were expended on " Mally, for her when

she had ye Smallpox"; Mary Davy received 2s. 6d., and
"oyntment for Mally's head" cost 6d.

The following year both children contracted "ye maslels,"
and were evidently considered to be far more ill than Mally
had been with smallpox. Dr. Lancaster made several visits,
remaining to dine and sometimes for the night in order to
diversify his professional activities with sport. Various neighbours sent messages "of a How-doe" (to enquire). After a
month in the house the little patients were sent out in "ye
Coach to take ye Aire," but later in the spring both were very
ill again.

That winter old Mistress Frances Blundell died at the age of
82; her body was borne in Nicholas's "coach carriage" from
Ormskirk to Little Crosby. It was escorted by her great-nephews
Blundell and Mountgarrett and by relatives and neighbours
among whose forebears she had lived through stirring times, and
was laid to rest in the Harkirk Burial ground where in her youth
she had seen funerals take place secretly at dead of night.[1]

The next patient was Nicholas himself, who gives the following account of his short and strange illness.

"March 27th. Rich Cartwright let me Blud.
March 28th. I sent for Doctor Lancaster. He gave me a vomit.
March 30th. Being extreamely ill of a continuall Fitt of
hekoping which lasted for about 15 hours without ever any long
intermission, both Dr. Will. Lancaster and Dr. Andrews came
to me. Mr Scarisbrick sent to see me. Parson Gerard Wairing
came to see me. I signed my third will. The doctors went hence.
Dr. Andrews came again and lodged here. Lord Molyneux sent
to see me. Pat. Maynard, Burton and Mannock came to see me."
(The last three named were priests.)
"April 1st. Doctor Lancaster came to see me, I being on ye
mending hand.
"April 2nd. I took a turn in the garden."

[1] *Cavalier.*

CHAPTER V

NEIGHBOURS

I

MOST of the Lancashire country gentlemen were recusants but they lived on the friendliest terms with their non-Catholic neighbours. Their houses were searched by officers of the Law, it is true, when there were rumours of an attempt by the Stuarts to re-obtain possession of the Throne by the assistance of French arms, for they were all reputed to be Jacobites. The order was carried out in a perfunctory fashion at Crosby by an acquaintance of the Squire's, on February 22nd, 1705 : " My Hous was slightly sirched for Armes by Mr Leigh,[1] Captain in Lord Derby's Regiment and by Dutton ye High Cunstable."

During this period there was much agitation throughout the country over the question of the Government's supposed leniency towards Dissenters, and the consequent weakening of the established Church. The Law already placed Catholics outside the pale of any concessions which might apply to other Non-Jurors; indeed their difficulties would have been rendered insuperable by the Act of 1699[2] had this been applied in the full rigour intended by its framers. The Diary, however, presents a picture of a tranquil society. Every hall (as manor-houses are invariably called in Lancashire) had its private chaplain who taught their religion to the children of rich and poor; when the sons and daughters of well-to-do families disappeared from their homes it must have been generally known that they were pursuing their education on foreign soil in direct defiance of the

[1] William Legh of Westhoughton.
[2] Appendix IV.

Law; many hundreds of pounds could have been collected by determined informers but in Lancashire they seldom showed their heads until the Stuart rising of 1715 took place. Perhaps the pursuivants hesitated to penetrate into a wild countryside of bogs and waste-land, where every farmhouse and cottage was prepared to shelter the priest if he was driven from the hall. The justices of the peace were also obviously unwilling to convict their Catholic neighbours who already paid double taxes on their lands.

Trouble penetrated even into this happy corner of an otherwise disturbed kingdom in 1708, when the invasion of Scotland was attempted by a small force of combined French and Irish troops in the service of James.

"March 19th. My Hous was serched for myself, horses and Armes by Edward Willoby[1] Esq, Lievetenant Tompson,—Orme[2] ye High Cunstable etc. They seazed upon two of my Coach Horses viz Jack and Robin, and they are to be sent to them tomorrow.

March 20th. I sent my two Horses as promised. They were returned to be forthcoming when called for."

The law forbidding a recusant to own a horse worth more than £5 had to be acknowledged by the justices at such times. Nicholas possessed more than two horses, but other friends were at hand to conceal them when the alarm was raised. He did not venture to send for them for a month.

"April 20th. I sent Henry Sumner to fetch home my two Horses Hobb and Buck, and sent Rob Tompson for Bess and her fole. I had sent them Abroad to be secured."

The exercise of a little bribery is suggested by the following item of expenditure during the month.

"Spent by my Servants in my business   ...   15s. 0d."

This is an unusually large sum to be included under that heading; the amount is seldom more than 2s. on less important occasions.

---

[1] Edward Willoughby of Shaw Place, Charnock, J.P., succeeded in 1712 as 13th Baron Willoughby of Pasham.

[2] Abraham Orme of Ormskirk.

Three days after the " serch " Nicholas is found peacefully
mending a spinning wheel.

" I took a wheele down out of ye Fals Roof and mended it to
spin Gersey with."

The false roof probably concealed a hiding-place. The upper
part of Crosby Hall has been much altered and added to since
the Diarist's time. There were two other hiding-places, one in
the thickness of the walls, and another in the partition between
two rooms. The existence of the first was only re-discovered in
1887 when a fire removed eight layers of wall paper and
damaged the oak panelling. The fire also uncovered some fine
Elizabethan tapestries in the same room under innumerable
layers of wall paper. Fortunately these were saved, although the
oak panelling was destroyed and we shall never know the secret
of access to the priest's holes. The Squire of that day
unromantically converted both into cupboards!

The solitary mention of a Protestant clergyman displaying an
unfriendly attitude towards his Catholic neighbour occurs in the
Diary on May 16th, 1708.

" Mr Plumb sent an Express to give me Notice concerning an
Information made against Mr Blundell of Ince by Parson
Ellison.[1] I went to Ince to acquaint Mr Blundell therewith, and
writ from thence to Mr. Plumb."

The same " Information " evidently threatened Nicholas and
others within a few days, for on May 23rd, he writes to his
cousin John Gillibrand at Chorley :

" One favour I have to beg of you, that you will act for me
as you doe for Yourself if you think it convenient, and I will be
accountable to you for ye Charge viz in Relasion to our conviction, for both our naims (amongst divers others) were
returned at ye Sessions as Non-Jurors, and since sent to London
as I hear, to be prosecuted against. If so my Opinion is, subject
to better judgment, that it were better to quench ye Fier ere it
begin to flame but as yet I hear of none that has endeavoured to
put any Stop to what may come upon us, and those I have spok

[1] Rector of Formby, then a small village on the coast four miles from
Crosby.

to are resolved to take their venter. However 'tis a thing in my opinion to be delibered upon and your Assistance therein will be a great satisfaction."

The affair, which had doubtless caused much anxiety, ended very merrily :

" July 26th. 1708. I went to Ormskirk Sessions where Mr Molineux of Bold, Mr Trafford,[1] Mr Harrington,[2] I etc., compounded to prevent Conviction. We appeared in Court before Sir Thomas Standley,[3] Dr Norris[4] and Mr Case,[5] all Justices of ye Peace. We Catholicks that got off our Convictions dined altogether at Richard Woodses. After Dinner we went to ye New-Club-Hous and then came back to Richard Woodses and drunk Punch with Sir Thomas Standley."

Lawyer Plumbe and John Gillibrand between them steered the case to this anti-climax at a low cost :

From the Disbursement Book :

" At Ormeskerk Sessions given to prevent my being convicted
To Lawyer Starkesy ½ a Guiney
To Edge ye clark[6] one Guiney
Court fees 18s. 6d., in all 2 10   9
Spent at Ormskerk...   4   0 "

Thenceforth the Crosby neighbourhood at least remained untroubled by the activities of either Jacobite or informer until the year 1715.

Some years earlier (in 1701) Lawyer Starkey had proved a good friend to the Diarist's kinsman Robert Scarisbrick, by advising him "to goe into Cheshire or Yorkshire or anywhere else out of the County," and so avoid an impeding summons for

---

[1] John Trafford of Croston was connected with the Blundells of Crosby through his wife Catherine Culcheth of Culcheth.

[2] Charles Harrington of Huyton-Hey. The estate passed in the female line to a branch of the Molineux family.

[3] Of Cross Hall, Ormskirk.

[4] Edward Norris of Speke had practised medicine in Chester before succeeding to the Speke estate upon the death of his brother William.

[5] Of Redhassles, Huyton.

[6] Richard Edge, Deputy Clerk of the Peace.

recusancy. His message was transmitted to Scarisbrick in a letter from a friendly Anglican clergyman.[1]

Nicholas had many friends among the clergymen of the surrounding parishes. The Diary abounds in such entries as the following:

"I went with Cousin Dick Butler to see Parson Richmond,[2] but he being gon to Leverpoole, we went to see Parson Marsden[3] who we found Ill of ye Gout. Coming home we called at Parson Wairings[4] and eat an Oat Cake and butter with him."

In 1706 Father William Gillibrand was sent to serve in Liverpool; he was the first Catholic priest to be established there after the Reformation. Father Poyntz, who succeeded him at Crosby, did not get on well with either the Squire or his wife and was shortly afterwards sent elsewhere by his superiors. Nicholas wrote to the Provincial of the Jesuits in England to ensure that no mistake be made in the next appointment:

"To Mr Barnes,[5] to be left at Mr. Nelsons an Apothecary in Great Wild Street London. Feb. ye 4th. 1706/7.

Sir,

Thô you be a Stranger to me yet I presume to address myself to you, being you are not ignorant of ye Subject I writ about wch is to desire you will, with what convenient Speed you can, furnish us with one of yours, that you think will be propper. You have formerly been informed how we desire he should be qualifyed, so shall be breef on that Subiect, only say in few words that we desire a Man of Wit and Conversasion, one that can preach well and is willing to take Pains amongst ye poore Catholicks, of which we have a great Many, and one that is of a good Humour and will be easy contented with tollerable good Fair. . . . Sir your speedy Answer to this would much oblidge.

Yours Humble Servant

Nicholas Blundell."

[1] Historic Society of Lancashire and Cheshire,, Vol. 88.
[2] Rev. Henry Richmond, Rector of Liverpool, 1706-1721.
[3] Rev. Thomas Marsden, Vicar of Walton.
[4] Master of the Merchant Taylors Grammar School, Great Crosby.
[5] The Rev. Peter Barnes was also known as Hammerton. Priests frequently adopted assumed names.

After the lapse of several months the chaplain who was destined to be the Diarist's closest friend for twenty-one years was directed to Crosby.

" August 7th. 1707. Mr Aldred's Portmantle was brought hither from Ormskirk."

The friendship would have been wrecked in its inception owing to Mrs. Blundell's difficult temperament, had not her husband taken firm and tactful measures. For three weeks Mr Aldred and he fished, rode, and went coursing together, but soon the peace was disturbed.

" Sept. 14th. 1707. Though it was a boysterous and stormy Day," writes Nicholas disapprovingly, " my wife went to Southward[1] upon a designe."

Sept. 15th. Mr Aldred and I dined at Ince. . . . When I came home I found an Express from my wife concerning Mr Aldred. Sept. 16th. I writ back to my wife at Southworth. I consulted Pater Gelibrand at ye Angel."[2]

Mrs. Blundell, however, did not return.

" Sept. 19th. I sent Walter Thelwall to Southworth with my second Letter to my Wife."

In this letter he evidently acquiesced in a proposal that Mr Aldred should move from the Hall and be provided with accommodation elsewhere in the parish. Perhaps this *modus vivendi* was tactfully suggested by Mr. Golding, and the Squire had been advised by his cousin to agree.

" Sept. 22nd. Mr Aldred went somewhere abroad. Mr Hammerton came to lodge here and to discours about ye cause of ye Separation."

Mr. Hammerton apparently advised them all to try to agree and to continue as they were. John Bannister the gardener was the bearer of another letter to Mrs. Blundell; he returned with an answer the next day and two days later was sent again.

Finally, after nearly a fortnight's absence, Mrs. Blundell came home, quite determined, it may be assumed, to have her own way, for her husband's letter to Mr. Barnes, written a few

[1] Southworth Hall, Winwick, then tenanted by a Catholic lawyer named Golding.
[2] The Angel Hotel still occupies its site in Dale Street, Liverpool.

months later, reveals that poor Mr. Aldred had been duly turned
out of the Hall.

"To Mr Barns. Feb. 17th. 1707/8.

I ought long since to have returned you thanks for the good
Man you sent us viz: Mr Aldred who is qualified according as
desired and is extreamely to my liking and gives very great Satisfaction to the Catholicks hereabouts who are very numerous, but
cannot say my Wife carries to him so sivilly as she ought, which
causes him to be dissatisfied and not willing long to continue in
my Famoly. However he being so well approved of both by
myself and all the Neighbourhood, I am not Willing he should
part far, so have taken care that another Hous not far distant
from hence be provided for him, and many of my Neighbours
have made their Petission both to Mr Babthorpe[1] and myself
that he may be fixed there, and that is now also my Petission to
you . . . the Neighbours have not only Petissioned for his stay,
but have on their own Accord promised considerably towards
his Maintonance which, with what I shall do, will I hope, maintain him Sufficiently."

Mr. Aldred now became parish priest, receiving a house and
£10 a year from the Squire, and further "considerable" financial
assistance from the yeomen and farmers who were all recusants.[2]
At first he lived in a cottage in the village known then, and for
generations later, as Ned Howard's House. Its exterior remains
little altered, a small iron cross on the roof indicating the attic
room in which Mass was said.

Nicholas actively assisted in getting the cottage ready.

"I helped Mr Aldred to work at his Hous both before and
after Dinner. . . . I helped Mr Aldred to place his Bookes. . . .
Mr Aldred went hence to live in ye Towne.[3] I looked out som

---

[1] Rev. Albert Babthorpe, S.J., was at the Jesuit House at Ince
Blundell known as New House from 1702 to 1714 and from 1710
was Superior over the thirty Jesuit priests ministering in Lancashire.

[2] Yeomen have unfortunately disappeared from the district, as from
the majority of English counties. The farmers and cottagers are still
all Catholics.

[3] The Diarist thus invariably designates the tiny hamlet of Little
Crosby according to ancient custom.

Linnen for him. I gave a Load of Hay. . . . I helped Mr Aldred to put up some Pictures. . . . I served Mr Aldred ye first time he sayed[1] in his new Chappell."

Thenceforth the happiest relations between priest and people are reflected in the Diary. Mr Aldred offered Mass, recited Vespers and taught catechism; he took part in sports with the Squire and his friends; now and again we see him interrupting these to carry out his priestly task :

" I went ye first time with Mr Aldred to fish for shoulers . . . As we were busy at ye Pit by candlelight Ned Hatten called Mr Aldred to help Philip Syer who was in danger of death. . . .

I found Sir Francis Anderton[2] and Mrs Blundell[3] at Mr Aldreds, but he was gone to help Ginnet Arnold to die."

Marriages were celebrated privately.

" J. Kerfrey and Elizabeth Pye came to be married, but Mr Aldred being gon to Lidiat . . . they stayed till he came after Supper and then were married."

Mrs. Blundell kept the peace for the next six years although Mr. Aldred really did ask for trouble when he suggested that her maid, Bradley, should do part-time work (there is a modern ring about this!) in his cottage. Bradley already made trouble enough by continually giving notice. This is the only occasion on which the Diarist's pen betrays irritation with his friend.

" Jan. 9th. 1708. Mr Aldred desired my Wife and me to walk down, and then he spoke about not cuting his hair and Bradley working Half her Time for him. Begon."

Perhaps Nicholas refrained from uttering the last word out of respect for the priest's cloth, and confided it to his Diary instead. Mr. Aldred may have justly considered his hair to be his own affair, but possibly indifference to his personal appear-

---

[1] The word *Mass* is omitted.

[2] Fifth Baronet of Lostock, near Bolton. He was deprived of his estate in 1715 for taking part in the Stuart rising of that year.

[3] Of Ince Blundell Hall, one mile from Crosby Hall. During the centuries in which the two families have lived on their adjoining estates, only one marriage took place between them. This was in the reign of Henry VI.

ance may have been one of the causes of Mrs. Blundell's
captiousness in his regard.

Hair-cutting was quite a family affair in the Squire's own
case. There was no need to be meticulous about it since a wig
covered all irregularities, but he carefully notes when it was
done. He usually cut his children's hair himself.

"I cut off Mally's Hair. My Wife and Mary Howerd[1] cut off
mine."

A few months later : "My Wife and Mrs Howet[2] cut off my
Hair."

Nicholas only once states that he performed the office for his
wife.

"It being near full Moon, I cut off my Wife's Hair."

II

Among the Diarist's greatest friends were "Parson Wairing"
and "Parson Gerard Wairing" father and son, who were successively Headmasters of the Merchant Taylors' School at Great
Crosby. Never a week, indeed scarcely a day, passed in which
Nicholas and the elder Parson Wairing did not meet until the
clergyman's death in 1711.

Nicholas was among others who "signed a Petission to ye
Company of Merchant Taylors of London in behalf of Mr
Gerard Wairing that he might suckseed his Father."

The appointment was duly made and the second Mr Wairing,
too, remained fast friends with the Squire through life. Amicable
controversy was occasionally indulged in.

"Mr Aldred and I . . . took Mr Wairing to Nick Johnsons[3]
and treated him to som little Discours about Priests not
Marrying.

I invited Parson Wairing to dinner. It was cheefly on

[1] A newly-arrived nursery maid.
[2] Wife of Thomas Howet Esq. of Ormskirk. She was staying at
Crosby.
[3] A tailor and smallholder.

G

Account of a Dispute formerly between him and Mr Aldred, but he could not come."

Parson Wairing indeed on one occasion "spoke ill of King J. 2nd." but he did not thereby impair his relations with the family at the Hall. France was then the traditional enemy of England, and the reliance of James upon French arms and money in his efforts to regain the Throne undoubtedly deprived him of the stout support of many Englishmen irrespective of their religion. If Nicholas was a Jacobite at heart, he did not risk confiding his views to paper.

"Great Nuse from Portugal. Maids dancing," he wrote on May 23rd, 1704, when the tidings reached Lancashire that Portugal had renounced her alliance with France and joined forces with England and Holland.

The Diarist designates as "cousin" everyone whose family had intermarried with his own, even if the connection had been made six or seven generations earlier. Meetings with one or other of these cousinly neighbours were of almost daily occurrence in summer and very frequent in winter. At racing and coursing-meetings, at "cockings" and bowling-matches, at the Wool Pack or the Angel he joined Lord Mountgarrett or Mr. Scarisbrick of Scarisbrick, or Mr. Molineux of the Wood, or of the Grange, or of Mosborough Hall, Mr. Blundell of Ince Blundell, Mr. Wolfall of Moor Hall or Mr. Eccleston of Eccleston or Mr. Gorsuch of Gorsuch, or many of these gentlemen together. He "wated of my Lord Molyneux" and "my Lord Derby" on suitable occasions; he thought it his duty to pay his respects to the Duke and Duchess of Norfolk[1] who passed through the county shortly after their marriage, on their way to Stonyhurst.

"July 28th. 1709. I met the Duke of Norfolk behind Ashton in their way towards Stonyhurst. I drunk at Ashton with the Duke, his two brothers, Sir Nicholas Sherbourn, Sir William Gerard[2] etc. . . . I wated ye Duke and Duches etc. to Wigan and supped at Totalls."

[1] Thomas Howard, eighth Duke, married Mary daughter and heiress of Sir Nicholas Shireburne, of Stonyhurst.
[2] Sir William Gerard of Bryn, fifth Baronet.

Very different from such a solemn social occasion, was the daily affectionate and intimate intercourse between relations, friends and neighbours.

"I went to Croxteth to wish good Suckcess to Mr Molyneux[1] 'ere he went a-courting."

The preliminaries for the marriage of Lord Molyneux's heir had of course been settled and the bride's dowry and jointure duly bargained for. It only remained for the young people to approve of each other which apparently they did. When the bride was brought home to Croxteth, Nicholas hastened to pay his first visit to "Mr Molyneux his lady." Were a friend travelling only into the next county his neighbours visited him a day or two before he started to wish him a safe journey, and as punctiliously welcomed him home on his return.

"May 6th. 1710. I went to Ince to wish Mr Blundell a good journey becaus I heard he was going out of this country for his Health.

Aug. 6th. 1710. My Wife, Dr Cawood, Mr. Aldred and I went in ye coach to Ince to welcom Home Mr Blundell and his Lady out of Yorkshire."

When Nicholas and his wife had been away from Crosby "Mrs. Molineux of the Grange, Ailes Tickle[2] and Mrs Betty Rigmaiden[3] came to Welcom my Wife home."

If the returned traveller was only a schoolboy, his arrival was not allowed to pass unnoticed.

"I went to Ormskirk to wate of my Lord Mountgarret's son, Coz. Richard Butler[4] who was come home from Schoole."

When a birth was expected in a neighbouring family a servant was sent "to see" the mother; in our phraseology, to inquire for her.

"I sent Walt Thelwall to see Mrs Scarisbrick who is lying in of Joseph her sixth son."

[1] Richard, later fifth Viscount Molyneux, married Mary, daughter of Lord Brudenell.

[2] The wife of a yeoman.

[3] Probably the wife of Thomas Rigmaiden of Ince Blundell who was descended from the Rigmaidens of Woodacre Hall.

[4] Son of Edmund Butler, sixth Viscount Mountgarrett.

On another such occasion—indeed on many another—
Nicholas and Frances visited the lady together.

"Oct. 17th. 1710. My Wife went to see Coz. Scarisbrick who
was lying in of her son Henry. I went with her. We dined
there."

As soon as Mally was old enough she accompanied her
mother to inspect the latest arrival in that neighbourhood of
densely-populated nurseries.

There were gatherings for christenings and funerals as great
then as now, in spite of the distances to be traversed with
limited means of transport.

The Diarist never recorded having failed to secure accommodation at an inn during all the years in which he kept note of
his movements. On a journey homewards from Yorkshire
accompanied by his wife, children and servants, he writes this
typical account of a day's travelling:

"We came to Henry Nowells in Duesbury where we dined,
it is an extraordinary dear Hous. Thence to the George at
Holcroft Head, thence to Samson Sunderlands the Black Lyon
in Rippondale where we lodged. Tis a very cheap Inn, and sivell,
oblidging People but ye Lodging very ordinary."

Nicholas travelled by night and at great speed when occasion
demanded.

"July 27th. 1714. There came an Express from Stockhild to
invite me to my brother Middletons Funerall. I began my
journey towards Stockhild about 11 of ye Clock at Night.
July 28th. I came to ye Swan with two Neckes in Bolton about
six in ye Morning, thence to Bradford where I lodged at George
Fletchers ye Signe of ye Black Swan.
July 29th. Came to Stockhild before Dinner."

The capacity of country houses of the day to provide
extensive hospitality at a moment's notice is as striking as the
enterprise of resolute travellers. A few random quotations illustrate this aspect of the general neighbourliness.

"Whilst I was out I was sent for home, being my brother
Langdale was come to lodg here. . . . Lord Molineux sent a
Servant to let us know he intended to dine here on Thursday. . . .

Coz. Scarisbrick sent to let me know his famoly and Croston
famoly[1] design to lodg here on Monday Next. . . . William
Ainsworth[2] came here betymes in ye Morning. He brought a
Present of Fish. He went a-Coursing with me. He lodged here.
Young Mr Trafford lodged here. . . . I sent a Cart into Lever-
poole for som Provitions for my Gests against next Week. . . .
Mr Trafford of Croston, his Lady and two Doughters, Mr
Scarisbrick, his Lady, son Francis and Doughter Betty, lodged
here."

The guests on this occasion remained five days during which
they were entertained according to their sex and tastes :

" Mrs Trafford and her Doughters, Mrs Scarisbrick and my
Wife went to Leverpoole. My Wife and ye two young Mrs
Traffords stayed to see a Play at Leverpoole and to danse. They
came Home next morning. Young Mr Trafford went a-coursing
with Some Leverpoole People at Great Crosby. Old Mr
Trafford, Mr Scarisbrick and I went out a-setting."

The Squire conscientiously ended this account of the day's
doings with the statement : " I finished Wheat-seeding."

A typical house-party is described in July 1707.

" Mr Livesley[3] and one of his doughters came to Dungen
Hall.[4] Mr Clifton of Lytham and his lady and 4 or 5 of their
children came to lodg there as did also Mr Walmesley of the
Lower Hall and his lady. . . . We dined in the great dining-
roome."

This universal hospitality was made possible by the prevailing
plenty. The Disbursement Book reveals considerable purchases
of groceries; sugar was bought in quantities, sometimes specified as " Lofe Sugar," sometimes as " Brown " or " Powdered."
A hundredweight cost £1 12s. in July, 1710, and in the following November 16s. 10d. was paid for a further supply described
as " Sugar of sondry Sourts." The average price was 4½d. per

---

[1] The Traffords of Croston Hall, near Preston.

[2] A tenant farmer.

[3] Probably of Ravenhead Hall, Prescot.

[4] Dunkenhalgh in the parish of Whalley, the original home of the
Walmesleys of Dunkenhalgh and Showley.

lb., at a time when a turkey "very fat" cost 2s. 6d. and a pig
"ready to kill" 4s. 6d. "Currans and Reasons, hard Spises,
Almonds, Vinegar, Carraway Comfits, Capers, salt Butter at
7d. per lb, Salt, 40 lbs for 3s. 4d." are items that figure in one
of Mr Ledbetter's quarterly bills. But the main foods and drinks
were home-supplied in quantities commensurate with the continual and often large-scale entertaining. The poultry yard was
well-stocked, as rents were partially paid in "Boone Hens."
On one occasion Nicholas sent 500 eggs to be sold in the
Liverpool Market, presumably without curtailing his household
supply. Meat was also furnished by the home farm and only
very small quantities of sea fish were purchased, either fresh or
salted. There is no mention of game being eaten in any
great quantity. Hares were coursed for sport but the small
number killed did not make a noticeable contribution to a larder
which had to be supplied on such lavish lines.

When an unusually large gathering was expected the mistress
of the house was assisted in her hospitality by gifts in kind from
housewives of all degree. Even on lesser occasions gifts of food
were helpful and usual:

"Thomas Syer[1] made me a hansom Present of Fish. . . .
Mrs. Blundell" (of Ince) "sent my Wife a present of a Bowle
of Brawn. . . . Margery Blundell[2] brought a present of a Rabet
Pie. I sent John Bannister with Pudings etc. to Ormschurch."

Tactful help was given to the priest at Little Crosby when he
invited his friends from the two neighbouring halls to spend
the evening with him.

"My Wife and I met Mrs Blundell of Ince and Mistress Anne
Blundell at Mr Aldred's. We had a cold Supper there brought
by both partyes."

Freshwater fish and eels formed a very important part of the
diet; the ponds on the Crosby estate were carefully managed
in order to provide at once good fish and good sport, while
neighbours greatly appreciated presents of fresh fish both alive
and dead.

[1] A yeoman.
[2] A tenant's wife.

"I put into ye New Pit in ye Oaklands 40 Carp Fry and 5 Mungrills, into ye Carthous Pit 30 Carp and 3 Mungrills, Wheat Hey Pit 18 Carp, Town Field Pit 22 Carp. I sent a good many Breame Fray of a present to Leverpool to Mr Ralf Marser[1] ... Mr Glegg brought me about 67 Carp from Hooton. . ."

Carp were the most prized of the freshwater fish, the waters being too sluggish for trout, although great efforts were made to keep the ditches between the pits open in order to drain the marshy land. The pits were methodically re-stocked.

"Notwithstanding that we had severall Disappoyntments with our Pump we drained ye Carthous Pit so as to get ye flat Fish and som Eles. We took six large Carp, one was 2 ft 4¾ inshe. Since we began to fish it this bout we got 9 Tensh, 7 of them were put in ye Horspoole, Carps 8 larg ones of which 4 were put in ye Pike New Pit and 2 into ye Horspoole, Breames got in all besydes small Fray, about 557. Breames stored in ye Horspoole 20 lbs, in ye Duck Coy 30 [lbs]. Eles got in all above 30 lbs."

Nicholas took his usual burning interest in the home construction of the chain pump, which was an affair of craftsmanship as shown by his Disbursements for it.

	s.	d.
"Pump Chaine at 3½d. per pound	10	6
Owler[2] Trees at 6d. per Yard for a Pump...	2	6
Booring 5 yds. of a Pump	5	0
Wood for ye Pump Frame and making it...	7	6
Smiths Work for ye Pump Tree & Wheele	6	8 "

Eels were extensively eaten. The nets used to catch them were also home-made.

"Hemp for a Snig[3] Net at 10d. per lb, spinning and twisting at 3d. per lb, kniting at 4s., in all 7s. 9½d."

An elaborate trap was constructed to take the eels in running

---

[1] The name is spelled indifferently Mercer or Marser in old Liverpool deeds, relating to West Derby.
[2] Alder.
[3] Lancashire word for eel.

water and so exclude the muddy flavour they acquire in stagnant water.

"Feb. 6th. 1712. I went to my Sniggary and gave Directions to Ned Hawkseye what compass ye Hous was to be over it."

Not until May was "ye Hous" ready for its roof.

"I begin to thatch my new Sniggary.

June 7th. I set my net ye first Tyme in my new Sniggary, having finished that Building except for a few Things that are to be don at no Great Charge.

June 22nd. Will Ainsworth went with me both in ye morning and night to my snigary. In ye morning I got 9 picks (pike) and about 9 lbs of eles and at night I got 21 picks."

This was rather too much of a good thing : immediate steps had to be taken if some good food was not to be wasted.

"June 23rd. I made Catherine Howard[1] order eles three different ways to try to keep them."

Catherine Howard got to work and her methods were duly entered in the Recipe Book. Her industry was all the more necessary because that very day 106 more pike and three and a half pounds of eels were taken in the Sniggery nets. Half the pike were given to a tenant who "designed to carry them home Alive to stoar in Pits."

Evidently coarse fish was not disdained in the days when the nation lived on what its own land and water produced. Now, in a hungry country, such cheap food is not utilised.

1706-1714

III

The social meetings alluded to up till now give but a very inadequate picture of the prevailing good fellowship of the Diarist's day and scene. He designates as " my neighbours " all who lived on his estate, whether as yeomen (of whom several rented land from him in addition to the fields they owned) tenants, or "workfolk." The Disbursement Book contains

---

[1] The cook.

monthly entries of small sums "given in Charitye." But if the recipient is not a stranger he writes: "Given to a poore Neighbour."

Good neighbourliness very seldom found expression in gifts of money however, for all lived on the land in a sturdy independence. If some were rendered very poor through sickness or other adverse circumstances, food was given to them, but not food ready for the table. "Corne to ye Poore" was dispensed regularly; the persons receiving it had to grind and bake it themselves. Oat-cake was the Lancashire countryman's staple food. Sometimes oatmeal already ground was given: " I weighed some Oatmeal for Anderton's Wife."

It has been seen that Mrs. Blundell called upon the ladies of her acquaintance after the birth of a child. She personally stood by less well-to-do mothers in their hour of trial.

" My Wife stayed till Morning with John Tickley's Wife who was in Labour. She baptised ye Chylde. Mrs Gill ye Midwife dined here. . . . My Wife intended to have been at Nanny Howerd's labouring but she was brought to bed ere my Wife came. . . . My Wife went to see Lawrence Blundell's Wife who was lying in of two Sons."

If there was no room for the midwife in the cottage she was accommodated at the Hall.

" My Wife went to see Thomas Swift's Wife who was in sharp and dangerous Labour. Mrs Moss, ye Leverpoole Midwife lodged here."

The Squire's advice was universally sought in his own domain, and he often undertook the part of peacemaker.

" John Tickley told me his Secret and his greatest Troble and advised with me about it. . . . Winny Scott was here to Consult about ye Misunderstanding as is between her and her Husband. I gave her my Advice and let William Weedon help to make them Friends. . . . I agreed a Difference between John Blundell and Margaret Field. . . . Ann Howard advised with me about her Husband taking Thomas Weedon's Son a Prentice."

The Diarist's willing assistance was forthcoming even in a minor difficulty such as that which beset a village mother when sending her daughter off to service in London.

"I helped Ellin Harrison to pack up some of her Doughter Jane's Cloaths that are to be sent to London as she says."

He also bestowed 2s. 6d. upon Jane.

In books about the period it is usually suggested that the Lady of the Manor was wont to act as medical adviser to those about her. But poor Mrs. Blundell was probably too much harassed by her own ill-health to concern herself with that of other people, for it was her husband who kept a stock of medicines, salves and other remedies, and provided himself with books describing how to make these, and their uses. He had implicit faith in the recipes which he and his friends and forbears had collected. Some of these are subscribed "Proved" in the Recipe Book—strangely enough, in view of their nature! "I made some Skull Powder for ye Convulsion Fits or Falling Sickness." The self-constituted physician took endless trouble to make up decoctions recommended for divers ills, and carried them himself to sufferers.

"I gave my wife two pills she was extreamely sick," he announces candidly on one occasion, and on others :

"I straned William Tompson's Medecine and finished making it for him . . . Charles Howerd's Wife was here. She showed me a Receipt for ye Convultion fitts which her Son is trubled with. I gave her som Herbs to make a dyet Drink for him. . . . I gave a poor Woman a doce for ye Falling Sickness and a Quantity of ye Same to take accourding to my Directions. . . . I took a bottle of Phisick with me to Ned Hatton's for his Doughter that was ill of ye Ague Fitts."

After Dr. Cawood's successful treatment of his eyes, Nicholas felt quite competent to take the oculist's place with regard to his neighbours.

"Thomas Medow's Sister was here to let me look at her eye as was not well. I gave her something for it."

Let us hope the prescription was as harmless as the one on which Parson Wairing depended :

"Parson Wairing called here as he came home from Ince Bowling Greene to beg some Rew to apply to his wrist to cuar his Eyes."

The amateur physician was ready to neglect a guest in order to attend a suffering " poore neighbour."

" Sir James Poole lodged here. I went to dress Ginnet Blundell's Legg."

A day or two later he admits : " I took in Hand to cuar Ginnet Blundell's Legg but she did not long continew my Pasient."

He tried to keep up to date in his self-imposed task :

" Dr. Cawood helped me to examine my Apothecary's Shop and to put it into Order. . . . I put my Scholasticall and Phisick Bookes into more regular Order. . . . I writ som Phisicall Receipts in my Recipe Book."

The Squire was very fond of skating and took advantage of the ice on every opportunity, but when a little village girl fell on it and was hurt, he took her home and attended to the injury himself.

" Richard Bridges' Doughter Mary cut her Eyebrow with a fawle on ye Ice. I came home with her and drest it."

He could be as hard as other men of his time in what he considered to be the interests of justice.

" Seaven Boyes of this Towne were beaten at my Lodg Gate with stirrup Lethers, som by their Fathers, som by their Masters and others, for stealing apples and other peevish Tricks."

Nevertheless a genuine love of children peeps out on many a page of the Diary :

" I helped to barr out ye Children's Master," (he was staying with friends). " We went to Nick Johnson's where we saw Will Tarlton's[1] son, a boy not four years of age, smoake a good part of a Pipe of Tobacco, I think about ye Quantity of Halfe a pipe, and when I asked him whether he would rather have a Pipe of Tobacco or a butter Kake he answered Tobacco. . . . I taught Joseph Sumner, Will Marrow, Rob. Tompson etc. to play at Penny Prick with ye Foot Balle."

The families living at hall, farmhouse and cottage mingled and enjoyed themselves together in thoroughly democratic fashion. It was not a case of the richer man invariably enter-

[1] A yeoman.

taining the poorer; they all went in and out of each other's houses; it is evident that Nicholas would have given offence had he not visited his more important tenants at times of festivity, in order to partake of the special fare provided.

"It being Crosby Goosefeast my Wife and I went to William Tarltons, then we went to Nick Johnsons. William Tarlton and his Wife were with us. Thence we went to Ned Hattons."

His noble kinsmen were not above taking part in rural merry-making.

"My Lord Mountgarret and his Son dined here. I went with them to Great Crosby Goos Feast. We eat at William Tarltons. We went to a rase on Crosby Marsh between a black Mare of John Gerards[1] of Garswood and a Baye Mare of Leverpoole."

Christmas merry-making took place on Twelfth Night, not on Christmas Day which was reserved for religious devotions. "Jan. 6th. 1712. We had a Merry Night. Rich Tatlock played here. We had a great many Danses. They dansed my Sword Danse. I played at Cut in ye Pantry with Joseph Blanchard of Lady Green, Rob Massam etc. . . .

Jan. 10th. I got my breakfast at Ellen Harison's, being I had not eat any Christmas Fare with her."

Shroveteide was also an occasion for merry meetings.

"We eat Pankakes at Richard Newhouses and Ralph Nelsons. Thence we went to Nick Johnsons and eat pan-kakes. . . . Severall of ye Neighbours turned the Pankakes here after Supper and dansed in ye Hall. Henry Kerfoot played to them. . . . Severall of ye Neighbours' Wives came here to eat Pankakes and be merry. I was amongst them."

Henry Kerfoot was miller and fiddler.

Family birthdays were celebrated. If it was the natal day of the Squire himself or one of his male cousins, or of Mr. Aldred, a bowl of punch was enjoyed with one or two cronies. There was always music and usually dancing in the evening.

"This being my Wives Bearthday William Anderton played here at night. We had carding also. I carded with them.

[1] Younger son of Sir William Gerard of Bryn, by Anne, daughter of Sir John Preston, Bart.

There was Abraham, Coxhead, Philip Syer, Walter Thelwall etc."

Abraham was a farmer, Syer a mason and Thelwall the steward.

"This being Mally's Bearthday, the Miller played to ye Servants after Supper."

Music was usually supplied by Richard Tatlock a fiddler, and William Anderton a piper. When the war with France was raging and supposedly indigent men were being indiscriminately recruited for the army, Nicholas came to the aid of his "Poore Neighbour" Anderton.

"It being my Bearthday . . . James Brown fiddled at Night. Anderton's Wife told me her Husband was pressed[1] at Wiggan."

On the same day Nicholas took up his pen on the piper's behalf.

"To Captain Bradshaigh. June 17th. 1704.

Though I have not the Honour of any great acquaintance yet the Relasion to your family makes me troble you with these few Lines on behalf of William Anderton who has for many Years past maintained his Famoly by his Industry and Care, and chiefly by playing on the Pipes, by which he has brought up Seven small Children and has never yet been troblesom to the Town he lived in; but in Case you press him not only his 7 small Children but also his Wife must be maintained as poor of the Town, which I conceive is a very great hardship. Wherefore I humbly desire you will not be so unkind as to ruin a poor Famoly who has ever lived in good Repute, but set the poor Man at Liberty."

The appeal seems to have been effective for there are frequent entries in the Disbursement Book:

"To Anderton one night   1   0"

The neighbourhood did not by any means rely for its enter-tainment solely on mutual hospitality and the large gatherings for such events as race-meetings and cock fights.

---

[1] For the Recruiting Acts of Queen Anne's Reign see *Reign of Queen Ann*, Vol. I. Trevelyan.

Strolling companies presented dramas in private houses and village barns, and the villagers themselves acted plays. The young men named in the following extract were all the sons of yeomen or tenant farmers.

"Feb. 25th. 1712. *The Souldiers Fortune* was acted at Mrs Ann Rothwells in this Towne. My Wife went with me both to ye Play and Gigg.[1] The Actors of ye Play were Thomas Farer *Sir David Dance*, William Marrow *Captain Bewgard*, Watty Thelwall *Sir Jolly Jumble* etc." The Company toured their neighbourhood.

"I saw *ye Souldiers of Fortune* acted in Richard Harrison's Barn. . . ."

A week later: "*Ye Souldiers of Fortune* was acted in my Hall. William Marser did not act." The following week: "The Actors of *the Soldiers Fortune* came hither and sung the Gigg."

In May 1708 "My Wife, Mr Plumb I etc. went to Great Crosby and saw *The Recruiting Officer* acted. Mr Syer of the Ford and his Wife, Mr Latham the landlord of the Woolpack and his wife suped here and after supper we went to Great Crosby and heard part of the Gigg."

In May 1709 "*The She Gallants* was acted imperfectly in ye Hall."

Nicholas and his wife went to the theatre in Liverpool twice in one week, in May 1706.

"May 13th. My wife and I went to Leverpoole and saw acted *The Earl of Essex*. Mr Plumb and his wife, Mr R. Norris[2] etc was there. We came home about 2 of the clock in the morning. May 16th. Colonel Butler . . . my wife and I saw *Ye Gamester* acted at Leverpoole."

In summer the coach and four could make the journey into Liverpool along the firm sands of the foreshore with compara-

---

[1] The humorous entertainment which usually followed a more serious play.

[2] Richard Norris of Speke, a prominent citizen of Liverpool. He was Mayor in 1700 and again in 1718, and Member of Parliament for Liverpool in succession to his three brothers, Thomas, William and Edward. The Norris Papers reveal that he was no friend to recusants.

tive ease, but this was not the case in autumn and winter. On one occasion disaster overtook Mrs. Blundell and her guest.

" Oct. 4th. 1712. My wife and Mrs Fleetwood Butler went to Leverpoole. Charles Howard overturned ye coach upon ye Leverpoole Rocks and damaged it very much, and hurt my wife and Mrs Butler. He brock it worse in Great Crosby Field."

A Liverpool surgeon of note was summoned.

" Oct. 5th. Mr. Yats [Yates] looked at my wife's shoulder as was hurt yesterday. He and Walt Thelwall drunk with me in the pantry.

Oct. 6thh. Mrs Molineux and Ailes Tickley came to see my wife upon account of her fawle in ye coach."

No great harm was done either to the lady or the coach for the family were soon on the road again, but this time six horses formed the team considered necessary to drag the heavy vehicle safely through the mire.

" Oct. 9th. I sent Charles Howerd with a letter to Mosborough[1] to let them know my Wife and I designed to be there next Monday.

Oct. 13th. My wife, Mrs Fleetwood Butler, I and Mally went in our Coach and six to lodge at Mosburgh. The water in Rainford was very high and came into ye Coach and wet some of our things in the Male trunk and boxes.

Oct. 14th. I sent William Ainsworth home with some of my horses from Mosburgh."

He probably sent four horses home and kept two for riding, as from Mossborough he hunted with the Garswood hounds and paid calls on all friends within reach.

Nicolas seems never to have failed to go to the house of any neighbour who was ill, or had had an accident or was merely " out of order," irrespective of the social status of the sufferer. It has already been seen that his neighbours were equally assiduous in their inquiries for him or any member of his family when ill. In fact the visiting of the sick was undertaken in general and as a matter of course.

[1] William Molyneux of Mosborough, Rainford, married as his second wife the Diarist's cousin Frances, daughter of James Gorsuch of Gorsuch.

"I visited ye Sick in Little Crosby" is an entry which occurs regularly in the Diary.

When Rob. Tompson fell from his cart while on a homeward journey with a load of slates and was run over, sustaining a broken thigh, he "stayed under Pothecary Barton's hands and lodged at Winstanleys in Ormskirk." His village neighbours travelled the ten miles to Ormskirk and back "to see Rob Tompson." When he had been laid up for a fortnight Nicholas reports: "My children went to Ormskirk to see Rob Tompson who was laim there."

Less than three weeks after the accident the Squire visited the injured man "who I found walking on his Crutches." Three days later: "I fetched home Rob Tompson from Ormskirk in a Cart."

Pothecary Barton must have been a fairly skilful bone-setter for there is no further information on Rob Tompson's case, and his wages are included in the usual quarterly list without comment.

In the spring of 1709 there was much sickness and many deaths occurred in the district. When an old retired servant living in the village was dying Nicholas writes:
"April 15th. I went after twelve of ye clock of ye Night to see Richard Harrison. I found my Wife there.
April 18th. Richard Harrison dyed about 3 in ye Morning he had been Servant about 18 years to my Grandfather. He was a truly honest Man of a very sound Judgment. William Starkey dyed about eleven of ye clock at Noone. He was my Cow Man and had been Servant in this famoly about   Years[1] and I think never a Meniall servant in my Father's time, nor of a great Will of mine, but towards ye latter end of his Time I maintained him at my own Hous with Apparall and all things necessary."

In that Catholic society of all ranks, the claims on a good neighbour did not cease with death. The Squire's "coach carriage" with its four horses was lent to rich and poor alike to carry their dead with dignity to the grave.

[1] The Diarist evidently intended to ascertain the exact extent of Starkey's service, but omitted to do so.

"I lent my Coach-Cariage to carry ye Corpse of Elizabeth Fareclough to Sefton."

On October 31st, 1711, the Diarist was at the funeral of Parson Wairing the elder. "Ye Corpse was carried on my Coach-Carriage."

If the distance to be traversed was too short to necessitate the use of a horse-drawn vehicle, Nicholas took his turn with other bearers in carrying the coffin.

"I helped to carry ye Corpse of Elin Bullen to ye Burial Ground. . . . I helped to carry Jane Starkey to her grave."

While the dead awaited burial Nicholas joined the throng of friends and relations—"neighbours" in fact—who gathered at the house of mourning to offer united prayers for the repose of the departed soul.[1]

"I called at Thomas Ridings and prayed there, he being to be buried tomorrow."

He always procured the offering of Masses for the deceased, and on the day of "The Month's Mind" or one month after the date of death, he resorted with others to the deceased person's home to pray and attend Mass; the same charitable gathering took place a year later.

"It being the Anniversary Day of Jane Bryansons, my Wife and I went thither to Prayers. We heard three and a Peece."[2]

It was not considered the privilege of the leisured class (if such could be said to have existed in that world of activity) to carry out these offices of charity to the dead.

"I went in ye Morning to my Burners in the North Hey and gave them Leave that had a Mind to goe to Ince to Prayers being Mr Blundell was newly dead. I also went thither to Prayers."

Thus did master and man still befriend their neighbours beyond the grave.

[1] This custom still prevails in Little Crosby.

[2] Masses are here alluded to.

CHAPTER VI

SERVANTS

IT was a far cry from the days when Pepys considered himself justified in kicking his "cook-maid" and the reigning sovereign did not hesitate to strike his footman,[1] to that in which the butler and housekeeper in a Victorian mansion were looked up to by their juniors as personages scarcely second in importance to anyone in the realm.

At Crosby in the early eighteenth century we find a circle of domestic servants living under totally different conditions from those of either of the periods mentioned. An interesting point about this household is the extreme independence of its members, who usually came from the farmhouses and cottages of the district. The men remained for years in the service of the Squire, leaving the continual arrivals and departures of maids to tell their own tale of an unreasonable mistress.

As a rule Nicholas makes no comment on what must have been an uncomfortable state of affairs for him, but occasionally a line or two conjures up the scene:

"Betty Atherton went away in a passion but returned again. . . . A grand Fawling out with Bradley, upon which she went out of ye Hous with an Intention to goe quite away but She came back Againe. . . . Catty Weedon went hence upon account of a Fawling out as had been . . . a Grand Fawling out with Eaves." (The next day) "Eaves left her Service."

Even the butler was once involved:

"A Fawling Out with Thomas Gower."

Thomas Gower however did not leave for another year. Before his departure he was nursed through a serious illness when priest and doctor were sent for, and William Anderton the piper "bludyed him three times."

[1] Agnes Strickland, *Lives of the Queens of England*, Vol. XI.

The following is a list of the maids who came and went within six months.

"Oct. 8th. 1709. Mary Bell came to be nursery maid and chamber maid.

Oct. 10th Anne Tarlton came to be Dary Maid.

Oct. 12th. Betty Harrison left her service.

Oct. 31st. Eaves left her service.

Nov. 16th. Catherine Carys came to be ye houskeeper.
(She remained less than three months.)

Nov. 24th. Margaret Charnock left my service.

Dec. 7th. Frances Howerd came to be ye houskeeper.

Dec. 8th. Margaret Jackson came to be ye cook.

Dec. 16th. Frances Howerd left her service.

Jan. 4th.1710. Catherine Carys left her service.

Jan. 10th. Mary Bell left her service.

Feb. 16th. Jane Walton left her service after one month pd 3/6."

It must be admitted that this was a period during which Mrs. Blundell was more than usually troubled with "attacks of ye gravell" or a "soar leg" or "paines in her back and her thigh." But the mistress of a house, sick or well, in any century, would surely be asking for trouble if she employed two house-keepers at the same time, the more so if her object was to ascertain which of the two was the best and most economical manager.

While their children were still young, Nicholas made repeated efforts to provide his wife with a companion, but none of the ladies who accepted the post for a salary, or came as "tablers," remained for long. At one time the Diarist's young cousins Fanny and Catty Gorsuch of Gorsuch Hall took it in turns to keep Mrs. Blundell company. The lady who remained the longest and with whom the final "fawling out" seems to have been the most bitter, was Mrs. Mills. We are told nothing of her antecedents but she first appears at the christening of Fanny, when she "stood for my Lady Gerard." Three weeks before the birth of their second daughter Nicholas and his wife stayed for a few days with Lord and Lady Gerard and may have made the acquaintance of Mrs. Mills at Dutton Lodge. She was a guest at Crosby for three months and then remained as a "tabler" for another five months. The actual parting between the paying guest and her hosts was amicable although the accounts were not entirely satisfactory.

"April 30th. 1707. I stated accounts with Mrs Mills. I nailed up her box which is to goe to London.

May 11th. Mrs Mills went hence to Warrington in order to goe by coach to London. My wife went with her to Warrington."

As Mrs. Mills was unable to pay the last 24s. she owed for her "bord" on leaving, she was asked "to return it in Coffy" to the same value, to be sent from London at her convenience. Nicholas thought this would be a good way out of the difficulty of sending such a small sum to pay for the coffee. Mrs. Mills also undertook to send some articles of apparel to her late hostess. Copies of the first letters exchanged between the ladies are not preserved, but the Letter Book contains an outburst from Mrs. Blundell which is evidentally part of an acrimonious correspondence carried on intermittently for more than two years.

"To Mrs Mills from my Wife
Madam

I wonder you should not be sensible of ye difficulty to Return small Sums up to London . . . for none of ye Merchants would troble themselves with returning any less than £10 and hardly so little a Sume as that but to a Friend . . . We have had too much troble already except we had more thanks than we must ever expect from yourself considering what favours you received at Crosby. I am very sorry you are put to such a pinch for Money amongst your own Friends and if you consider well, you will find we cannot be reconed amongst ye least of your Friends when you had not onely Mr Blundell's horses for your Service, his Servants to do you Service, and his Purs at your command, when your own friends would not supply you, besides the Favour you found in having 3 Months dyet etc given you, and ye moderate rate we demanded for ye remaining time not being above half ye Common Rate of Tablers & all this without ye least Obligation to you. You know very well you are in debt to Mr Blundell and whot you have layed out for me I know not so pleas to state Accounts & if anything be remaining it shall be honestly payed, for Mr Blundell has Occasion to return a good Parcell of Money to London so may add yours among ye Rest but would have Accounts adjusted first for ye greater ease to both sides. You have been a long time a-sending down my Stayes & Cap, I could have had them in half the time from another, and thanks to boot, but if you do not send them soone you may keep them."

The Squire's indignation was as great as his wife's when the stays and cap arrived without the coffee.

" To Mrs Mills I suppose I writ it about Oct. ye 20. 1708.
Madam,

... had you at first desired your Trunk I should not have made ye least difficulty of sending it, but your refusing to send ye Coffy thô you are more indebted to me than it comes to, makes me unwilling to send your Trunk until I receive my Money, for you being ye first in making ye return. It was a great Disapoyntment not to send ye Coffy, first because it is considerably raised, Secondly because for want of it I bought at ye Shops as I had occation, and lastly had it come along with ye other things I should have payed little or Nothing for ye Carriage, for ye box being so larg and yet light they were not content to take pay by ye Wight. . ."

The trunk remained at Crosby for nearly two years and was then claimed by its owner in a letter to which Nicholas replied with undiminished, and it must be admitted, with unworthy rancour.

" To Mrs Mills at London   July ye 12th. 1710.
Madam,

In yours to me you brag you have more honour than I because you propose paying ye Money to Mrs Brid. Butler,[1] you would have showed your honour much more by disposing of it in Coffy when desired, & then Accounts would long ere this have been adjusted so thank yourself that your trunk has been so long in ye Country . . . I know of no occasion as I shall have for anything to be bought by Mrs Butler, so desire you will pay ye 24s.

[1] Sister of Edmund, sixth Viscount Mountgarrett.

to Mr Baker at ye further end of Kings Street Near Bloomsbury Square, & upon advice from him that 'tis payed your Trunk shall with all Speed be sent to you . . ."

Sometimes the mistress of the house had legitimate cause for complaint.

"Catty Howerd and Nanny Blundell should have set up in ye Night with their Sweet-hearts, but they were discovered and prevented . . . John Blundell came and chaptered his Doughter Nanny for her last nights Proiect."

The Disbursement Book raises a suspicion that the Squire's tight hold on the purse strings may have had something to do with the fallings out. For we find Mary Scot, the nursery-maid who succeeded Mary Bell, presently promoted to be "Head maid, nursery maid and chamber maid" but with no corresponding increase in wages. In 1707 the dairymaid and housemaid were each receiving 10s. per quarter, but from 1708 onwards the two offices were rolled into one, and 10s. per quarter was paid to "Mary Howerd *chamber-maid and dary maid*," and to her many successors. Sometimes the cook is described as "cook and brue" but her wages remain unaltered.

The tale of the disgrace and dismissal of Richard Ainsworth, the ploughman, will presently be related. When Henry Sumner was promoted to replace him from being merely coachman to "Coachman Groom and Ploughman," his wages actually were advanced from 10s. to 15s. per quarter. After a year or two he asked for a further increase; this not being granted he left. Charles Howard then undertook his combined jobs for 12s. 6d. per quarter.

Richard Cartwright followed Thomas Gower as butler, but when he left that office was vacant for some time. Then we find John Bannister the gardener described in the wages list as "Gardiner and Butler," at the same salary as before the double job was imposed upon him. He was first engaged at 15s. per quarter in 1704 and his wages were raised to 18s. 9d. at the end of a year. Thereafter he served for eleven years for the same pay, but he as gardener *and* butler, and Sumner as ploughman *and* groom, were favourably placed to add to their earnings by the receipt of "Vales." The servants were tipped not only by the numerous guests who stayed in the house for visits of varying length, but also by casual diners. Nicholas never gave less than 1s. to the bearer of " an express " from one of his relatives or friends, while to a gamekeeper or head gardener who brought a present of value, such as a haunch of venison or a quantity of fruit, 2s. 6d. was not unusual. Such gifts considerably enhanced wages at a date when, according to Blundell's Disbursement Book, two quarters of beef could be bought for £1 13s. and a dozen pounds of candles for 5s. 3d.

The men who went out with the coach contributed to the cost of their liveries which were very expensive.

" Feb. 1713. Outside lining etc for a livery for			
Robert Tompson	3	4	6
Part of a livery given to			
H. Kerfoot	3	4	6
Two hats for my livery servants		5	0
Silver lace for my livery hats ...		15	0
Blew livery stockings		1	2
Making two suits of livery at my bord		9	0
Taylor's work, more		1	0
" August 1713 For two liveryes			
Gray gersey for two coats and britches at 3s. 8d. per yd	1	18	6
Blew serge for was-cots at 2s. 4d. per yd ...		15	2
Blew serge for facing at 2s. per yard ...		6	0
Mettle buttons for two coats at 10d. per doz.		5	0
Ditto for wastcots and breetches 2½d. per doz.		1	8
Mohair, silk, canvice etc		5	9
Fustian for lining at 11d. per yard		8	3
Skin for some pocket			6
Silver lace for two hats		15	2"

Thus the liveries cost £13 6s. 2d. in one year.

Henry Kerfoot, the miller's son " paid part of his viz £1 13s. 8d." Robert Tompson must have contributed 15s. for his wages are reduced from 15s. to 12s. 6d. during the six following quarters.

For several years Richard Cartwright occupied a position of trust in the family. This trust was not based upon skill in the upkeep of silver, management of the cellar, care of his employer's clothes and direction of a houseful of underlings, as was the firm position of those butlers whom a few of us can still remember. No, Richard Cartwright was in the first place skilled in "letting" the blood of his master and mistress, an office he was called upon to perform as part of his ordinary duty. After he "left his service" to enjoy an independent existence as a butcher, he was, as has been seen, engaged to carry out the treatment as required at an economical fee.

The butler no doubt carried the meals to the table although *waiting* at table was unusual;[1] he may have cleaned the much used pewter vessels, brass candlesticks and the very small amount of silver possessed by the family at that date. Such routine matters obviously would not be noted in the daily record of the master of the house. But what he does tell us of his butler's work would rouse disapproving astonishment in a latter-day manservant. Your Victorian major-domo uncorked the bottle and poured the wine: the eighteenth century butler first helped to create the drink and later served it. And when bidden to enquire how my lady of a neighbouring manor did when lying in of her son John or her daughter Anne, no inhuman telephone awaited Richard Cartwright's hand. He mounted a horse and, leaving behind the dull care of "putor and chinea," he rode across country to the Hall in question. There, having accomplished his errand, he received a "vale" and while subsequently comparing the beer or mead with which he was regaled with that of his own brewing, he will have collected all the deliciously intimate items of news concerning neighbouring families brought by the midwife—titbits to be conveyed back to his fellow-servants. Indeed his life could not be described as monotonous:

"I sent two panniers of Apples by Rich. Cartwright to Lever-

[1] *English Home Life*, Christina Holes.

poole to be sold. . . Rich. Cartwright climbed som Chimneys for young Swallows. . . Rich Cartwright and I took some bees on ye granary stayres. . . Rich Cartwright curled my wigg which I designe to give to James Houghton. . . I and Rich. Cartwright pitched and stopt the window on the stairhead to hinder ye wet from coming through. . . I sent Rich Cartwright to Croxteth to see Madam Molineux who was said to be in labour. . . I sent Rich. Cartwright to ye Grange to bottle of ye wine that was between Mr Rich. Molineux and me. . . We began to bord ye parlour. Rich. Cartwright brought some sheet lead for ye gutters from Leverpoole."

John Bannister was also frequently called upon to ride hither and thither on jobs quite outside a gardener's calling.

" I sent John Bannister to Leverpoole with bills of £235 to be sent by post for my brother Joseph and my Sisters at Gant. . . I helped John Bannister to redy[1] ye dining-room and to carry ye nets and some other things into ye store-hous, we also redied other Plases and layed up some things and hung Pictures in different plases. . . I sent John Bannister to Mr Plumb with a swan as a present. . . John Bannister layd some bottles of Green Gooseberries in a Hole in the Ground. . . John Bannister and two of my maids went towards Holly Well."

Pilgrimages to Holywell were frequently made by one of the men and two of the maids in company. They were absent three days, two being occupied in the outward and homeward journies and one in devotions at the shrine.

Recognised holidays were of course unknown, but there are many references in the Diary to the goings and comings of the servants to their own homes, and also to feasts, fairs, merry nights and " ye play." They often danced in kitchen or barn :

" The Miller played of his Fiddle to ye servants etc after supper till Pritty late. . ."

The same merry atmosphere prevailed in greater houses. When Lord and Lady Gerard were entertaining guests at Dutton Lodge " John, my Lord's brewer played on his Pips in ye kitchen and some of ye Servants dansed."

[1] To put in order.

Wages were low, hours of work unrestricted and probably very long; Nicholas describes himself as selling turves "before 4 of ye clock in the morning," and on one occasion notes that he and his wife came home in their coach from Scarisbrick, where they had been staying, "before seven of ye clock in the morning." They must have left Scarisbrick at 5 a.m. and the men will have had to feed and attend to the horses before that early hour. Nevertheless dependents, both men and women, lived very much with the family and took part in any pleasure within reach.

"Most of my servants, if not all, went to Ince to ye Merry Night . . . Some of Ince servants came hither to eat Christmas fair. . . My children and ye three maids went in ye coach to Formby [Hallowtide]. . . My wife, Moll Butler[1] and I went after supper to ye Mill. We dansed in ye kill[2]. . . My wife and Bradley walked to Lidiat and back. . . Mr Aldred and I skaited at Farmosspoole. There was with us . . . [among others] Mary Howard[3]—Mr Aldred and I made up a shod-sledg or trenow. My wife, Bradley etc went with us to Farmosspoole and rid in it . . . Mr Aldred fixed a back to ye sledge or trenow. We went to Farmospoole with it. The maids came with us."

In short the maids shared in the fun incidental to a hard frost in the country. When the excitement of draining the Long Pit and catching the fish at the bottom was afoot "the maids were with us part of the time."

The "rearing" or raising of the roof-tree of a building was always celebrated by dancing as well as by drinking.

"I went to Ditton, thinking to have been at the rearing of my new barn, but it was reared yesterday notwithstanding it was a most extream wet day. I drank at Mrs Travises with William Atherton,[4] severall of my workfolk etc. Will Atherton went home to ye Bank House. I went thither and dansed with ye neighbours." [Later in the same year 1708] "I went to Ditton after dinner. I lodged at ye Bank Hous. After supper I showed William Atherton, Philip Syer etc some tricks of legerdemesney

[1] The nursery-maid.
[2] Kiln.
[3] The housemaid.
[4] His chief tenant at Ditton.

and I set some of ye workfolks upon playing of tricks such as leaping of ye Rouling Pins etc."

Nicholas evidently greatly prided himself on his conjuring tricks and frequently records how he entertained people by their means.

When Fanny was six years old she was sent to stay with the Athertons at Ditton for change of air. After she had been there a fortnight Betty Harrison, the chamber-maid and dairy-maid, and Catty Howard, the cook " went towards Ditton to see Fanny. They designe to lodg at Leverpoole and goe on their journey tomorrow."

The two maids evidently walked all the way, and were absent for three days. Two months later :

" My wife rid behind me to Leverpoole. Betty Harrison and Catherine Howard walked there. We saw ye play acted called *Ye Earl of Essex*. . . My wife and I came home in ye wet between 4 and 5 next morning but it was so excessive wet that our maids came not home till afternoone."

When horses could be spared Nicholas mounted the maids as well as the men, for all could ride.

" I lent horses to Nanny Gorsuch and Jane Harrison to go to Leverpoole. It was a day of thanksgiving and great rejoicing for a victory obtained by the Duke of Marlborough. . . I lent Mary Woodcock a horse to ride on to Leverpoole. Eaves and she went together. . ."

On other occasions horses were lent when the maids rode together to have teeth extracted in Liverpool, or on the happier errand already alluded to of carrying eggs and butter to market. They stayed to sell their produce, thus agreeably varying their usual work.

" Nanny Blundell and Catty Howard went to Leverpoole with eggs, chees, fresh butter & salt butter. They sold almost all."

Hospitality was extended to friends and relatives of the men and maid servants as well as to those of the family.

" Bradley had been at her Father's. She came back hither. Her brother came along with her. He lodged here. . . Mr Aldred,

Bradley's brother and I layed fish lines. . . John Bannister's
half-sister lodged here. She fidled here. . . Thomas Tickley my
late Gardiner dined here. . . Ann Scot, her child, and her Brother
John lodged here. Nelly Sergeant's Mother lodged here. Nelly
Sergeant's Kinswoman Betty Bolton lodged here. So did Peggy
Jackson. . . John Bannister's Father lodged here. One Man and
two Women Acquaintances of Mary Molineux lodged here. . .
Dorothy Chaddock, an old Servant here, came to see me and
look about her. . . Dorothy Chaddock lodged here."

Even maids who had departed after " a fawling out" counted
upon hospitality at the Hall if they had occasion to pass that
way :

"Moll Butler, who had formerly been a nursery-maid here,
made a Visit hither. She came from Chester."

Cock-fighting was a sport ardently shared in by master and
man.

"Hen. Kerfoot took som cocks with him to Leverpoole and
fought two of them there. He fed them in my Pens. . . I weighed
my Cock and some others as are up in my Pens. . . Jo. Whitley
brought me a Cock which he lent me against my Cocking on
Easter Munday. . . I made a match with John Rose to play my
Ditton Cock Clumsey against one of his. . . Will. Ainsworth
brought me a Cock from Will Atherton of Ditton. I designe
to feed him against ye Cocking as is to be at Mrs Anns on
Easter Munday. . . I was at a Cocking at Mrs Ann Rothwells,
there was there my four Push-Ploughers, Rich. Webster our
Smith etc." Easter Monday : "We had a great cocking at Mrs
Ann Rothwells. They played Battle Victory. I had two Cocks
in ye Battle, and one of them got two battles. There were nine
Battles played this Afternoone. Mrs Blundell[1] and Mr Turbour-
ville[2] made a Viset here, but I came not to them from ye
Cocking."

The Diarist was as ferocious towards poachers as any squire
of later times when game was more extensively preserved. He

[1] Of Ince. She was daughter of Sir Charles Anderton of Lostock,
second Baronet.
[2] Rev. John Turberville, S.J., was chaplain to Lady Anderton.

constructed what he described as a "Duck coy"[1] at considerable expense and great was his wrath when trespassers took advantage of it to help themselves. He made an example of one:

"I began my journey towards Lancaster in order to try Thomas Hartley for destroying game in this township. . . I lodged at Marshalls ye Signe of ye Queens Arms. I suped there with Mr Darcy Chantrell. . . I had my tryall with Thomas Hartley & cast him."

The prosecution cost him a great deal: he fee'd two lawyers and paid them and their clerks £3 18s. 9d. besides the expenses of the journey, bringing a witness, and staying four days at an inn with a servant and three horses. Indeed Nicholas appears in his least amiable light when he brings a dishonest servant to justice, although doubtless the inhuman laws of his day seemed to him necessary and just. When he and Mally on one occasion "saw the drummer's wife whipt for stealing" in Liverpool he probably thought the sight an extremely wholesome one for his eight-year-old daughter, as a warning of the fate of the wicked.

Rich Ainsworth, his ploughman, must have been an ingenious fellow to make, or get hold of, a key to the cellar. The story of his first fall from grace is related in the Diary in the course of a week:

"Thelwall told me of Rich Ainsworth's key of ye cellar. . . I gave Warning to Rich Ainsworth that I would part with him owing to his having a Key of the Seller. . . Rich Ainsworth delivered me ye Key of the Seller which he had long time made use of much to my Damage."

Richard Ainsworth however remained in the neighbourhood, and two and a half years later he roused the Squire's wrath to a degree not to be placated. Here is the whole history:

"June 1st. 1708. A masty dogg, more meat, all absent things stolne. Twas Pater Aldred's advice.

---

[1] In the *Victoria History of Lancashire* it is stated that only two famous decoys are known to have existed in Lancashire, and a full description of the decoy at Hale is given. It occupied five acres of land, was most elaborately constructed, and was still in use at the beginning of the present century.

June 4th. I sent Thelwell to Leverpool to get a Warrand to serch R. Ainsworth's Hous etc. which William Weedon ye Cunstable did. He had for his Assistance John Gregory ye Slater and W.Marser. I and Thelwall also helped to sirch.

June 5th. I went to Leverpoole and had R. Ainsworth examined for Robing me before Mr Rich Norres ye Maior, Sir Thos. Johnson,[1] etc.

June 7th. I told R. Ainsworth I would send to fetch Away ye Goods he had Stolne from me.

June 8th. I and Thelwell went with William Weedon ye Cunstable to Rich Ainsworth's and Brought Home in a Cart some Boards, iron etc as he had stolne from me.

July 11th. Rich Ainsworth desired I would Pardon him before ye Assizes. I ordered him to meet me at Leverpoole.

July 12th. I went to Leverpoole to meet William Gray[2] and Rich Ainsworth. . . I spoke to Mr Plumb about Rich Ainsworth.

Aug. 4th. Rich Ainsworth desired to know whether I would Pardon him before the Assizes. I told him ' noe ' and advised him to make what Provition he could against his tryall.

Aug. 13th. It was first proposed to me to let Rich. Ainsworth contribute to enlarg Mr Aldred's Hous and not to take him to Lancaster. I sent for Richard Jump and discoursed him about what he knew of Rich. Ainsworth robing me.

Aug. 14th. I went to Leverpoole and discoursed Mr Plumb about Richard Ainsworth. He, William Weedon, T. Kerfoot etc were present. It was at ye Wool Pack in ye Dining-roome.

Aug. 15th. I went after Dinner to Scarisbrick and discoursed Lord Mountgarrett, Sir William Gerard & Coz. Robert Scarisbrick about Rich Ainsworth and we considered whether it were better to try him or Compound with him.

Aug. 17th. I examined my Diurnall to find out ye Dayes of ye

[1] Sir Thomas Johnson was one of the prominent citizens of Liverpool who, first as Mayor, and subsequently as M.P., contributed most by his energy, power and influence to the development of the town and port during the early part of the eighteenth century.

[2] Gray and Weedon were Blundell's tenants and Weedon was employed by him.

month which I thought most Materiall for me to be ready in against I went to prosecute Rich Ainsworth at ye Assizes.

Aug. 18th. I went to Lancaster to Prosecute Rich Ainsworth for Robery.

Aug. 19th. I dined at my Lodgings with Mr Roughley and one or two more of ye Grand Jury. I and Walt Thelwall were examined by ye Grand Jury against Rich. Ainsworth. Sir Thomas Johnson was ye foreman. I heard Judg. Trecy give his Charg.

Aug. 20th. Rich Ainsworth was found guilty of Robery before Judg. Trecy.

Aug. 21st. Rich Ainsworth and two Others were burned in ye Hand."

From the Disbursement Book:

"What followes is ye Charges I was at in prosecuting R. Ainsworth at Lancaster and for my own expence. Some little more was spent by Thelwall of himself & Witnesse:

	s.	d.
Drawing of ye Inditement	2	6
Bayliff	1	0
Swearing 4 witnesses & to ye pourter ...	1	8
Mr Plumb's fee at ye tryall	6	8
Dore-keeper to ye Grand Jury		6
Meat & drink for myself from home to Lancaster & back again	8	2
Horses	6	0
Proofses three	1	0
Oates		10
Witnesses Robinson 10/- Wm Weedon 7/-	17	0 "

To the above items had to be added those included in Thelwall's accounts.

	s.	d.
"Geting a Warrand for R.Ainsworth & Spent	2	6
Spent going to Ri. Robinson	1	10
Spent by Thelwall at Lankaster on himself and in part on witnesses	12	4½ "

It all amounted to the total of £3.6s.½d., while the wages of the defendant had been £4 per annum. But where there was any question of dishonesty Nicholas seems to have been unforgiving, except in one case when his wife intervened:

"Oct. 9th. 1714. I intercepted a Peece of Beef as Margaret Ridgat was sending to her Mother for which I turned her out of my Hous for this Night, but upon her great Submission I took her again next day."

His suspicions of worse depredations were however roused.

"Oct. 21st. I went to Leverpoole and got a Warrand to Apprehend Margaret Ridgat. I serched her mother's and her Brother John's hous in Great Crosby, Rob. Johnstone ye Cunstable."

Evidently nothing was found and his wrath subsided.

"Oct. 22nd. James Davy ye Cunstable came hither to carry Margaret Ridgat before Sir Thomas Johnson, but my wife beged me to Pardon her."

Probably the culprit's services could not have been dispensed with conveniently, and husband and wife saved themselves trouble and expense by forgiving her.

Timber was scarce and the purloining of wood constituted an offence not to be condoned, as has been seen in the case of Richard Ainsworth. Another offender was summarily dealt with.

"I turned off Ailes Davy from Working for me becaus she took some Wood more than I gave her."

We are afforded sad glimpses of Joseph Massey, ploughdriver,[1] who received £1 2s. 3d. for his first six months' service.

"I sent Joseph Massey to Leverpoole for a Pennance becaus he refused to fetch a Mugg of Butter out of ye Towne. . . I was told Jo. Massey had robed me. . . I sent Weedon to Leverpoole to get a Warrand upon Account of Things stolne by Jo. Massey . . . Ellin Massey's Hous and some Others were sirched for Things supposed to be Stolne by Joseph Massey. I searched Joseph's Chest where I found some Things he had Stolne. . . Weedon ye Cunstable seased upon Joseph Massey and I turned him out of my Service."

[1] A boy who drove the oxen while the ploughman directed the implement.

It is to be feared that Joseph received the usual sentence for minor thefts, namely a public whipping, for the cost to the Squire of bringing him to justice was insignificant.

"Charges spent in punishing Joseph Massey, in all 7s. 7d."

Many years later Massey appears upon the scene again in an unfavourable light.

"The Overseer of Ince brought Joseph Massey and his Wife into this Towne. Being this is their Settlement we accepted of them but they doe not come yet to Live here."

By the Act of Settlement[1] of 1662 each parish was bound to find accommodation for the persons born within its boundaries and to support those unable to support themselves. Joseph Massey seems to have been turned out of the township of Ince as an undesirable resident.

Nicholas might, with more reason, have acted with corresponding severity towards his steward Walter Thelwall who had been trusted by three generations at Crosby before the Diarist discovered that "his accounts were not quit adjusted." He pointed this out to Thelwall and they agreed to part. The steward retired to his own holding which had been granted to him for his life by William Blundell the Cavalier, who had remitted the usual deposit or "fine." Nicholas had included his son's life in the lease of three lives also without taking a fine. "I hoped," he writes in the Tenant's Book, "he would prove a good Servant and sinceir Friend in advising me (who was then young and ignorant) to Manage my affairs and to know what Fines to demand of my Tenants by informing me of ye Price of each Teneament. But he proved Otherwayes. . . Walter Thelwall did not whilst he was my Servant carry himself as if he had received any Favour or Kindness from this Famoly, and after he left my Service I had no Reason to look upon him as a Friend to me or a Well-wisher to ye Township of Little Crosby but much otherwayes."

Yet the two men remained outwardly friends.

"Most of my Servants went to Great Crosby to drink Walter Thelwall's Farewell."

---

[1] See Trevelyan, *History of England in the Reign of Queen Anne,* Vol. I.

I

A few days later the dismissed steward was assisting his late employer in an awkward job.

" I burned some of my Beas[1] in ye Hornes, this being ye first Time I began to mark them in ye Hornes. Mr. Aldred, Thelwall etc. helped me."

Thereafter Thelwall is constantly in the picture in all matters connected with the tenants for he was a useful, able man, much above his neighbours in education. Five years elapsed before the Diary reveals a contemporary's bad opinion of him, but without comment :

" Edmund Tristram[2] said he could prove Walt Thelwall a Rogue."

[1] Thus he invariably spells *Beasts*.
[2] Yeoman of Ince Blundell. *Non-Jurors.*

CHAPTER VII

WORKFOLK AND CRAFTSMEN

I

NICHOLAS differentiates between "my servants," who were the men in his regular employment, and "my workfolk," these last constituting the far more numerous contingent of casual labourers both men and women, who weeded, reaped, sheared sheep, "push-ploughed," burned the moss or "fleas" skinned from the surface of the undrained fields by the push-plough, grubbed up gorse, cleaned ditches, and spread mole-heaps. The majority had their own holdings and eked out their livelihood by such seasonal employments, or paid their rent in part by boon work.

The Squire associated with his workfolk daily, and frequently helped them with the task in hand:

"Philip Syer began to lay a Cundit[1] overcross ye way between ye Long Garden and ye Bleaching-Ground. I helped to carry a Great many of ye Stones. . . I was most of ye Afternoone in ye Next North Hey, helping ye Workmen up with two great Roots of trees out of ye new Moss pits. . . I helped to Winnow some of ye worst wheat with ye Fann. . . I was in ye Winter Heys with my Workfolk. There was a great thunder Shower and all or most of us took Shelter. Thence I went to see John and Jane Bryanson who were ill. . . I went betymes in ye Morning to my Burners in ye Winter Heys and after Dinner I stayed with them till Night and gave them a Sillibube. I had 32 Hands working for me at my Water-Cours. . . I went to them in ye Morning and brought them some strong Drink and Bisket, and went againe after dinner and brought some more strong Drink. . . I was most of ye Afternoone with my Burners in ye Winter Heyes. I

[1] Conduit.

sent them Two large Pailes of Whey which was very acceptable."

During the harvest Nicholas went busily from one group of reapers to another; thus of one day he writes:

"I went to my Mowers in Nicholas Hey. I was also with my Shearers of Barley in ye Pike and with my Leaders[1] of Otes in ye Little More Hey."

The demand on the boon worker's time was not heavy, "cottage boons" usually amounting to six days in the whole year. The hardship must have lain in being summoned to work for the landlord in good weather when the boon-worker could have harvested his own crop had it not been for the Squire's summons. There are many entries in the Diary announcing that its writer had been in person or had sent his steward, "to Warne Boon-workers for tomorrow," and only one to the effect that men so warned had refused to present themselves. It seems to have been understood that the tenant had no right to choose the days on which to give free toil as part of his rent. He was however entitled by his lease to pay 6d. per day "in lieue of reaping" and 3d. per day "in lieue of Cottage Boon" which included such jobs as cleaning ditches. Rent and Boon Tallies of the Cavalier's day show that smallholders paying a yearly rent of 3s. to 5s. were called upon to do three days' boon shearing[2] and three days boon carting or ploughing, the work to be "due upon warning." Farmers of a more considerable area had to do two or three days' work with their own teams, according to the size of their farms, or to pay 1s. for each day. The part payment of rent in hens was an easy method for both cottager and farmer who grew their own poultry food or obtained it largely by gleaning. A hen for this purpose was valued at sixpence; six birds were usually paid on the Crosby estate and were demanded in winter when meat was scarce.

"Dec. 9th. 1709. I went to ye Morehouses and ordered most of ye Tenants to bring som Boone Hens."

[1] Carters.

[2] The Diarist uses the word *shearing* for cutting corn as well as in the ordinary sense.

When a new tenant took up a holding he paid a preliminary deposit or "fine," in consideration of which the family enjoyed undisputed possession during the lives of the three persons mentioned in the lease. The agreement terminated at the end of ninety-nine years, even if one of the three were still living. This system pressed very unfairly on the tenant's family in those days of uncontrolled epidemics and practically non-existent medical help, when life was shorter and more uncertain than now.

An fine of £12 was paid for a cottage at Ditton with Right of Common and two roods thirty-two perches of land; the rent was 7s. per annum paid in two instalments at midsummer and Martinmas, and one day's boon reaping or 3d. and one day's breaking of flax or 3d. The lives in such leases were usually those of husband and wife and son or daughter. When one died the remaining two usually sought to increase their security by paying a smaller additional fine to add another life to the lease. A very considerable family effort must have been required to save £12, owing to the small wages earned and the consequent necessity of subsisting on the produce of the holding; but it secured possession of a home possibly for three generations.

In that independent age housing shortage in the country was easily met, although the disgraceful housing of the working-class in the towns was already a blot on the land. The following account of the erection of a cottage is taken from among others in the Diarist's "Tenants' Book."

"Farrer, Edward has A.D.1717 or thereabouts erected a cottage built with stone containing two good Bays[1] by consent of me Nicholas Blundell, upon the Waist opposite to his Brother's hous. Edward Farrer has also inclosed a long Garden Spot and a pretty little croft upon ye Waist adjoining to his Hous, in consideration of which he is to pay me yearly 2s., to do one day Reaping yearly or instead thereof to pay 6d. He the said Edward Farer is to enjoy the said Hous, Little Croft and Garden for 99 years determinable upon the life of Edward, Ellin his wife and James their son, and being he was at the sole charge of building ye hous I did not demand any fine thô think

[1] A bay was a division of a building—especially when timber-framed —generally 15 to 20 feet in length.

perhaps hereafter a small Fine may be demanded and perhaps he may have Liberty to enclose a little more of ye Waist."

So Edward Farrer, by his own industry and enterprise, provided himself with a home at a ground rent of 2s. per annum and one day's reaping.

The last sentence in the above-quoted lease and many others like it, were for the guidance of the Diarist's heir, written with the calm assumption of the eighteenth century countryman that the world would go on as he knew it for ever. Indeed in the Diarist's day he and his neighbours were still paying feudal Chief Rents.

"I sent Walt Thelwall to Mosborough with three pound of pepper for rent," he wrote on March 21st, 1705. Two years later, when renewing a lease, he inserted a clause binding Nicholas Abram, the tenant, to pay yearly "on ye 21st. December one pound of Pepper to Mr Molyneux of ye Wood[1] upon Account of ye Pepper Fields for which I have good old deeds to show."

Nicholas received Chief Rent from the head of another branch of the Molyneux family.

"Mr Molineux of ye Grange came hither and paid me his tenpenny rent."

II

"Charr-women" are sometimes mentioned in the Disbursement Book, and on a solitary occasion "A Drudg" appears in the person of William Fisher, who received the relatively large sum of 15s. at a single payment. His unspecified work must have been of an out-door nature, otherwise "ye hous" is always mentioned. Thus:

	s.	d.
"Charr Work in ye hous	1	7"

[1] This branch of the Molyneux Family originated in Thornton, one mile from Little Crosby. It had moved to The Wood, Melling, in the reign of Edward III. The Diarist's relative and neighbour, although still designated "of the Wood," was in fact living at Mosborough Hall, St. Helen's, which had descended to him through the female line from the Lathoms.

An intriguing casual worker constantly figures on the pages of Diary and Disbursement Book as "Darby Wife." Darby himself accomplished such divers jobs as mending a pair of shoes, or breaking up old bricks. He is mentioned among the sick visited by the Squire. There is a disapproving note in the following two entries in the Diary which suggest that he was not addicted to regular work and did not control his son.

"Dec. 7th. 1709. I found Darby and Skinner Blundell playing at Tables at Ailes Davy's after eleven of ye Clock at Noon. They had been playing all ye Night.

March 2nd. 1710. I called at Darby's and discoursed him and his Wife about their Son Katching Rabets."

But "Darby Wife" is shown repeatedly through the years in the capacity of a trusted messenger. The usual entry in the Disbursement Book is: "Darby Wife for gong Arrants at 4d. per Day."

The enterprising woman seems to have been ready to stay away a night or two whenever her destination was too far to allow of her return on the same day. There is no record of expenses for a horse or public conveyance on any of her journeys which must therefore have been accomplished on foot. "March 9th. 1709. Darby Wife brought me from Mosborough 138 Carp Fray, 8 Tensh, Carp, Mungrills and 22 Roach."

It was a journey of twenty-four miles, with a burden probably of two cans of water containing the fish, on the homeward way. We find Darby Wife taking a present of fish to Lord Mountgarrett at Ormskirk, a distance of twelve miles, or of black puddings to Mr. Plumbe in Liverpool. On one occasion she carried a bass-viol to Ormskirk for Richard Butler, Lord Mountgarrett's schoolboy son, who had been staying at Crosby and evidently could not convey the musical instrument on horseback. Her furthest recorded journey was "into Cheshire." She may have been away for two or three days, since for this single excursion she received 3s., an amount nearly equal to a month's wages for a housemaid.

A privileged casual worker was Ned Howard, son of John Howard, concerning whom William Blundell, the Cavalier, left the following emphatic instructions in his Tenants' Book, dated January 15th, 1663.

"I do strictly charge and conjure my Heir and as far as lawfully I maye, I do oblige him hereby in strict Justice that he do regard ye Heir of John Howard according as he regardeth or ought to regard his antient Tenants. And I do further desyre my Heir to show sometymes unto ye said John and his children some marks of particular favour which may be known to be chiefly don in memory, and gratitude, for ye long and faithful service of his Uncle Edward Denton performed to my Grandfather and myself."

As a result, no doubt, of these injunctions the Diarist and Edward Howard had evidently grown up in friendship. Howard visited Nicholas in his bedroom when he was ill, and often "smoaked a pip" with him and also, on one occasion at least, with Lord Mountgarret when he was on a visit to Crosby. He helped the Squire not only with his writings but with some of his more delicate tasks : "Ned Howard was in my Closet most of ye morning making Skull Powder."

Howard was away from his home in service when Mr. Aldred was established in his house, which presumably had been unoccupied as there is no mention of a family. In April, 1713, he returned to Little Crosby and immediately set about improving the chapel, a work in which the Squire and his neighbours assisted him :

"April 3rd. I discourced Ned Howerd about enlarging ye Chappell and promised him somthing towards it.

April 13th. I gave Ned Howerd £3 towards inlarging his Chappell.

April 18th. William Thelwall[1] brought me a long Ash-Tree for which I am to give Ned Howerd an Oak Beame for his new Building.

April 20th. Yester Night and this Morning I took a Doce of Pills. Ned Howerd dined with me in my Roome."

Ned Howerd now found he was short of room for himself

---

[1] A carpenter, son of Walter Thelwall.

and had evidently come to consult the Squire about it. The matter was swiftly and simply dealt with.

"April 30th. My two Teames and four others led some Slates for Ned Howerd for the enlaging of his Hous.

May 4th. Ned Howerd began to build a Chamber for himself."

III

The craftsmen employed for special jobs were possibly not included by the Diarist in the category of Workfolk, for they were themselves employers of labour.

"Masons' Work at ye pillers before ye Gallery Window 140 dayes and ½, besides Meat, drink & Lodging. Ye Master Workman had 9d. per day, some of his men 8d., others 6d.: pay'd £3 16s. 4d."

Work in connection with the mill was probably the most important in this category. Earlier generations of the Blundell family had depended largely upon the mill for their livelihood, and even in the Diarist's day it was all-important to the economy of the countryside. The obligation "to grind at my mill" was inserted in every lease, payment for the work being made in "toll corn" which contributed considerably to the Squire's income. It was not with a disinterested eye that he surveyed the field operations of his tenants.

"I went into Thomas Syers Corn Fields and took account of what numbers of Threaves[1] he had in each field."

The interior of the mill was a scene of great activity when the wind was favourable, but when the creaking and groaning of the turning sails was stilled during calm weather, it afforded space for dancing or a village meeting. It could be a comfortable place in those days, when there was no machinery to keep up incessant noise.

"I sat some time in my Mill," writes Nicholas more than once, and on one occasion when he was indisposed: "I went to ye Mill and took a Nap there."

[1] Twenty sheaves equalled one threave.

After the harvest, when work was heavy and the autumn winds provided plenty of power, the Squire's butler was called upon to undertake night shifts at the mill in addition to his already multifarious duties.

Consternation must have reigned when the mill was out of order; expert workmen were summoned in haste:

"Dec. 3rd. 1710. I sent my Miller for ye Mill Rights, my Mill having suffered very great damage in ye Sales and Shaft this last Night by ye Winde."

The millwrights worked in a family team.

"Dec. 5th. Rich Dauber came to repair ye great Loss I have suffered in my Mill.

Dec. 6th. Henry Dauber ye Mill Right and his Nephew James came to mend my Mill, and ye two Sawyers Richard and Joseph came to do ye Sawing Work for it. I helped Henry Dauber to see whether I had any Tree growing about ye Hous proper for a Mill Shaft.

Dec. 7th. I felled an Oak Tree between ye New Orchard & the New Grounds for a Mill Shaft.

Dec. 11th. Charles Howerd brought me Home two Fir Ballks for my Mill from Thomas Hurst.

Dec. 21st. I put up a new Mill Shaft.

Dec. 23rd. I paid off ye Sawers, and ye Mill Rights went hence.

Jan. 9th. 1711. My Mill was set a-going, it being ye first Time it went since it was so ill Brocken."

Mill-stones were brought from a distance and cost £4 each.

"Hugh Whitley brought me a Mill Stane from Whitly[1] Hill. I paid him for it."

When new sails were required or the old ones needed repair, a tailor carried out the work on the spot, after various local craftsmen had manufactured the cloth mainly from locally grown materials.

"November 1712. I made one half of a new sail Cloth for each of my six Sailes and put them upon ye driving and following sides, some of it was Lincy Wolsey woven Twill way & a full yard broad, it lay me in 18d. per yard viz 7d. per Pound for ye

[1] Whittle-le-Woods, near Chorley.

Wool when it was Spun, Teer of Hemp Spun fine at 10½ per pound; Weaving 26 yards at 4d. per yard, and all outcast was paid for; Winding ye Teer of Hemp at ½d per Pound. Totall Lincy Wolcy when Woven lay me in £1 19 0. Holland Duck 2 Foot 6 Inches wide 21d per yard £1 0 ½d. Rushton Yarne supposed to be woven licke Pole Davy, some of it was above 2 Foot wide at 9d per yard, some Not so wide at 9¼d 15s. 10½d. Hare Cording at 8d per Pound, Tarr Cording at 4½ per Pound ye Cording cost 11s. 5d. Holland Thread two Pound 1s. 8d. Making ye six half Sailes at 6d per Day and Meat to ye Taylor 4s. Part of some of ye above mentioned things was left so that ye six halfe Sailes lay me in £4 7s. 1d.

Spinners were engaged to work in the house by the day as required. The village weaver converted home-grown flax into linen for payment which varied according to the quality and breadth of the materials he was ordered to produce. For "fine Flaxon a full yard wide" he received 2½d. per yard, and 1¼d. for a lesser width. A spinner boarded in the house received 7d. per week. While the weaving of camblet cost 6d. per yard, 12s. was paid for weaving 8 yards of "Fine Flaxon. It was most extreamely Troblesom." The weaver received 2d. per ell for his work on "cours Flaxon for ye Servants' Sheets," but when Nicholas bought "Flaxon for Shirting" he gave 1s. 3d. per yard for the finished material. For "bucking and bleaching fine Flaxon Yarne" 1¼d. per lb. was paid, and 3½d. per yard to the village forerunner of modern dyers and cleaners for "scouring, dying and Callendering Camblet."

Home-grown wool for country clothes was also dealt with in the neighbourhood from the moment it left the sheep's back. The shearer, if not a boon-worker, was paid 2d. per sheep; 3d. per lb. was the rate for spinning the yarn and 1d. for bleaching it.

In 1712 the Squire noted with evident satisfaction the economical cost of a suit for himself made out of his own wool.

"They began to spin this Year's Wool to Make me a Sute of clothes on. . I had a Webb of Druget made for my own Wearing. It made one Coat, a Wastcoat and two pare of Britches.

	s.	d.
Reckening my own Wool and Spinning to utmost it Cost per Yard. Some of ye Particulars as followeth:	2	4

	s.	d.
Weaving 15 Yards of druget	5	1
Woosted yarne 3 pound	6	0
Woolen Yarne 1 pound	1	0
Dying and Walking 12 yards of Druget ...	4	6
Buttens, Silk, Shammy etc for making up my first Hom-made Sute of Clothes ...	16	6"

Tailors often stayed in the house while they worked on the Squire's "sute," liveries for the menservants, or "mantews" and petticoats for Mrs. Blundell and her daughters. The cost of their "bord" was reckoned, as in the case of other workers, at 4d. per day.

	s.	d.
"Making two Liverys at my Bord	9	0
Making two Mantews and two Petticoats and one Apron ...	1	6
Leting out my London Sute ...	2	0
Making Mally's Coat here	5	0
Altering my gray Sute ...	1	0
Altering my Wives Mantew ...	2	0"

Workfolk and boon carts were much employed in the transport of both coal and turf.

"I led Turves with 12 Boone Carts. . . I sent my Carts to ye Cole Pits. They brought Home about 20 Baskets.[1]

"I led one work of Coles with my own two Teames and four Boones. . . I brought Home two Cart Lode of Cannell from Sir Roger's Pits."

Sir Roger Bradshaigh of Haigh, Blundell's cousin, had developed a great trade in coal from his estate at Wigan. The cannel coal was so hard that it could be cut and polished like marble. Favourite presents from inhabitants of Lancashire to their friends were objects made from cannel.

[1] One basket equalled two bushels.

The "provision of Cole for ye Winter" was always made in summer when the roads were dry. The Crosby Hall teams and the boon carts went to all the pits within reach. The Disbursement Book sets forth the following entries, all under one date, September 29th, 1709.

> "Coles from Hightown[1] 13 Baskets at 2d per
>   Basket they were one Load   ...   ...   2s.   2d.
> Coles from Sir Thomas Standley one Work
>   and 36 Baskets they were nine Load & cost 12s.   0d.
> Coles from Whiston one Work and 36
>   Baskets they were eight Load and Cost ... 13s. 10d."

A number of Coroner's Inquests[1] held towards the end of the eighteenth century revealed haphazard conditions in the coal pits which will have been even more primitive in the Diarist's time. Children were let down into the pits "to draw coals" by a rope on a windlass, which anybody who happened to be in the neighbourhood was permitted to work, with the result that fatal accidents were frequent.

Nicholas was brought in touch with another group of craftsmen when he was elected churchwarden of the beautiful parish church at Sephton. Catholics were no longer refused burial[3] there although priests who died in the neighbourhood, and a small percentage of layfolk, were interred in the Harkirk burial ground in the Diarist's time. Mistress Frances Blundell was probably laid to rest there by her own wish. The last person to be buried there was the Rev. Peter Williams S.J., in 1753.

In the eighteenth century churchwardens still had many duties which were not identified with worship in the edifice concerned, and a heavy fine was imposed on anyone who refused to undertake them. The Diarist's final consent to act, after at first refusing and subsequently seeking advice in the matter, may have been dictated by the secret hope, shared by many of his neighbours, that the church might be restored to Catholic worship if a Catholic king ascended the throne. Little Crosby, which

[1] Huyton, near Prescot.
[2] *Historic Society of Lancashire and Cheshire*, Vol. 86.
[3] *Cavalier's Note Book.*

is now a separate parish, was then included in that of Sephton. Nearly all the land covered by the parish was owned by members of the Molyneux family who, with Lord Molyneux at its head, were all Catholics, while a very large percentage of the country folk clung to the ancient faith. On one side of the church was the chantry known as the Blundell chapel, on the other the Molyneux chapel where the heads of the respective families were buried of right even in the worst days of persecution. Before the Reformation the Blundell family had of course attended Sephton parish church.[1]

In the spring of 1714 Queen Anne's health was failing so rapidly that the question of her successor could not remain for long undecided. Her ministers were secretly intriguing with James Stuart who would have encountered little opposition on landing in England had he been willing to forswear his religion. Jacobites of all religious views openly anticipated the peaceful triumph of their cause, and recusants hoped for a coming deliverance from the oppression of the penal laws.

The following letter, addressed by Nicholas to the Superior of the many Jesuit chaplains in the neighbourhood, seems to hint at this possibility. Priests and parsons were in the habit of meeting amicably at a social club in Sephton. Father Babthorpe thought this should be stopped; the Squire thought otherwise.

" To Mr Babthorpe   June 14th, 1715.
By some of yours abstaining from harmless and good company as upon occasion they have with a great deale of innocency kept, and by words as by the by I have heard, I do conjecture (pardon me if I mistake) that it is by your orders. But this refusall of their usuall conversation I know is taken very henously and not without reason, especially by some parsons who have often been checked for being conversant with some of yours and have, notwithstanding these rebukes, still desired their company because they find them men of parts, good company and conversation & free from all manner of vice; but now to refraine their company at this juncture they say is onely becaus ye priests must caball amongst themselves and at ye least pros-

[1] The Catholic church at Little Crosby was not built until 1847.

pect of change, contemne those who wish them well and have suffered Reproach for Speaking well of them. And if these sivell Parsons in whose Power it was to doe an Unkindness be exasperated, I am afraid it may be of Ill consequence. . . I suppose ye Occasion hereof may proceed from ye Insinuasion of som who perhaps may Spend their time less innocently than those who meet with Parsons and some of ye Best of ye Parish once a week, to keep up good Conversation and correspondence and to divert themselves at ye Expence of 6d per week."

On a later occasion Nicholas deliberately averted his election as churchwarden at Ditton by arrangement with his friends and tenants there, while his neighbour the Squire of Ince enlisted his help " to prevent his being chosen Church-Warden."

But to return to the spring of 1714:

" March 30th. . . went to Sefton to ye Parish meeting but all business was over and found ye Parish had chosen me to be their Church Warden.

April 1st. Went to Ormskirk and advised with Mr Brooks[1] about my being Chosen a Church Warden of Sefton Parish.

April 2nd. Went to Sefton and told Parson Letus I would not stand as Church Warden.

April 5th. I lodged in Chester at Mr Pantons[2] ye Signe of ye Whit Bull out of Norgate.

April 6th. I acquainted Mr Bourchier that I was chosen Church Warden of Sefton and advised with him about it. Mr Panton went with me to look at Severall flower Gardens in Chester. I bought some Gloves for my Wife of Mr Edward Glegg[3] and left my Lether Britches with him, to get washed since which time I have received them very well done."

Mr. Bouchier's advice evidently coincided with the Diarist's own wish, and he now proceeded to devote himself with his usual whole-heartedness to the business involved in his new

[1] A lawyer.

[2] The Rolls of the Freemen of Chester for 1732 cite Charles Panton, goldsmith, as " son of Edward Panton, innholder."

[3] The Rolls (as above) for 1709-10 name Edward Glegg as " son of William Glegg of Whitby, Co. Chester, gentleman, apprentice of Thomas Jackson of Chester, skinner, defunct."

rôle. The protestant yeoman, Thomas Syer, distinguished from
the recusant of the same name by the designation "of the Ford,
was chosen to act with him, and Nicholas seems to have been
empowered to delegate some of his duties.

"April 16th. I went to John Sumner[1] and agreed with him to
act in part as Churchwarden for me.

April 21st. I met Thomas Syer at Harsnops;[2] 'tis the first
time we met to consult of ye Parish Affaires since we were
Church Wardens, we caused a Chest over ye Church Pourch to
be brock open as had not ben opened of very many years.

April 30th. I met Thomas Syer at Leverpoole. We being ye
Church Wardens bought two Locks for ye use of ye Church and
promised Rich. Eccleston that he should do ye Plumbing and
Glaizing work at Sefton Church. Thomas Syer and I looked at
ye Legasy Table in ye Old Church in Leverpoole.

May 1st. Thomas Syer and I met at Harsnops to receive ye
Church Leyes[3] through the Parish from ye Cunstables but few
of them came, we looked to see in what Repaire ye Leads were
in and ye Windows, we drunk at Harsnops with Parson Letus
Thomas Bradley etc. Thomas Bradley was here in ye Morning
I signed a Petission for him to show to ye Bishops Court about
geting a Seat in Sefton Church, he suckseeded in it."

[1] Probably the son of Sarah Sumner of Thornton, widow, who was
possessed of a house in Thornton and another in Little Crosby. The
Sumners were tenants of the Little Crosby estate in the Cavalier's time

[2] Roger Harsnip was landlord of the Church Inn.

[3] The Leys were the Rates of the day.

"The Oxlay is used for provision of oxen for the King's Majesty'
Household.

The Maimed Lay is for the relief of sick, hurt and maimed soldier
and mariners.

The Prisoners Lay is used for the relief of poor prisoners in the
King's Majesty's prison at Lancaster.

The Soldiers' Lay or County Lay is for the mustering, arming o
furnishing soldiers for the King's Majesty's wars, or for the trained
bands or for the repair of bridges or any other use or purpose within
the said county."

From a manuscript written for the use of John Yates, the County
Treasurer, in 1716, and published in Gregson's *Lancashire*, 1824.

So great was the demand for accommodation in church in those days that when a protestant tenant at Ditton was unable to obtain a seat in Farnworth church, Nicholas took the matter to the Bishop's court, claiming that a " pue " in the church had belonged to his family from time immemorial and that it was within his right to allot it to his tenant. As he obtained no satisfaction in the Bishop's court the case was tried in the law courts at Chester and was won by Nicholas. He now consolidated his claim.

" May 13th. I was at ye Bishops Court in Ormskirk, the Chancellor gave me leave in ye Presence of Mr Roberts and Mr Sankey to put Doars without locks to my Pew in Farnworth Chappell. Being Thomas Syer and I are ye Church Wardens we dined at ye Talbot in Ormskirk with Parson Letus, Parson Wairing etc."

During their term of office Nicholas and Thomas Syer directed Richard Eccleston's work on the leads of the church roof, Richard Webster's repairs to the font, Richard Heaton's and John Melling's mending of " ye Bell Wheele," and William Abbot's construction of " stayres for ye Pulpit." One Master Hunt " desired he might writ out some of ye Olde Church Wardens accounts if they were to be Writ out for Hier," but the job was given to Walter Thelwall whose fine handwriting, with its great display of flourishes, is much in evidence in the Tenant's Book and the Recipe Book at Crosby. Richard Eccleston's bill was not passed by the two churchwardens :

" I went to Leverpoole there Thomas Syer and I discoursed Richard Eccleston and made him give us a more moderate Bill of work done by him for Sefton Church."

A few days later : " Thomas Syer and I had Richard Eccleston and the Clark under examination about the Plumbers Bill before Parson Letus at his own Hous."

Presumably a compromise was arrived at under the guidance of Parson Letus for the matter is not mentioned again. Nicholas next relates :

" I discoursed William Abbot about making Stayers for ye Pulpet of Sefton Church."

K

The construction of a hearse for the parish was entrusted to Richard Heaton and William Abbot.

"Oct. 5th. I went to Great Crosby and spoke to Thomas Syer about Parish Affairs. Then I went to Rich Heaton's and Will Abbot's to see how they went forward with the Corps Carriage and Pulpit stayres."

The hearse was not finished until the following year; throughout the winter Nicholas, sometimes accompanied by his little daughters, made visits of inspection to the workshops of Abbot and Heaton; in the spring Glaziers were engaged to mend the church windows.

"Feb. 20th, Thomas Syer was here. I showed him ye Table of Fees I had drawn up and ye Orders as I intended to propose for the good of the Parish.

Feb. 27th. I put ye Harnish as were fited up and bought for the Parish Hears, on two of my Horses and drue them in ye Harnish and rectifyed what was a Miss.

March 21st. Thomas Syer and I met at Harsnops to hear the Cunstables make their Presentments to the Assizes. Some of us went into the Church and layed one Church Ley and then went into a Roome from ye rest of ye Company except some as came to us.

April 6th. I went both before and after Dinner to Will Abbots to see how ye Painters went forward with ye Parish Hears. I went to Sefton Church to see what ye Painter had don at ye Pulpit.

April 9th. We brought ye Parish Hears from William Abbots to ye Church and there set it up.

April 12th. Thomas Syer and I met at Sefton, we ordered how ye Table of the Benefactors was to be hung and gave the Painter orders about it. Thomas Syer computed what Timber was used about ye Pulpit Stayres, we examined part of Will Abbots Bill.

April 13th. Thomas Syer dined here. He and I were extraordinary busy both before and after Dinner drawing up our Parish Accounts against Easter."

Finally on April 19th: "Thomas Syer and I delivered up our Account as Church Wardens they were read in the Church and severall Stints were set for the better Regulating the Affairs of the Parish, there was present Parson Wairing, Thomas Bradley etc. I gave Parson Letus £5 towards the Augmentation of ye Parish Stock."

During the months in which the Diarist accomplished his duties as churchwarden with characteristic thoroughness, England passed through one of the most decisive periods in her history. It has already been noticed that Queen Anne's death is not even remotely alluded to in Blundell's Diary. He gave considerable space however to his account of a great storm in the following February.

"The first day of this month there was a most Prodigious great Wind which did a bundance of Damage in some parts of England though others suffered little or nothing by it. I am told that in one Parish of Lancashire it blowed down 14 Barnes and it is not to be imagined how many Barnes were blowed down in ye County and many of them were built of Brick & in good Repair, of which mine was one. The chief Dammage was upon Barnes, to say nothing of ye great quantity of Thatch as was blown off Houses & Barnes which made Straw in some Plases above three times ye Price it formerly was, and so scarce that severall were fourced to lay on their old Thatch & cover it over with Sods of Earth. They say in Cheshire and Wales this Wind did more Dammage than in Lancashire. Some sayes this Wind was a greater loss to the Country than one year's Land Tax."

On the day on which the tempest took place Nicholas states that "it did more damage in this Town than has ever been knowne done by Wind here. James Davy was blowne of his Hous and very ill hurt. The Salt water was carried with this Wind to Holland near Wigan, as some have told me, but it is undoubtedly true that ye Hearts and Leaves in my Gardens were Salt with the Sea Water."

CHAPTER VIII

THE FIELDS

THE average landowner of the eighteenth century whose rents were paid partly in boon work and boon hens, depended for actual cash on the fines received at irregular intervals, and the sale of his own cattle and produce. Circumstances therefore compelled him to be a practical farmer. The Diarist bred most of his own horses and cattle but bought Manx and Welsh bullocks for fattening as occasion offered. In 1706 he paid £20 for "83 good sheep." He tried to improve pastures by the purchase of good seeds. In 1712 he ordered 230 lb. of grass seeds from London, sowed some on his own land, and sold some to tenants; he bought "Bookes of Husbandry" and studied them:
". . I transcribed ye use of some Grass Seeds and ye Ground proper for them . . Mr Aldred and I had a great deal of discourse about Fatoning Kattle and Sheep in ye Beyond-Sea manner."

An experiment in growing Maize afforded Nicholas much interest but evidently no profit for he did not again attempt to cultivate "Indian Wheat" as he called it. He cautiously essayed "fatoning one small hogg" at a time respectively on acorns and potatoes, and satisfied himself that these economical foods were not adequate substitutes for corn.

The great number of horses and cattle maintained to ensure means of transport and food for man and beast, necessitated resolute cultivation of the land which the Squire kept in his own hands. The belt of woodland which now surrounds the park had not yet been planted, and the wall encircling it was not built until three generations later. From his door therefore Nicholas looked across fields to "ye waist" of Crosby Marsh, now long since enclosed and built upon, and beyond to the sandhills at the mouth of the River Mersey. Where acres of modern roads and avenues with their houses and gardens now spread out from the little old township of Great Crosby, not a single building stood. Nevertheless the bare wind-swept countryside was alive with human beings and their animal companions.

" I went to the Great More Hey to Thomas Syers Shearers of Wheat. . . He had 22 good hands besides 4 that were indifferent, and he was to overlook them."

The cluster of cottages which formed "ye Towne of Little Crosby" were doubtless little better than hovels, but from them, and the small widely-scattered farmhouses, emerged large families who streamed across field and waste, busily occupied with the production of food for their own consumption and of wool, flax and leather for the making of their own clothes.

The system of agriculture pursued by the village community was that of the single Town Field. From the beginning of the Diary to the end the dates are recorded on which either cultivation was begun in "Little Crosby Towne Field" or "Ye Towne Field was turned common"—that is left fallow. Operations in Great Crosby Town Field are also noted. Although the rotation of crops through the cutivation of roots was not yet understood, Nicholas grew cole[1] presumably for animal feeding; "turnops" and "pottatows" were only produced as garden crops. The Diary affords no indication that south-east Lancashire was becoming one of the main potato-growing districts of England. Neither does it reveal the gradual improvement in the quality and quantity of livestock which followed the draining and more intensive cultivation of the land begun during its writer's lifetime. Nicholas farmed on the same lines as his grandfather, who left some records of the animals slaughtered in his day.[2] They compare very unfavourably with the weights of bullocks, etc., of the next century and of our own.

The difficulty of providing winter fodder in the days before feeding stuffs were imported, necessitated the utmost use being made of pastures. Even working horses had to find much of their living in the fields far into the winter.

"Dec. 15th. 1714. I lay'd 3 of my Coach Horses in ye Hous to

[1] Rape.
[2] Appendix V.

ly in onely in ye Nights. I do not intend to give them any Hay, onely Bean Straw for the present."

Nicholas always alludes to stabling whether for horses or cows as "ye Hous."

The unclipped, underfed and often overworked coach-horses, dragging the heavy vehicle along deep ruts and through deep hollows, must have presented a very different appearance from the satin-coated, round-flanked prancers of a later day.

The Disbursement Book announces expenditure only on hay when the horses were put up for a few days away from home. Doubtless a few feeds of home-grown oats formed part of Henry Sumner's baggage. On long journeys such as an excursion into Yorkshire, coach horses were given hemp as well as oats.

The Diarist bred most of his own horses, making use of any stallion that happened to be in the neighbourhood. There is never any suggestion that care was taken to select a pure-bred animal. The fee paid varied between 1s. 6d. and 2s. 6d. The Squire took a burning interest in the progress of the foals which were named at birth. Statements are scattered through the Diary such as :

" Bonny Buttocks fowled a Filly ye last night. Tis to be called Bonny Lass. . . . We removed my three youngest colts into ye Park. . . . I wained my three Colts Buck, Snowball and Steele."

On the comparatively rare occasions when horses were bought, Nicholas indulged his fancy in the matter of names, regardless of the steed's sex.

" I bought a grey Mare . . . I call her Punsh. . . . I bought a paising Gelding. I call him Paisient Grissel."

The horses were broken in at the age of two. An expert was often engaged to "pace" a youngster and farrier's bills find a place here and there in the Disbursement Book. The following is an especially heavy one.

" Buck, drinks and Purge	...	...	...	4	6
Stagg drinks and Purge	...	...	...	5	6
Hobb Saves and Powder	...	...	...	1	6
Doctor two Drinks ...	...	...	...	3	0
Ginson, a Drink	...	...	...	1	0
Farrier for coming 5 times hither ...		...	...	5	0 "

In the same month (October, 1719) the Diarist records a death :

"My good old Coach-Hors Jack dyed, I suppose last night."

Needless to say the care of a sick animal was taken in hand by its owner.

"I showed Henry Sumner how to take a Web off a Horse's eye. . . . I sent William Ainsworth twice to Leverpool to get something for Snowball and when he came with it I helped to dress her for ye Farcey. . . . I gave my Horse Stagg a comfortable Drink."

Indeed the Recipe Book contains almost as many prescriptions for equine as for human ailments.

The only fertilizers known apart from animal manure, were lime, ashes from the burned moss of undrained land, seaweed and marl, the last named being considered the richest. Consequently among specialized agricultural jobs perhaps that of the marler was the most important. The custom of marling portions of the land in rotation every twenty years dated from very early times. In the "Great Hodge Podge" at Crosby, a manuscript volume containing odds and ends of data from Elizabethan to Victorian days, there is a record of the marling carried out by five generations of Squires during a hundred and fifty years. Nicholas reckoned the heavy cost in his time to be at the rate of £12 per acre; it was, however, considered to be in the nature of capital expenditure since the marl was supposed to renew the fertility of the soil. One area in Little Crosby and one in Ditton were marled during the period covered by the Diary. The process took place so seldom, and the results expected from it were so vital, that it was followed throughout with interest not only by the landlord but by his neighbours, and ended in a sort of ritual triumph. The sequence of proceedings from the day on which boring for the marl was inaugurated until that of the concluding festivities, is set forth in the Diary for the year 1712. Marlers went in groups from one estate to another, contracting with the landowner to bore for the clay, dig it out, and spread it in the agreed proportion upon the selected land. Carts and carters were supplied by the owner.

Two companies of marlers were engaged by contract six weeks before the work began, and the site whence the clay was to be produced was marked out.

"April 12th. Will. Ainsworth and Hen. Ashcroft board for Marle.

April 14th. I set some marling to John Darwin, Thomas Westhead and their partners, and to Charles Stevenson, John Harrison and their partners, and we signed artickleys of agreement of each side. Some of ye Marlers went with me to ye Great Morehey where we set out ye Marle Pit.

May 29th. Tenn of my Marlers came and shot the two paises of my new Marle pit.

June 3rd. The Marlers' drink was tuned.[1] I computed how many Quarts a day it would be for ye Marlers.

June 8th. I computed how mony Inches there was in a Marl cart and what Number of inches were lost if ye Carts were an insh or more too little.

June 12th. I began to marle ye Little Morehey and Pick, out of a pitt made in ye Great Morehey. I had two companys and each company consisted of three Hewers and four Fillers. There was twelve Carts, four Spreaders and one Water-bayly. They got out 754 lode. I was with them soon after three of ye clock in the morning.

June 13th. My Marlers got out 8 hundred Lode or more. I mesured most of my Marle Carts to see whether they were big Enough."

The number of loads dealt with in a single day indicate that the work, begun at earliest dawn, can have ceased only at nightfall. The many presents received by the toilers were certainly well earned.

"June 14th. I was pritty much with my Marlers. They got out 8 hundred & 23 lode of Marl. I turned off John Tarlton's teame becaus his Horses were supposed to have ye Scab.

June 16th. Severall of my Ditton Tennants, and some as were not, came along with them to see my Marlers. They were tenn and I suppose all of them gave Something to my Marlers. They all dined here afterwards and I drunk with them in ye Hall.

[1] Tunned.

June 23rd. Charles Stevenson, one of ye Lords of my Marle Pit was hurt by a small Fall of Marle.

June 28th. William Ainsworth helped me to Mesure ye Ground that was already set with Marle to see whether it was set according to ye Propourtion as I intended.

June 30th. Dr. Cawood, ye children and I were at my Marlers.

July 8th. Pat. Wofold[1] and Rich. Tickley gave Money to my Marlers."

The whole neighbourhood took part in the preparations for the final celebration.

" July 3rd. I made a Sword Dance against my Marlpit is flowered.

July 4th. Some of ye young folks of this Town met those of ye Morehouses[2] and Great Crosby to consider about ye flowering of my Marl Pit. Some of them met at Weedons and others at my Mill.

July 7th. I was very busy most of ye after-noone shaping Tinsall etc for the Garland of my new Marl-pit, and after Supper ye Women helped to Paste some things for it. I began to teach the 8 Sword Dancers their Dance which they are to Dance at ye Flowering of my Marl-pit. Dr Cawood played to them.

July 8th. I was very busy making Kaps etc for my Marlers and Dansers, severall of Great Crosby Lasses helped me. The young Women of this Towne, Moorhouses, and Great Crosby dressed ye Garlands in my Barne. I tought my 8 Sword Dancers their Dance, they had Musick and Danced it in my Barn.

July 9th. I was extremely busy all Morning making some Things to adorn my Marlers Heads. My Marl-pit was flowered very much to ye Satisfaction of ye Spectators, all the 14 Marlers had a Particular Dress upon their Heads and carried each of them a Musket or Gun. The Six Garlands etc. were carried by young Women in Prosestion, the 8 Sword Dancers went along with them to ye Marl-pit where they dansed, the Musick was

[1] Rev. T. Wolfall, chaplain to the Molyneuxes of the Grange and brother of the Diarist' friend, Richard Wolfall of Moor Hall.

[2] An outlying portion of the Crosby estate adjoining the modern village of Hightown.

Gerald Holrold and his son and Richard Tatlock, at Night they Danced in ye Barne. Thomas Lathard of Leverpoole brought me to ye Marl-pit a Dogg Collar against my Bull Bate as is to be in ye Pit.

July 15th. I Baited a Large Bull in ye Bottom of my New Marl-Pit, he was never baited before as I know of, yet played to admiration, there was 8 or 9 Doggs played ye first Bait and onely two ye 3rd bait, I think there was not above two Doggs but what were very ill hurt, I gave a Coller to be played for but no Dogg could get it fairly, so I gave it to Richard Spencer of Leverpoole, being his Dogg best deserved it.

July 18th. Mr Aldred began to make some Kaps for some of my Sword Dancers against ye Finishing day.

July 22nd. I went early in ye Morning to my Marlers, thence to Great Crosby. . . . William Kennion, Christopher Parker and their wives, Sara Atherton John Mather etc. dined here. They came, some of them to give to my Marlers and others to present my wife against ye Finishing Day of my Marling. I went with them to my Marl pit. John Mather & Rob. Atherton lodged here.

July 23rd. I had my Finishing Day for my Marling and abundance of my Neighbours and Tennants eat and drunk with me in ye Afternoone. Severall of them had made presents to my Wife of Sugar, Chickens, Butter etc. All my Marlers, spreaders, water-balys and carters dined here. We fetched home ye May-powl from the Pit and had Sword dansing and a Merry night in ye Hall and in ye Barne. Richard Tatlock played to them."

The last of the marl was reserved for future use.

" July 28th. One Company of Marlers got out ye Remainder of my Marle viz. 4 hundred and 13 Lode. I layed it in a Heap by ye Pitt, not having occation for it at Present."

The marl pits filled with water which was sometimes utilized in incidental field-work :

" I ploughed some Water Furrows in ye Little Moss Hey to let ye Marle Water runn over ye Meadows."

The wide shallow pond whence the marl was taken, with its

sloped bank to allow access by the carts now lies behind the park wall. The Great Moor Hey and the Little Moor Hey still send their generous crops to the Liverpool market. But over the Oaklands, marled by the Diarist's father, a building estate is advancing, while a group of prefabricated houses already crouches on the Further Oaklands.

The finish of "a great breaking of flax" was also celebrated with festivities. Flax seems to have been grown in the swampy fields, not as a normal crop, but as required. Nicholas does not record growing it very often, probably only when linen for the house and the family wardrobe needed renewal. In general his land was devoted to grazing and food crops, and the production of fuel in the form of turf, as peat was called.

Only at long intervals does the Disbursement Book record expenditure on "rippling," "scutching," harvesting, "swingling," "breaking" and, finally, weaving flax. All these operations depended upon casual labour. The crop was "rippled" by being laid in water to steep; "scutched" by beating the stalks to part the wood from the fibre; "swingled" to separate the coarse and fine fibre, and "broken" to extract the flax from the tow. Primitive machinery in the form of the "gigs" mentioned by Nicholas, already existed for "breaking," but the other processes were accomplished by hand with wooden implements.

"I had a great Breaking of Flax, there was 12 Breakers, 12 Scutchers, 11 Slansers, 4 to tend two Gigs and one to take up ye Flax, in all 40 Persons. I gave a Good Supper to my own Breakers and Swinglers. Tatlock played to them at Night, we had 4 Disgisers, and a Garland from Great Crosby and a deal of Dansing."

Tatlock was evidently a fiddler of repute for he received 4s. 1d. for one night's playing, while a lesser man was only paid 2s. 6d. and Anderton the piper but 1s.

Work on the flax harvested in summer was not completed until the following spring.

"March 14th. I began to swingle with 10 Hands ye Remainder of my last Year's Flax which was onely Scutched over ye last Summer.

March 16th. I finished Swingling my Last year's Flax and paid off all my Swinglers at 6d. per Day."

Push-ploughing was another field operation carried out by contract.

"I set ye Middle North Hey to Nat. Worthington and two partners to be push-ploughed. I am to give for pushing it £3.15/-."

The small light plough with a shallow share, skinned the mossy surface off the poor, undrained soil. It was slow and arduous labour, only to be undertaken in suitable weather. During a frost or heavy rain the work had to be abandoned. In the year cited (1711) the three men started to push their plough and gather up the thin sods on February 20th, and they had not completed their contract by the end of May.

"May 28th. The Push-Ploughers finished working for me at this Bout. I paid them for finishing part of ye Winter Heys."

They only received £2 10s., however, and an additional gratuity of 2s. They returned in the following April to resume their task.

The burners followed the push-ploughers.

"I tryed a Day or two since to see how ye nearer North Hey would burn, but today I began to burn it in good Earnest with 19 Hands before Dinner and three More after Dinner. I was with them a good part of ye day."

The fine ash produced from the burned turf was much prized as a fertilizer.

"I led Muck and Turf Ashes into ye Cross Field with 4 Carts."

Cultivation was started as soon as the burned land was cleared.

"I began to plough and sow my burned Ground in that part of ye Winter Heys which now I intend to call Ye Slip."

The first crops were buckwheat, designated by the Diarist as "French Wheat," and barley.

"Burning in ye Slip" cost more than double the amount paid for push-ploughing it, but many more hands were employed in the second operation.

Turf-mosses were valuable as a source of income to the landlord. The fuel belonged to him even when it existed on a tenant's holding, "thô by custom," writes Nicholas in his Tenants' Book, "they have Liberty to get in their Tenements enough for their use, paying 3d. per Lode."

A tenant who cut his turves above the normal size was called to account:

"I spoke to Charles Howerd about his Turf being too larg but he submitting, I took onely 4d per Lode from him."

The Squire personally supervised sales of turf on the actual site on which it was cut.

"June 3rd. 1715. This being ye first day of Selling Turves this year I went betimes in ye Morning to Thomas Marrow's Moss and sold some to Henry Watkinson, Mary Molineux etc, then I went to ye Morehous Moss where I found George Abbot[1] who had sold some Turves to William Eccleston, Rich. Molineux etc ... Coming home I met old Rob Bootle[2] and went with him to Flealand where I sold him 3 Rood of Fleas."

The fleas, or mossy sod above the more valuable turf, was sold at a cheaper rate, to be cut and removed by the buyer himself.

The Disbursement Book yields full accounts of the work of turf-getting and its cost.

"Turves got for my own Use AD1708

"For feying 46 Roods at 5d per Rood ...	...	19	4½
"Delving 44 days at 12d and 9½d per day	...	2 4	0
"Wheeling 44 days at 7d per day	... ...	1 5	8
"Dressing 396 Loads at 10d per Score of Loads		16	3

"Turves got for Sale in Marrow's Ground

"Riding Gors where ye Mospit must be		...		10
"Feying 41 Rood at 5d ...	...	...	...	17 9
"Delving 29½ days ...	...	...	...	1 9 6
"Wheeling 29½ days ...	...	...	...	17 2½"

[1] George Abbott, whom Blundell engaged as his steward on November 20th, 1714, had suffered imprisonment in Liverpool in 1689, when in the service of William Molyneux later fourth Viscount. See *Abbott's Journal*, the Cheetham Society Vol. LXI.

[2] Yeoman, of Thornton in the parish of Sephton.

Turf was still the main fuel of the countryside although the well-to-do burned coal. At Crosby turf seems to have been used mainly in the mill and kiln, while coal was burned in the house.

It has been seen that part of the estate upon which the rural community at Little Crosby depended was barren land. The turf mosses were still undrained and uncultivated, and the sandhills along the Mersey estuary, now used extensively by the military, golfers and holiday-makers, were then inhabited by foxes which have long since disappeared.

"There were some Hunters in ye North Hey and Little Eases. I heard it was Mr Molyneux of Wooton hunting ye Fox. My Wife, I etc went up into ye Leads to look at them. . . I went very early in ye Morning to look for Foxes in ye Great Crosby Warrand. We thought we found ye Pricks of two but we saw not One Fox. . . seaven young Foxes were taken in a Denn in my Warrand. I think they will bring them all alive to Wooton to Mr Molyneux."

Kites, now among the rarest of British birds, only existing under strict protection in remote corners of our island, then soared in numbers over "ye waist" and the cultivated land alike.

"I hurt my face with shooting at a Kite. . . I shot one Kite and 13 Crows. . . Betty Swift sent me a Mare to lay[1] to shoot Kites at."

In later years, when Nicholas had probably given up shooting, the Disbursement Book contains regular entries "for killing Kites and Hawks."

The huge birds must have committed serious depredations among the poultry which were so important to the country's economy. But they will also have been attracted by the snakes, unwelcome intruders in farmyards where they congregated to breed in the warm manure. According to the Diary a hundred and twelve adders were killed in the Crosby Hall outbuildings in June 1711. In the summer months of each year entries such as the following occur:

"July 3rd. 1708. There were 72 adders or longworms taken in ye miding on ye backside of my stable and ye double stable in

---

[1] i.e., a carcass to attract the birds of prey.

about two hours time, 22 of which were baired and killed with lifting up only one pitchfork of dung or old straw; some others were killed in other places about this hous today and yesterday. When they were all together they were 81 in count, those of the longest size were about 3 feet and $\frac{1}{2}$, the generality upwards of 2 foot 10 inch. They were in weight 45 lbs."

A few days earlier he had sent " a present of 22 adders to ye doctors of ye Low."[1]

The fact that there is never mention of any person or domestic animal being bitten by the reptiles, taken in conjunction with their size, suggests that they were in reality harmless grass snakes.

---

[1] The district of Liverpool now known as Everton. Doctor Fabius lived there among others.

TWO FATEFUL YEARS

I

WHATEVER may have been the political views which Nicholas discussed with his friends at Harsnips in Sephton, or Ann's in Great Crosby, or at the Angel, the Golden Fleece and the Woolpack in Liverpool, he was careful to commit none of them to paper. Too often in its history had Crosby been ransacked by pursuivants for evidences of supposed treachery in his father's[1] and grandfather's[2] days, to say nothing of members of the earlier generation[3] who took refuge in the fields while Queen Elizabeth's cooks occupied their home.

In 1714, when a crisis of the first magnitude was obviously about to confront the nation, the placid current of life at Crosby was momentarily disturbed by the fear of informers.

"May 22nd. Pat Aldred lodged here upon account of a fals Allarrum that there were some People Searching at ye Grange for Pat Wofold."

The Grange, like Crosby Hall, was equipped with a priest's hiding-hole.

The alarm seems to have proved groundless for Nicholas proceeds with his chronicle of daily happenings without alluding to it again.

". . . I saw ye Morris Dansers of Sefton as were going their round in order to rear a Maypole at Sefton . . . I was at Leverpoole. I saw a Beast something like a Cammell with two large Bunches on its back."

The churchwarden's activities were interrupted for a few weeks in the summer of 1714, in order that he might escort his

[1] *Cavalier.*
[2] *A Cavalier's Note Book.*
[3] *Crosby Records.*

wife and little Fanny into Yorkshire where Mally had already
spent some months with her aunt Middleton.

" June 11th. I sent some Things to Leverpoole to goe by York
Carrier for my Wife.

June 12th. I went to Leverpoole and bought a Sute of Cloths
from Mr Hurst except some little thing as I had by me towards
Making it up. . . My wife came to Leverp after me. She rid
home behind me. . . At night she had a most sevear Fit of ye
Gravell or Stone.

June 13th. My wife being very ill of ye Gravell, she kept her
Bed till after Dinner.

June 15th. Rich. Cartwright let my Wife Blood in her Arme.
He took about 13 ounces of Blood from her."

Poor Mrs. Blundell can hardly have looked forward to the
journey but the preparations proceeded inexorably, and two days
after the skilful Richard Cartwright had bled her so profusely,
she was on the road.

" June 16th. I was very busy giving instructions how to saddle
and fit Horses against my Wives journey tomorrow.

June 17th. My Wife, I and Fanny began our journey towards
Stockhild, we called at Tho. Places in Ormskirk. He gave us a
drink at the doar. We baited at Fletcher's, ye Signe of ye Bucks
Heads in Brindle, thence to Gisburn where we lodged at John
Yates, ye Spotted Hind.

June 18th. From Gisburn we came to Skipton where we dined
at Gilbert Johnsons ye Signe of ye Spotted Horse, thence we
went to Stockhild where we lodged. We found my Lord
Langdale there.

June 19th. I sent to York for my Trunks of Apparrell but they
were not come."

Mrs. Blundell must have been highly indignant at the non-
appearance of her fine clothes, for dinner-parties and visits filled
their days during their three weeks' sojourn among their Yorkshire relatives.

Father Joseph Blundell, the Diarist's younger brother, now a
professed Jesuit, was at the time serving the Yorkshire missions.
He joined the family at Burgwallis where they again broke their
homeward journey as they had done eight years earlier.

L

As Nicholas entered his disbursements for the month, it may be surmised that he compared the expenses of his late journey with those of the former one made in his coach, and discovered that he had not achieved a noticeable economy by dispensing with the vehicle.

" Spent when my wife and I went into Yorksire and came back with our Children, in travelling expenses for ourselves, Servants and Horses £2 18 7
Carriage of our Luggage backwards and forwards
     and charge in getting it   ...   .   1 3 9 "

Father Joseph Blundell spent a short vacation at Crosby after an absence of many years passed, first as a schoolboy at St. Omer College, and subsequently in the Jesuit seminary.

Together the brothers visited the neighbours, took part in bowling matches, inspected the eel nets at the Sniggery, and met the friends of their boyhood at the taverns of their choice. " Bro. Jos." made a pilgrimage to Holywell with Mrs. Blundell and Mally; he also exercised his priestly functions.

" July 11th. My brother Joseph held forth at Mr Aldreds and then went to dine at Ince,
August 7th. My Brother Joseph Married Michael Mackdaniell to Catherine Taylor."

During that fateful autumn conflicting news, with attendant rumours, travelled about the country but the Diarist makes no comment upon them, neither does he record the arrival of a foreign king to mount the English throne.

II

Mally was now ten years old. Such education as she had thus far received included only lessons in reading, writing, sewing and dancing. Her father notes her advance in needlework when she " began to quilt." She was sent away from home to pursue her studies in 1715.

" April 23rd. My wife and Mally went to Leverp. she left Mally at Mrs Meginnis to be taught by her."

On the following day a curious treat was provided for Fanny, possibly to console her for her sister's departure.

"April 24th. Fanny went to the Sea-side to see a Man as was cast up.

April 26th. Being Mally is to stay at Schoole at Mrs Maginnis, I sent her Cloths to her.

April 29th. I went to Leverpoole cheefly to see Mally at Mrs Maginnis."

Mrs. Maginnis's terms for a boarder were 5s. per week. The same amount was paid monthly to the dancing master for each pupil.

Obviously Nicholas missed the constant companionship of his elder child. In less than two months he brought her home "for a few nights." These holidays were repeated at frequent intervals during the summer. Whether Mally's progress was unsatisfactory, which it might well have been in view of these interruptions, or whether she was unhappy at school is not explained. But on August 25th her brief career under Mrs. Maginnis was terminated.

"Mally came home with my Wife. She is come quite away from Mrs Maginnis."

It is possible that plans for taking both little girls to a convent school abroad were already afoot. Nicholas was very busy drafting "Artickleys of Agreement" between himself and the yeoman Thomas Syer "to set part of my Demesney to him," and also receiving money and paying debts.

"August 4th. I put up some goods into my Ovall Trunk and into a dale Box."

A week later the Diary records the first indication of the coming trouble.

"August 10th. The Constables John Sumner and James Scarisbrick summonsed me to Appear at Ormskirk on Friday next to take ye Oaths."

However there is no mention either in Diary or Disbursement Book of a journey to Ormskirk. One shilling was paid for "an express" from Mr. Plumbe who presumably succeeded in arranging matters for his client and friend.

During the following month, while the clans were gathering

in Scotland to welcome and fight for James, and while in England the king who could not speak English was becoming more and more unpopular, the Jacobites came further into the open. Riots and disturbances were taking place in all the great cities, but the Diary reflects at least outward calm in rural Lancashire, considered the stronghold of Stuart sympathies.

On September the 6th, the day on which the Earl of Mar raised the Stuart standard at Braemar, Nicholas went to Prescot " and gave Lawyer Blundell directions to draw a deed for ye further settling my Estate."

This and other entries stating that he had made his fourth and last will, support the suggestion that an unusual family movement was planned. But as the month wore on, with all the commotions in the country at large which led to the hurried passing of the Riot Act through both Houses of Parliament, Nicholas writes of a sick cow and gives a detailed account of the subsequent post mortem on the animal. He " began to make a stack of hay behind ye stables," he " agreed with the Tith-men Tarlton, Westhead and Edward Hatton "[1] and gave them £4 5s as part of his tithe, he " bought 20 Geece," he began to teach his " Doughter Frances " to write, he and Father Aldred " decided ye difference as was between Roger Neal and Margarit Ridgate."

Toward the end of September more emphatic hints of an impending change appear.

" Sept. 27th. I went to Prescot and heard Lawyer Blund. read over a Deed of Settlement as he had drawn for me, in case I have no Son nor a Grand-Child.

Sept. 30th. I gave warning to four of my Men-Servants as I shall part with."

October opened with another visit from the officers of the law.

"The Cunstables James Scarisbrick and Jo. Sumner showed me their warrants for getting the Militia Armes in order."

Yet weeks passed peacefully at Crosby while rival forces were engaged in Scotland and the supporters of James were quarrelling as to what course to pursue.

---

[1] All three collectors of Tithe are named in *Non-Jurors*.

" Oct. 3rd. I was very busy most of the day clensing and redying my Closet and perusing some papers concerning my contributing to ye Milicia Hors. We tuned some very strong Aile as Betty Farer had brued for me. I designe to bottle it."

During these fateful days for Britain Nicholas was teaching his " Grewhound Whelp, Buty, to lead," he helped John Banister " to lay up Apples in Wheat Straw in ye Dining-Roome"; he was measured for " a pare of boots."

" Oct. 16th. It being Crosby Goos-Feast, my Wife and I went towards evening to James Rigby's. I sent to Croxteth of a How-doe-you.

Oct. 17th. My wife and I dined at Thos. Syers with James Tristram and his Wife, a Son and Doughter of Thos. Fleetwood etc. . . Thence some of us went to Thos. Hesketh where some of us dansed. Thence Edward Tristram & I went to Dukes where we drunk with Atturney Berry, Parson Wairing, Derbyshire etc . . . Mally lodged at Thos. Syers and Fanny at Rich Newhouses.

Oct. 19th. Duke let my Wife blood in her Arme.

Oct. 20th. Lawyer Blundells man Rich. Holrold brought me some writing which his Master had drawn for me."

The bill was a stiff one—£9 to the lawyer and 5s. to his clerk. " Oct. 24th. I had five Hands all day sorting & laying up Apples in ye Dining-Roome. I began to make Thumb Ropes of Hay to bind Beans in. My Wife began to drink her Dyet Drink from Doctor Lancaster. Parson Letus, William Tarlton etc. were here a-beging for some in the South as had lost a great deale by the death of their Cows."

The general unrest had not put a stop to the organised collection of subscriptions from one section of the agricultural community in favour of another hard hit by ill-fortune. The drought of the previous year is thus described in the Diary.

" This Year has been remarkable for fair Weather all over England and in some parts so great want of Water that ye Cattle were fourced to be driven severall Miles to Water . . . a very great Mortallity amongst Cattle especially amongst Milk Beas near London which was supposed to proceede through want of Water and by their eating Graines. The Publick News gave us frequently account of[1]   or more as were burned in one day becaus neather the Milk nor ye flesh was wholesome. I am very well assured that there were severall Persons in London that for some months eat neather Beef, Mutton, Veal, Milk or Butter. The whole number of Cattle as dyed this year on this unusuall Distemper (as a Breef for beging Charity for the Relief of those who had lost Cattle gave Account) was 5418 Cowes and 439 Calves; the Loss as the same Breef gave Account was computed to amount to £24598—14s besides what the Government had given towards each Persons Loss."

Only on October 29th, 1715, does the peaceful scene at Little Crosby darken :

"We expected the Hors Militia to come Serch here. My Children should have lodged at Thomas Bannisters but I thought it not proper."

The Squire's priest friends and relatives still came and went freely. His cousin, Father William Gillibrand, was staying with him and during the next few days he and Father Aldred visited Ince, went out coursing and otherwise behaved as though they had nothing to fear. But on October 31st Nicholas writes :

"I was with Edward Hatton when he was sowing Wheat. I came not in till dark Night, expecting a call."

These lines suggest that, had any inquiring stranger presented himself on Yeoman Hatton's land, Nicholas would have posed as a farm-labourer.

During the next few days life went on as usual at Crosby : Mally took a vomit, Mr. Plumbe dined and gave his opinion about the Squire's will. But known Jacobite leaders were now being arrested throughout the country and although Nicholas was not in this category, he was connected through his wife with active supporters of James Stuart. His brother-in-law Marmaduke Langdale was married to the daughter of Lord Widdrington who commanded a regiment on the Stuart side, while the wife of Lord Derwentwater, one of the leaders in the whole adventure, was daughter of Sir John Webb. Crosby therefore could not hope to escape the suspicious attentions of those res-

---

[1] The meticulous Diarist evidently intended to look up the " Publick News " and insert the correct number.

ponsible for carrying out orders sent from London. While the Diary proceeds with its chronicle of everyday doings, it gradually reveals a serious state of affairs for its writer.

"Nov. 5th. They began to fortify Leverpoole by Kasting up great Banks for fear of my Lord Darwinwater. I placed some barrels in my Seller to be ready against I make syder.

Nov. 8th. John Gregson brought me a Pair of new Boots. I paid him for them and for some Shoes for my Wife & Children. I finished making Syder. We pressed yesterday and today 37 Bushells and a half of Apples and made of them almost one Hogshead and a half of syder, we made ye great Lead full of Bumperkin[1] and there will be a Barrell more to be made tomorrow.

Nov. 9th. Pat. Gelibond helped me to paste some papers on my Boxes.

Nov. 12th. I applyed ye Cobra Stone[2] to a Cut. The Fight at Preston was begun.

Nov. 13th. We drank a Bowl of Punch. This Hous was twice serched by some Foot as came from Leverpoole. I think the first party was about twenty-six."

Preston is only twenty miles from Crosby; perhaps the bowl of punch was directly connected with the arrival of news that a Jacobite Force had entered that town. Nicholas usually announces the consumption of punch in connection with a family festivity. The good news (from the Jacobite point of view) was speedily followed by the tidings of the capitulation at Preston. A more rigorous search for Stuart adherents and for arms was now carried out.

"Nov. 16th. Mr Martingall and Mr—— were here. My wife lent them my Grewhounds. I sat in a Streat place for a fat Man."

While the Squire took refuge in the priest's hiding hole, his wife diplomatically disarmed unwelcome visitors by offering them a day's sport. Their suspicions were evidently not allayed. We are not told how Mrs. Blundell conducted her defensive campaign during the next few days, but Nicholas remained in the "streat Place," only seekng his bed for an hour before dawn.

---

[1] A small barrel.
[2] Copperas-stone, iron-pyrites or marcasite.

"Nov. 17th. I took a Nap between four of ye Clock and five, and then went to seek my Lodging."

Confinement and boredom drove him to the, for him, most unusual course of reading books.

"Nov. 18th. I made an end of reading a Book called England Jests.[1]

Nov. 19th. I made an end of reading the Book called ye English Rogue.[2] It was ye fourth part of it I finished today. This Hous was sirched today by some from Leverpoole. Mr Huson and Mr Robinson amongst them.

Nov. 20th. I was in the Boys Chamber and heard him talk. I had a bedfellow."

We are left guessing as to the identity both of the person heard talking and of the bedfellow. The former can have been no friend to the Squire. Canon Gibson suggests that the bedfellow was probably Father Aldred but it seems more likely that he was a fugitive from Preston, as he left the next day.

"Nov. 21st. My Bedfellow and I parted. I began to read the Unparalled Adventures[3] writ by R. Burton."

The next day, the immediate alarm being over, Nicholas emerged from hiding.

"Nov. 22nd. I brought Sawny home, and got some Plumbs and Whit wine."

"Sawny" was probably a good horse which he had confided to friendly hands to be preserved from seizure.

"Nov. 23rd. I heard some Writings read over but they were not signed. I took ye best Screen out of ye Frame."

And now, following on this record of business preoccupations and minor activities, comes the abrupt announcement of sudden flight without preface or comment.

"Nov. 24th. I rid over in ye Boat at Runk:Horn and did not

---

[1] *England's Jests Refined and Improved*, by Humphrey Crouch.

[2] *English Rogue; a History of the Most Eminent Cheats of both Sexes*, 4 vols. 1665.

[3] Probably *Unparalleled Varieties, or the Matchless Actions and Passions of Mankind*, by R.B. (Richard Burton, pseudonym of Nathaniel Crouch), 1683 and later editions.

light till I came to the Ail Hous where we baited, thence we went to Cole:Brook where we lodged at Robert Pickerings, ye Signe of ye Cock."

His farewell to Crosby, his wife and children under these uncertain circumstances must be left to the imagination for he makes no allusion to it. He rode his own mare Ginny all the way to London, and was accompanied by Thomas Gower. His lively interest in the small doings of the countryside remained unabated.

" On Dellamere Forest there are some very small Brows which if you cut a large Sod of ye Top and walk round that place, you may tread up a sort of Slutch which when tis dryed will burn well & is a Tollerable good sort of Turf; they also make some Turves by claping & working them with their hands, but most of ye Turves, excepting ye top Turves or Fleas, are made by spreading a sort of Moss-Slutch upon ye Ground about 4 Inches thick and when it grows pritty dry they cut into peeces lick Brick & turn them & dress them for use. . . Coming on ye Rode I observed some things viz : Cabbages buried in ye Ground with their Stalks upwards to keep them. In or near Abingdon a pair of Stocks with a building over them, two Parish Churches within a Bow Shoot of each other. I came past severall Houses as are for ordering Flax they call them Tutering Houses."

He was nine days on the road including two spent at Water-perry. He interrupts his account of his journey to insert his usual summary of the month's weather.

" This month has been seasonable enough thô generally very cold, especially the latter end of it."

In bitter winter weather therefore poor Ginny, who had not had a single day's rest on this long journey, pressed on, London being the goal where Nicholas planned at once to lose himself in the crowd, to see his friends, and to transact his private business.

"Dec. 1st. From Water-Perry I went to Higher Wickham where I lodged at Widdow Winshlows the Red Lyon.
Dec. 2nd. From Wickham I came to London and set up my Mare at Mr Ogles the Signe of ye Whit Hors at ye end of Little

Wild Street. I dined at Mr Aldreds[1] and lodged at Captain Stevens near Grays Inn Passage."

III

During the next few weeks Nicholas, far from his home and kindred, became an insignificant member of the London crowd; it may be surmised, from his gregarious disposition, that he enjoyed this sortie from his remote native heath into all the life and movement of the Capital.

With one or another or several together of his cousins and friends the Eyres, the Gorsuches, the Culcheths and other members of the Catholic community, he "smoaked a Pip in Vair Street" or "took a glass of Wine at the Wine Tavern in Holbourne," or "drank at John O'Gaunts." He dined and "suped" now "at a Cooks Shop in New Turnstile," now "at Cliftons the Bull and Gate Holbourne." At the Cock and Hoop in the same district he "drank good March Beere"; he "eat asparagus at Covent Garden" and Oysters at Jefferson's coffee house. He saw the sights of town too, which included "St Paul's Church," "The Wax Work and Beace in Fleet Street," "The Antilop and other Beas in Holbourne," "A Shew of Monstures viz a Whelp with 8 Legs and Feet and one Head etc" and "Ye Moving Images[2] in Shanlow Street the first time they were Shewed." He bought "a Hamburgh Lottery Ticket at ye Signe of ye Woolpack in Cornhill near Stocke Market"; he saw "five men and two women carted towards Tiburne there to be executed," and "a Woman whiped at ye Carts ars twice round Red Lyon Square"; he saw "ye English Opera acted called Dioclesian"; in "ye New Exchange" he was shown "a Looking Glass as was in one Peece 86 Inshes long and 44 Insh wide Valewed at £130."

"Dec. 9th. I saw ye Preston Prisoners come into town. I made a visit to Lady Darwendwater in Lester Street."

The more important prisoners taken at Preston were loaded

[1] Father Aldred's brother.

[2] See the description of the Moving Images and Pictures shown in London in *Social Life in the Reign of Queene Anne*," Ashton.

with ignominy on their journey South, and were insulted by an immense mob as they entered London on led horses with their hands tied behind their backs. But nevertheless considerable sympathy was felt for Lord Derwentwater who was of the same age as the young Chevalier and had been brought up in France in close companionship with him. The loyalty of a young man to the friend of his boyhood, whom he now acknowledged as his King, touched the imagination of many besides his fellow Jacobites.

"Dec. 12th. I received a Letter from my Wife. Tis the first since I came to Town.

Dec. 13th. I writ to my Children for Thomas Gower to take with him, and to my Wife by the Post. I began to burn my own Candles. I mended the Clock upon ye Stayres at my Landladys."

When Thomas Gower returned to Crosby Nicholas decided to sell his mare. Ginny may have been lamed by her hurried journey south for her master found it difficult to dispose of her.

"Dec. 16th. I went to Cliftens, the Bull and Gate in Holbourn and to other places to sell Ginny but to no purpose."

He himself had no better success in Smithfield, but the "Osler" finally disposed of the animal there.

The purchase of new clothes was rendered necessary by so much movement in London Society.

"Dec. 31st. Mr Aldred went with me to buy a new Surtute but I licked none of them."

So he sought female advice.

"Jan. 3rd. 1716. Mrs Ann Aldred helped me to buy outside and Lining for a Surtute at that Shop in ye Strand as is now called Doyleys.

Jan. 5th. Naylor the Taylor brought my Camblet Surtute. I began to wear it."

It was an exceptional winter.

"Dec. 21st. There fell a great deal of snow."

1716

The snow lay for a month although there was a partial thaw on January 1st, 1716.

" Jan. 4th. I went to Southerwick and saw Severall walking upon the Ice above ye Bridge.

Jan. 12th. I sat in ye Chear of State upon the Thames.

I danced on ye Thames in a Booth, and at ye Warwickshire Booth I got a Dish of Sausages Fryed. I walked over the Thames from Temple Stayres to Southerick and back againe.

Jan. 12th. I writ out a deal of News in ye Coffy Hous."

The news was stirring enough, for James Stuart had arrived in Scotland and had been proclaimed as James VIII throughout the greater part of that country.

" Jan. 19th. I was upon the Thames and there saw an Ox Rosting. I eat a part of it as I saw cut off ye Spit, they say there were two Oxes rosted on the Thames today.

Jan. 20th. I made a visit to Mrs Bond and gave her some of my Rosted Beef.

Jan. 21st. It began to thaw and continued to be a very fine and mild thaw without much rain.

Jan. 30th. This is the first day since ye Frost as Boats passed safely over ye Thames above London Bridge."

Nicholas kept the lenten abstinence whether in town or country.

" I bought some eggs and eat my Dinner at Mr Aldreds. . . I got my Collasion at Mr Aldreds."

The Disbursement Book contains the information that on Dec. 24th Mrs Blundell at Crosby paid William Atherton 9/4 " for a Chees to go to London." Her husband was duly notified of its dispatch.

" Jan. 7th. I went to ye Castle & Falcon for a Chees as was to come by ye Carrier but it was not then come.

Jan. 12th. I gave a very large Chees, most of it to Mr Aldred and a small part of it to Mrs Stevens."[1]

But more serious matters were preoccupying the father of a family. Nicholas was in debt and had been obliged to mortgage part of his estate.

" Jan. 16th. I went to Counsellor Eyre and took some notes for a Settlement to be made for paying my debts.

Jan. 26th. I told Counsellor Eyre ye whole Truth."

[1] His landlady.

It is not revealed whether "the whole Truth" concerned his debts, or the proposed sojourn of himself and his family on the continent with the object of procuring Catholic education for his children in defiance of the law. His own journey may have been advanced owing to the Act, hurriedly passed through Parliament thus early in the new reign, to compel all Catholic recusants to register their lands and possessions " to the end that by paying largely to the late great expenses by them brought upon this nation they must be deterred, if possible, from the like offences for the future; and that this nation may have the benefit of His Majesty's gracious condescension in giving his interest in the two-third parts of all the Papists estates which are already forfeited to him by law, for the use of the public, either by seizing the said two-third parts of their estates for the public service, or by laying some tax or charge upon their estates in lieu thereof". . . Many landowners thus threatened with immediate ruin may have seen a loophole in the added proviso " that if any person required to make such registry as aforesaid, shall be beyond the seas upon the eighteenth day of June 1716, then such person. . . shall procure his name and estate to be registered in such manner as aforesaid at any time within six months after the twentieth day of May 1717."

Nicholas, and many another who now fled to the continent, probably hoped that the storm would blow over within the fifteen months' grace allowed, especially as the Stuart arms had been defeated in Scotland. The Diarist adopts the tone of the public press on the solitary occasion on which he refers to the brief war there :

"Feb. 5th. Mrs Lloyd brought News that the Pretender and the Rebells were fled from Pirth."

Nor does he permit himself any comment on Lord Derwentwater's death on the scaffold.

"Feb. 24th. Lords Derwintwater and Kenmure were executed. I made a visit to Mrs Standleys.

Feb. 27th. There was High Mass for Lord Derwentwater at the French Envoys severall Persons of note were there."

As the recent Act specifically penalized anew "every person who is or shall be educated in the Popish religion," it was obviously not the moment for a party including two little girls to set forth for a destination in a Catholic country. Mrs. Blundell and her daughters remained at Crosby while Nicholas, in London, began to learn French and to acquire more clothes in preparation for embarking on the new scene.

"Feb. 6th. Mr Barton came ye first Time to teach me French. March 3rd. Mrs Ann Aldred helped me to buy a Roclore[1] and a Tissue Waistcot of Thomas Stevens, ye Signe of ye Duke of Ormonde on Horseback."

The arrival in London of Mr. Plumbe must have been very welcome to his old friend at this juncture. The lawyer's son followed his father's profession in the capital. Between them they may have found means to facilitate the granting of a pass to Nicholas to leave the country.

"March 5th. I received my Pass. I paid my Way to Mr William Plumb at John o Gaunts. I took part of a bowl of Punsh at Mr Jeffersons.

March 6th. I went out to see ye Apparition in ye Aire lick Clouds of Fier and Smoke.

March /th. I signed a deed for ye Payment of my Debts. I took my leave at Mr Aldreds. I was at Mr Rodbourns near ye Ship in James Street Covent Garden. He paid me my Annuety[2] as will be due the 25th of this month. I drank my farewell with Counsellor Eyre and his two Brothers and Mr John Culceth at ye Castle Tavern in Holbourne near Fullers Rant. I sat up all night prepairing for my journey tomorrow."

Nicholas did not omit to reckon up his expenses in London before his departure.

"Expenses for one Servant and two Horses for above a fortnight and for myself 15 Weeks viz from the time I left Crosby till I left London; for Meat, Drink, Lodging, Washing, Candles and Vailes, Tavern and Coffee-Hous Expences, seeing Plays, Shoes, Coach hier and gaiming, Paid to my French master, Post Letters and Charity to the Poore £25-3 -2."

[1] Roquelaure, a knee-length cloak.
[2] Bequeathed by the Dowager Lady Webb, now deceased, to Mrs. Blundell.

CHAPTER IX

FLANDERS

I

1716

NICHOLAS decided how he would deal with the difference between the calendar used in England and that of the continent, before he left London :

" When I come to Flanders where they recon by the New Stile I shall set the day of the Month according to that account at the end of each day but shall keep on the old Account in the Margent as formerly."

He adhered to this resolution,, inserting the date according to the continental calendar at the end of each day's record.

His ultimate destination was Gravelines where his wife and children were to join him as soon as circumstances permitted.

The journey, made under the exceedingly uncomfortable conditions of the period, cost a trivial sum even when allowance is made for the current value of money.

" Spent in my Travell from the time I left London till I settled in Graveling, being almost five Weeks £3 11s. 8d."

The first excursion across the Channel since his schooldays must have been fraught with interest for this middle-aged man who, with all his capacity for the enjoyment of good company and novel sights, had hitherto lived within so narrow a circle.

" March 8th. I came from my Lodging in a Coach to Billing Gate where I stayed a while at ye Blew Bell and then came in ye Tilt Bote (in about 3 Hours and a half which is twenty Miles) to Gravesend where I lodged at Michael Baylys, ye Signe of ye Hen and Chickens. Tilbury Fort is just the other side of the River.

March 9th. I dined with Mr Dodd[1] & my Landlord, they and I etc played at Whiste awhile. I played with Mr Dod at Cribbage. If ye Wind had served we had gon off today.

March 10th. Mr Dod and I walked up to ye Wind Mill, it was a fine prospect. He and I dined together in my Roome, then we went to his Roome where we played at Cards. I lay in his Roome in an other bed.

March 11th. I dined at my Lodging with a Dutch Captain and Lieutenant as were come out of Scotland.

March 12th. I went on Bord ye St John of Bridges,[2] a Smak of 50 Tunn, Jo. Docas Roby Master, we sailed at Seaven in ye Morning and cast Ancor at Margarit[3] about half an Hour after three in ye after Noone.

March 13th. We weighed Anchor at one in the Morning and Sailed till 4 at Night. We cast Ancor two or three times today.

March 14th. We lay at Anchor over against France for about Seaven Houres.

March 15th. We landed at Ostend before 12 o' ye Clock at Noone we were at Sea Three Nights and were under Saile onely 36 Hours . . . I lodged at ye Signe of ye Shipers Hous. The Slew-Bridges were opened and shut with Coggs and Rings. Tis a poor place but very well fortified with Mud Walls. XXIV."[4]

Nicholas obviously followed the British custom of adapting foreign words to his native pronunciation :

"I came in ye Barge to Brudges and lodged at Nicho. Egars in Gray werker Straet. I made my first visit to the Austin[5] Nuns."

---

[1] Probably the Rev. Hugh Tootell, alias Charles Dodd, author of *The Church History of England*, was on his way from Mossborough Hall where he had been chaplain to Robert Molyneux, to France where he collected material for his work.

[2] Bruges.

[3] Margate.

[4] The date according to the new calendar will not be added to future quotations.

[5] Augustinian.

During the next few days he saw the sights of Bruges. . . . "Went to ye Dominican Church which is remarkable for ye Carved Pulpit which is hung, or at least ye Top of it, with wood carved lick Ropes. . . .went to ye Archers Hall where I saw two silver Bowes and two Arrows of Silver, their Butts are about 8 Rood, the Bird they shoot at for King is made of Leather. The Exchange has a very handsome and High Tower as high as most Spier Steeples."

Wherever the Diarist went he found friends and acquaintances among the religious orders, sons and daughters of the numerous families with which he was connected by blood, and Jesuit fathers who had been his schoolfellows at St. Omer.

He alludes frequently to "ye 3 Merchants" but does not explain their identity. In their company he attended Mass at one church, "Sallew" (thus, in his best French, he rendered Salue, or Benediction) in another; he walked to "ye Coome where ye Ships lie;" in Holy Week he witnessed "the Procession representing Our Saviour's Passion" which took fifty minutes to pass; he bought a share in half a Brussels Lottery Ticket under the pseudonym *Prove Well.*

His one-time servant, Watty Thelwall, son of Walter Thelwall, appears on the scene at Bruges; it will be seen later how very many English Catholics found employment in the extensive society of recusants harbouring in Flanders. "Watty Thelwall made me a visit" is all we are told on this occasion.

Nicholas did not omit his self-imposed task in the midst of the distracting foreign scene.

"March 21st. I kept my Chamber most of ye after noone Transcribing my Small Diurnall Papers into my Small Diurnall Book."

He invested in "a New coat and Breeches trimed with silver" before moving on to Ghent; the journey, made in a barge, took about eight hours. Here he made haste to visit his sister Winnie, now a member of the Benedictine community known to his generation as the Benedictine Dames. Later he frequently "dined at ye Grate[1] at ye Daimes."

[1] Grille.

M

From her side of the grille Sister Winny must have asked many questions about the home and kindred she was never to see again, while on his side her brother enjoyed the community's hospitality in the convent parlour.

At Ghent Nicholas saw much of his wife's cousin, the widowed Lady Gerard of Gerard's Bromley;[1] he also fore-gathered with Lord Waldegrave[2] and Sir Walter Blount[3] who were all staying in the town. With priest friends he went out fishing, witnessed the making of snuff, and accomplished much sight-seeing.

"April 1st. Pat Daniell[4] went with me to ye Monks at St. Peter's Hill. They have been settled there 1000 Years and have about twenty villages belonging to them. The Monks now there are in Number only about 25."[5]

The story of this momentous month is conscientiously concluded with the never-to-be-omitted comment on the weather:

"There were severall very cold days this Month so that it may well be called very cold for ye Season."

At Ghent Nicholas was regaled by his landlord with "Leomond Tea", a beverage which he must have found anaemic indeed by comparison with the good ale, mead, and punch of his native land.

On April 4th, he returned to Bruges.

"April 6th. I walked quite round Brudges upon ye Rampers. April 7th. I came from Brudges in ye Barge to Newport where I lodged at ye Armes of France. I made a visit to ye Carthu-

[1] Daughter of Sir John Webb of Odstock, Wilts., and widow of Charles, sixth Lord Gerard of Gerard's Bromley.
[2] Third Baron, married Mary, daughter of Sir John Webb of Haythorpe.
[3] Sir Walter Blount, third Baronet of Sodington, Worcestershire. He died at Ghent the following year.
[4] Reverend Richard Daniel, confessor to the English Carmelite nuns at Antwerp, was a member of the Lancashire family of Daniel of Durton.
[5] The Benedictine Abbey of St. Pierre de Gand was founded about 610 and is described in Les Délices des Pays-Bas (published in Liége in 1769) as Un des plus riches et des plus illustres Monastères des Payes-Bas.

sians.[1] They are 16 as belongs to that Hous. Their Church is very small but most extreamely neat and pretty but not costly. April 9th. Pater Hunter came to my Lodging and helped me to change my Money and was most extreamely oblidging and ready to serve me. I hiered a Shais and came from Nieuport to Dunquerk."

The Jesuit Father Thomas Hunter was at the time engaged upon a vigorous reply to the attack upon his order by the Rev. Charles Dodd.[2]

Two of Nicholas's sisters and his aunt Alice were Poor Clare nuns at the Dunkirk Convent. He was entertained by the community, before he proceeded further into France.

"April 9th. I came from Dunquerk in ye Barge with 2 or 3 from ye North, we dined together at Burbruck and thence I walked to Graveling where I suped at ye Poor Clayres.

April 12th. I opened my Male Trunk and put my Things up in order. I took Account of what Linnen etc. as I had and set all things down.

April 15th. I saw ye Church Yard blessed because there had been a good quantity of Human Blood shed there in a Quarrell which had so profaned ye place as no one was to be buried there till it was blessed.

April 16th. I began to learn French of Peter Garde, he is in Colonel de Leons Rigeament. His Military name is Le Anglais.

April 17th. I saw 15 Companys of French viz: forty in each Company drawn up in ye Market Place, which made one Batallion of 600 men. I also saw a Batallion of Swiss drawn up, viz three Companies each consisting of 200 Men.

May 1st. Mr Simpson cut the hair off my Head. I writ most of my Disbursements since I left home fair over in my small Account book."

After these practical matters had received attention Nicholas went by boat to stay at his old college of St. Omer.

[1] The English Carthusians had been given asylum in Flanders upon the dissolution of the monasteries in England in 1537.
[2] For this controversy, see Guilday, *The Secret Policy of the English Jesuits.*

"May 3rd. I was at the Schools when the boys were had their places given them and Premiums. Mr Carroll[1] being to leave, gave his schoolfellows the Returritions[2] a treat."

On a subsequent visit to St Omer Nicholas was evidently intrigued by the college mill which was independent of wind-power.

"The Cogg Wheel is about seaven yards or more in Diamiture, the millstones I think a little above four Foot. One Hors will grind six hours per day and do some other little work besides. He will grind near 3 Bushells of Wheat in an Hour."

Brewing for the college was also done on the premises.

"In Bruing they Burn 500 Fagots before ye Water is rightly set on Boyling. They Boyle their Beer 14 hours and at Graveling their Beer is Boyled 22 hours."

The Diarist next visited the noviciate house of the English Jesuits at Watten, where his brother Joseph, and his uncles Nicholas and Thomas Blundell[3] had pursued their higher studies. During June he established himself in lodgings at Dunkirk where he beguiled the days of waiting for the arrival of his family "smoking a pip," with one friend, playing whist and trente quarante with others, learning and teaching tricks of "legerdemesney," and earnestly pursuing his study of French.

II

At Crosby Mrs Blundell was making preparations for the great adventure of conveying herself, children and maids across England and the sea to join her husband.

Nicholas occasionally received letters from her, but it is unlikely that she would have ventured to mention the troubles which had fallen upon Lancashire. He must have heard of these however from the friends and connections who were pouring into Flanders.

The Commissioners for Forfeited Estates now included in their investigations a search for money and property owned by,

[1] Probably a member of the Sussex family of *Caryl*.
[2] Rhetoricians.
[3] Sons of the Cavalier.

or in trust for, "Popish Priests." The new law allotted to informers a fourth part of the property which they could prove to have been used for "Superstitious Purposes" by its owners. The remaining three-fourths were forfeited to the Crown. Crucifixes, chalices, vestments etc. which were often of great value, were included in the category of property to be confiscated, as well as money and land. Informers in plenty appeared upon the scene throughout the country and Lancashire no longer escaped their attentions. Chief among them was Hitchmough, a renegade priest who had abandoned his calling and his flock to embrace their lucrative profession.

"This day Mr Hitchmough came to me and produced the enclosed Information which he was very earnest I should transmit to you," wrote Chambers Slaughter, chief accountant to the Commissioners, on January 8th, 1716. "He has brought me an account of £1000 held in trust by Thomas Golding, William Tarlton and others for the use of the Popish Secular Clergy at Douay College."[1]

Lawyer Golding and Yeoman Tarlton were among the Diarist's friends, as were many more whose names appear in the relative documents signed by Slaughter or Hitchmough— Fleetwoods, Gerards, Dicconsons, Culcheths and Cliftons among others. In their cases the informers were interested only in reporting the discovery of money and property devoted to the interests of the Catholic Church: they were not now investigating the movements of real or supposed rebels against the new King. Ruin and imprisonment therefore menaced both squire and chaplain in the homes of practically all the Blundells' neighbours in the North. Priests were concealed by their parishioners, moving from hall to farmhouse, from cottage to barn and back again to the nearest hiding-hole.

At Little Crosby anxiety for Father Aldred's safety must have been great, but he stuck to his post; no doubt he took refuge in the "streat place" when occasion required, while Mrs. Blundell saw to it that vestments and sacred vessels used for the

---

[1] English Catholic Non-Jurors. English seminarists were educated at Douay College in Flanders and sent from there to minister to their Catholic fellow-countrymen.

celebration of Mass were stowed in the "fals roof." Father William Gillibrand temporarily disappears from the scene, leaving to his brother John the charge of the accounts at Crosby. Indeed the preparations for the journey of Mrs Blundell and her children seem to have been made mainly by John Gillibrand.

The Disbursement Book reveals a good deal of what went on at Crosby in the interval between the Squire's flight and the family re-union at Dunkirk eight months later. Mrs Blundell inaugurated her solitary reign with very good intentions, for the entries during the first weeks are made in her own pretty, sloping hand-writing in which many recipes are copied into the "Book of Recipes." One line runs: "To Doctor Lancaster for Mee 10s.-0." But in a few weeks she either tired of this exertion or began to doubt her own ability to manage the money left in her hands. There are a few scrawled entries in large crooked letters which suggest that Mally had tried to help her mother; if these are samples of her writing when nearly twelve years old it is to be feared that her father's tuition in caligraphy did not provide very successful results. But soon the columns display the neat, small writing resembling the Diarist's own, which John Gillibrand may have learned in the same school of St Omer.

Items of expense hitherto almost unknown to the Disbursement book illustrate the fact that the home farm was let. Butter, meat, cream, rabbits, eggs, even "milk at times," now had to be bought.

When John Gillibrand took charge it was evidently agreed that *all* money should be administered by him. For such entries occur as:

	£.	s.	d.
"To Mrs Blundell herself			8½
To Mrs Blundell for Hous use		1	9
For Madam Blundell's Stays	2	4	0
For blooding Mrs Blundell		1	0"

Mally, who seems to have been in constant ill health during her childhood, was carried off by Doctor Lancaster for a fortnight's treatment.

"Feb. 22nd. 1716. Pd Dr Lancaster's Bill for Miss Mally Blundell with a fortnight's Dyet at his house   £1 15   6"

On June 14th, William Weedon was sent to Chester to pay a deposit for places in the London Coach.

To Boat hyred[1] going to take Coach ...	2	6
To Charges in Chester and back again	3	6
To half pay for 4 Seats and half in Chester Coach £4	10	0

When the party finally started on what must have been a momentous journey for them, John Gillibrand and his servant escorted them to London.

"June 16th. Spent at Warrington and Chester, ourselves, Servants and Seven Horses   ...   . £2   8   4"

The travellers were four days on the road between Chester and London, "5 in the Coach" writes Gillibrand, "and my man on the Box."

Their expenses for food and lodging on the road amounted in all to £4. 10s. 8d. while "the later moiety of Coch Hyre" was £5. 10s.

Boxes had been sent in advance at the cost of a guinea, but one of them having been "broke to pieces by ye carrier," 4/6 was paid for a new one.

In London Mrs Blundell and her children stayed with Mrs Anne Aldred, but bought their own food. Much shopping was accomplished and small payments "to Mrs Blundell's Pocket" occur very frequently, while Mr Gillibrand's man was paid £1. 9s. 1½d. for "small beer and odd things" purchased by him for the Crosby party. Mally had a new gown at the cost of £1. 1s. 6d., Fanny was set up with a nightgown for 13s. and "a Mantu & pettycoat with ferret, & a bag made" for 9s. 6d.

On July 4th, the second half of their journey was begun.

" Coaches to Billingsgate	4	6
Porters there	1	0
Boat to Gravesend	6	0
Supper at ye Inn at Gravesend	7	6"

[1] To cross the Mersey.

They took lodging for a fortnight at Mrs Savil's in Duke Street for which they paid £1 15s. 8d., including 3s. 8d. for milk. This was evidently a precaution in case they should have to wait upon wind and tide. Fortune favoured them, however, and the very next day saw the bustle of departure.

Everyone except the youngest member of the family received "money for her pocket" on John Gillibrand's relinquishing his office of steward of their resources. Mary Woodcock, the maid, was given £1 1s. 6d. "to make account for to her Mistress"; Mally received the large sum of £5, while 10s. was paid "to Mrs Blundell's pocket," and she was given charge of £63. 4s. in French money "in a purs". The last-minute rush is discernible in the acquiring of "leather bags for od things on shipboard and for present use"; roasted fowls for the journey were not forgotten. They stayed one night at Gravesend and on July 6th they were off. Nicholas announces their arrival on the same day. "July 6th. My Wife and Children came in Harvey's Ship. They landed today at Dunquerk. I came to them. My Wife and I lodged at the Poor Clairs, and the Children and Maids lodged in ye Town."

The girl who passed as their second maid was in reality their kinswoman Betty Gorsuch; she had joined Mrs Blundell at Gravesend on her way to become a Poor Clare nun at Dunkirk.

Meanwhile John Gillibrand returned to Crosby and carefully prepared accounts to be presented at a future date to his cousin. "June 16th. Mrs Blundell with her two daughters left Crosby. After their going, found in the Hous in Gold and Silver £150 19s. 0d."

All money received for rents, interest on loans and sale of produce, was paid in cash. Nicholas had left £254 11s. to be accounted for by his cousin, but of this amount £210 had been lodged "by bill" in London "payable to Mr Blundell as he calls for it." John Gillibrand included this sum when, on reckoning total disbursements, he found them to amount to £322 1s. 9d., so that he was owed £67 10s. 10d. He recouped himself from Mrs Blundell's hoard:

"Which said £67 10s. 10d. I payed myself this 16th day of November, 1716."

During the next fifteen months the Diarist and his family explored the country now incorporated into the kingdom of Belgium, by "shais", "bote", barge, and by a vehicle described by Nicholas as a "caraba"—the forerunner of our familiar "chara".

"July 25th. My Wife, I and Children came from Dunquerk to Newport in a Shais, and there took bote towards Brudges, but being ye River was almost dry near ye Town, we were forced to come some miles by wagon and twas so late we could not get into Brudges so my Wife and I lodged near ye Town at ye Golden Crown, a good Hous, my Children and Mary lodged at another Hous.

July 26th. My Wife, Children and I came in ye Barge from Brudges to Guant, where we lodged at ye Looking Glass."

After a short preliminary tour Mally and Fanny were placed as boarders in the Benedictine convent school at Ghent. They inaugurated their career as schoolgirls by being very ill. The complaint is unspecified but they were immediately "let blood". Their mother obtained special permission to enter the enclosure and "waike", or sit up at night, with her children. Five days after having been "bludded for the first time," Fanny was "bludied with a Leetch." In three weeks both children had recovered from the malady, whatever it was, and the effects of the treatment, and "came to the Grate" to see their father. In September they were taken on a holiday trip to visit their various aunts and cousins in convents at Bruges, Dunkirk and Gravelines. Finally Fanny was left in the care of her aunt at the Poor Clares Convent in the last-named town, while Mally, after a further tour, returned to school at Ghent.

Nicholas and his wife continued to move from place to place. He was at one time "very ill of his eyes," at another he had recurring attacks of ague which did not altogether yield to the available remedies.

"Mrs Waldergrave[1] applyed som thing to ye Little Finger

[1] Anne, daughter of Edward Waldegrave and his wife Mary King. She was a member of the community of English Canonesses at Liége.

of my Left Hand to cure me of the Ague Fits, notwithstanding which I had a Fit and they still continued with me."

The remedy which gave him the most relief was supplied by the Benedictine nuns at Ghent.

"I took ye Nunns Receipt for the Ague and had an easier Fit than ordinary."

The malady might drive him to bed early or cause him to get up late, but it did not put a stop to indomitable sight-seeing. From church to church they went, from convent to convent of English communities presided over by ladies who bore well-known names. Such were Madam Sheldon of the Augustinians at Antwerp, Lady Waldegrave of "Ye Daimes" at Brussels, Lady Swinburne of the English Benedictines at Cambrai.

Nicholas and Sir Walter Blount went on a short trip together during the summer.

"Sir Walter Blunt and I came from Guant in a Shais to Antwerp, tis 11 Legues, we dined at ye half way Hous, ye Star, and lodged at Antwerp at ye Red Tun in the Mair, a most noble Street which is hollow from one end to ye other so as Boates may pass lengthways under it and under the Jesuits Church,[1] coming along I observed very little on each side of ye Rode except great Plenty of Buck Wheat, Otes and Clover there being little els to be seen, especially Buck Wheat, or, as we call it, French Wheat; the most part of the Rode was planted with Oakes on each side as are to be croped for Fagots and in

---

[1] I am indebted to the Rev. W. Koch, S.J., of Antwerp, for the following information on the old waterways of Antwerp: "An old map of Antwerp shows the Meir with water at one end and some sort of tunnel running from there in the direction of the Cathedral. From the Meir Bridge a canal, which has been covered in for centuries, passed beside the church of St. Ignatius (now the parish church of St. Charles). This canal was nearly at right angles to the Meir, and was uncovered lately when new buildings were erected in the vicinity. These canals and many others were the moats of the first precincts of the town and now form part of the drainage system; some are said to be still large enough to admit of the passage of rowing-boats."

The church was the first in the world to be dedicated to St. Ignatius. It was built 1614—21, was struck by lightning in 1718 but re-built the following year.

severall Places where the Rode is broad 3 or 4 or sometimes more Rows of Oak Trees with Cart ways between each Row, ye Rode is deep Sand most of ye way; Antwerp stands upon the Skeld, a noble River, and formerly a Town of great Trade. In the Jesuits Church is a Statue representing Humility so well carved that ye King of France preferred for it its weight in Gold . . . and six or more originall Pictures of Rubins and Vandike. . . . I was in their Region of the Dead or Seller where they bury, which is very Neat, and in their Museum or Studi-Place where they are writing ye Lives of all ye Canonical Saints, this work was begun about 90 years past by Pater Bolandus & is now carried on by Pater Ianingus and three others, they have finished the end of June and writ twenty-four Folios. . . . Aug. 17th. We were in ye Sitadell which is very Strong and has very pretty Houses in it for Souldiers to lodg in. The Town is also well fortified and has ye finest Walls of any Town I have ever seen, part of them so broad that four Coaches can go in a Brest upon ye Rampers, and Noble fine Trees growing upon those broad Rampers."

The tourists went from Antwerp to Mecklinberg, where they dined at the Kettle, and proceeded the same day to Louvain where they lodged at the Golden Cup. After two days sight-seeing they went on to "ye Signe of ye Green Wood" in Brussels.

Incidentally, what a pleasant flavour there is in the names of the hostelries of those days compared with "Grande Hotel de l'Europe," "Hotel d'Angleterre" etc., of our own times. Besides the Inns already mentioned we come upon The Large Golden Apple at Ruisbruk, The Golden Head at Ypres, The Chase Royal at Dunkirk.

Some of the sights of the roadside, casually mentioned, were gruesome enough:

"When we came near Brussels we saw 8 or 9 Men hanging on one Gallows, and as many lying upon Wheels, and not far from thence were severall more both on ye Gallows and on Wheels."

"In the Town-Hous," writes our Briton firmly of the Hotel

de Ville at Brussels, "which is a most noble building, I saw severall curious fine Rooms with delecate Pictures and a great quantity of extraordinary good tapistry and two Tables of Marble with Maps most incomparably painted on them."

From Brussels they went to Alôst where they dined " at the Indian Kings, an extraordinary good Inn ", and returned the same day " along the Strightest Rode imaginable and all paved and set on each side with trees, to Guant."

The Lancashire Squire was profoundly interested in the canals and locks which facilitated travel and commerce in those busy provinces. He comments on the exact measurements of the new canal at Mardyke with its " Great Sluce " and its " Little Sluce " and " ye Island between them ". Windmills naturally caught his eye : he inspected the interior of one at Dunkirk; at Lisle which he describes as " the most butifull and fine town, and clearly ye best in Flanders," he counted " looking out of the Diligence on one side, 36 Windmills at once. I was told," he adds " there were 120 Windmills or thereabouts belonging to that Town, a great many of them were for making Rape Oyle."

The Disbursement Book contains a summary of the family doings during the 15 weeks following the arrival of Mrs Blundell and her children at Dunkirk.

" Meat, Drink & all Travelling Expenses and carriage of our goods for myself, Wife, two Children, and one Maid from ye time my Wife & Children came to Dunquerk till ye Children were settled and we began to table at Dunquerk, being about 15 weeks during which time we all went to Guant and stayed a good while. I took a toore into ye Country, so did my Wife and her maid at an other time; some other Journies we took, sometimes one, two or more of us at a time and spent in all things these 15 Weeks (apparall of all sorts, Physick and Doctors Fees excepted) the Sume of £57-1-1."

IV

Nicholas and his wife, after inspecting houses and apartments at Ghent, Gravelines and Dunkirk, finally hired an apartment in the last-named town.

"Feb. 4th. We took Possession of our own Apartment at Andrew Vanderburk's and began to keep hous there."

They bought some furniture and table linen, and with Mary Woodcock as cook, settled down for the next fifteen weeks, to a life of extreme sociability. The Diary shows an exiled community making the best of things. Members of many families who then still adhered to the ancient faith but whose descendants are no longer found within its fold, were among Mr. and Mrs. Blundell's friends. Their circle included the Lacys of Wiltshire, the Hindes of Lincolnshire, Lord Waldegrave, Sir Edward Blount,[1] Lord Rivers,[2] Sir John Webb and his wife; priest members of all the families so constantly mentioned in the Diary,—Talbots, Cliftons, Scarisbricks, Fazackerleys, Langdales, Middletons—were among those who came and went; their sisters, aunts and cousins were visited at "ye Daimes", "Ye Poor Claires", "ye Austin Nuns" and other convents.

Sometimes the Blundells entertained friends at their apartment with "a dish of tay"; on special occasions coffee was provided.

"This being Mally's birthday, she treated us with coffy. . . . This being my birthday I gave my Sister etc" (the Poor Clare nuns) "a Pot of Coffy and Tay at ye Grate."

Often small card parties took place at the lodgings of one or another of the layfolk.

As soon as he was established in his own quarters Nicholas provided himself with beer.

"February 11th. Mr Lacy went with me to ye Brewers to bespeak some Drink for me, and shewed me ye Method of getting it.

Feb. 12th. The Brewers brought me half a Tunn of Beer."

Members of the English circle seem to have made no contact with the people of the land which gave them hospitality. Even

[1] Fourth Baronet. He succeeded to the title upon the death of his uncle, Sir Walter Blount, in May, 1717.

[2] John Savage, fifth and last Earl Rivers, was a priest. He succeeded to his cousin, Richard, the fourth Earl, in 1712. He refused to accept the large fortune bequeathed to him on condition that he renounced the Catholic faith.

the shop-keepers with whom they dealt were English; no doubt exiled Jacobites were among them. "Fodergills ye Yorkshire Hatters" maintained their business at Ghent; Mr. and Mrs. West sold "Callicows and Holland" at Dunkirk; Nicholas bought "a silver Cheane" for his watch of Mr. Sutton in the same town. Joseph Thelwall kept a livery stable at Gravelines. The Diary frequently mentions short "journies" made in Joseph Thelwall's "Caraba" or of a "shais" being provided by "Jos." Fanny was brought from school to spend Easter with her parents in Thelwall's "caraba"; by the same vehicle Nicholas sent a present of oysters to the nuns at Ghent, and on another occasion made use of it to forward "a large Trunk of Cloths to Graveling to be ready there for us against we go there." Whether Joseph was a member of the Thelwall family of Little Crosby is not stated.

On February 9th Nicholas writes, without comment as usual : "Mr. Hind brought me some newspapers to read."

The news must have made sad reading to members of that north-country society who were nearly all interrelated and all looked upon each other as neighbours in the wide sense. At that very moment the assizes were being held in Liverpool at which Richard Chorley of Chorley was to be condemned to death for taking part in the rising. His son Charles, aged 21, was in the Liverpool prison where he died. Mrs. Blundell's nephew Edward Swinburne, and Richard Butler of Rawcliffe in Lancashire, also died in prison. Lord Widdrington and Sir Francis Anderton of Lostock escaped the death penalty but their estates were forfeited, a light punishment compared with that meted to members of the rank and file whom they had led. These only purchased their lives by petitioning to be transported : their petition was granted.

" Many of the prisoners were left to the merchants of Liverpool to be transported to the plantations of America."[1]

In plainer words, they were sold into temporary slavery.

Travellers from England, among whom was "Edward ye poore Claires Gardiner" must indeed have brought distressing tidings to convent " grates " and exiles' lodgings, but in spite of

[1] *Lancashire Memorials,* Chetham Society. Vol. V.

these the Squire of Crosby busied himself, in the midst of the foreign scene, with familiar and congenial occupations.

"Feb. 2nd. I went into ye Convent Garden and trimed some Wall Trees etc. I shaved Fanny's Head."

Each time he visited Fanny at school he performed this office for her.

"I sowed above a dozen sorts of Flower Seeds in Pater Francis' Garden. . . . I sowed severall Sorts of Flower Seeds in Antony Tevenet the Taylor's Garden. . . . I went into ye Clairs Garden and helped to prune and nail some of their Vines. . . . I helped to plant some Trees to ye Wall in ye Claires Garden and to plant those we took from thence in other places. . . . I began to trim an Apricock Tree in ye Claires Garden as was grown out of Shape."

His thrifty mind was evidently perturbed on noticing the damage done by rats and mice in "ye Claires Garden."

"I made some Mous:Traps for the Clairs Garden. . . . I showed Sister Clare John how to set the two sorts of Mous Traps."

He also set a rat trap in the garret of his lodging.

At Dunkirk he found a self-provided task greatly to his liking:

"Feb. 27th. Mr. Lacy and I began to paint the Clairs Church and with some help we finished it ye first time over.

March 2nd. I began to paint ye Clairs Church with ye second Colour."

Father Francis later joined the painting party:

"March 4th. We four painted ye most part of the Clairs Church with ye second Colour, part of it not being done thick enough before, we mended it today."

Nicholas must have been greatly disappointed when ague drove him to bed on the day on which their labours were almost completed.

"April 2nd. I went to bed ill of an Ague and burned all night. April 3rd. Mr Lacy and his Wife and Pat. Francis finished painting ye Clairs Church."

The indefatigable Diarist was hardly on his feet again before he and his wife were off on a tour. They went by coach to

Ypres, the road being all " Causey way, and the Country open and Champion."

The good road evidently did not continue for they travelled on to " Lisley " in a " Wagan ". From Lille they went once more along a " Causey way in a dilligence to Douai," and the next day had to take to a " Wagan " again to reach Cambrai, " the Rode extreamly bad ". Here they put up at the Guest House of the Benedictine " Daims ". At Cambrai they found Mrs. Blundell's sister, the widowed Mrs. Middleton with her son Jackie; Mrs. Langdale was also in the town, and possibly other acquaintances and connections for Nicholas writes :

"April 22nd. My Sister Middleton my Wife and I etc. went into ye Town to make Visets but we were disappointed in two Places."

Among others called upon was M. Blondel, a member of the French family whose arms differ little from those of the Blundells of Crosby.

Much sight-seeing was accomplished at Cambrai. " The Cathedral " writes Nicholas in conclusion of a long description of its interior riches, " has a great deale of Antiquity and Grandour in it "; he found the Church of St. Sepulchre, " new-built of most delicate fine whit Free Stone handsomely carved " to be " ye most Butifull Neat pritty Church," he had ever seen. They visited St. Julian's Hospital, staffed by the Augustinian Nuns, the forerunners of modern hospital nurses.

The travellers inspected the " sitadell " on a pleasant green hill which Nicholas describes as " ye strongest place I have ever been in." Cambrai was one of the chain of fortified places which had figured so largely in the Peace Treaties of Ryswick and Utrecht.

Douai was the next objective. Here was the famous college which was founded by Cardinal Allen in 1538 to educate young Englishmen for the priesthood. In its early days many of its sons died in the prisons of their native land; others perished on the scaffold, havng been condemned for exercising their calling which in itself ranked as high treason. English seculars now had their own Clergy House, and Clergy College in the town.

Scotch Jesuits and English Friars were also visited in their flourishing houses. As Nicholas was suffering much from recurring fits of ague he may have been glad to see his temporary home at Dunkirk again after three weeks of strenuous travel. In the midst of all the distracting fine sights he did not fail to notice one of interest to the agriculturist. The Diary for April is thus concluded:

" In this our journey I observed more than once four Horses drawing in a Brest at one Wooden Harrow and severall times I saw three Horses in a Brest."

Another journey was undertaken for a definite motive: they had evidently been informed of the beneficent effects of the hot springs near Liège upon childless couples.

" May 26th. I took places in ye Coach for Brussels.

May 27th. My wife and I went from Guant in a Coach and three Horses to Allost where we dined at ye Whit Swan, the Tillage on each side was chiefly Rye and cole Seed; thence we came to Brussels where we lodged at ye Queen of Swaids.

May 28th. From Brussels we went at four in the Morning in ye Diligence to Louvain where we changed Horses, thence to Tirlemont where we changed our good Diligence for one with two wheels, thence to St Trone where *I* dined and got my Trunk mended, and so to where we lodged at ye Whit Sheep."

There seems to be a hint of a tiff having taken place between the couple in the two-wheeled conveyance, for Nicholas underlines the pronoun *I* in the above passage, as though to stress the fact that he had dined alone.

" May 29th. I advised with ye Doctor about going to ye Spaws for a Son . . . I saw ye famous Miroir of Steel burning Glass which I saw melt Iron and Stone etc. in a Minnet's Time as I think, and set Timber on Fier in a Moment."

At Liège the Diarist found St. Paul's Church "very light and clean," St. Martin's "little and dark," and the Dominicans' " in my opinion a Conceipted Sort of a Building."

They travelled on to Chaudes Fontaines by an " extreamely long flat-Bottomed Bote, it was drawn by a Hors as waided in ye River a good part of the Way, it had no Rudder but the man guided it with a Bord about half a yard squair fixed at ye end of a Powl."

N

Nicholas makes no remark on the comfort or lack of it, in this boat, but, again underlining the pronoun, concludes "*I* dined at the Ordinary."

After taking the baths for a week—the water was made "very warme" when poor Mrs. Blundell was suffering from her usual complaint "ye gravell"—the couple returned "by ye common Boat" to Liège. Here they remained until the end of June, sight-seeing and meeting friends. Besides visiting 52 churches (and he does not omit to mention that he could have seen as many more) Nicholas made notes on the activities of the population. Perhaps many more crafts would still flourish in these days if less expensive means for the transport of small amounts of goods existed, especially if our waterways were kept clear and utilised. Nicholas thus describes a small mercantile raft:

"I saw a sort of Hurdle made of small Powles tyed together with Withys, it is to carry som sorts of Merchandize in, upon ye Water, instead of Boats."

He was interested in rates of pay too:

"I was in that part of the Town where they Twig Bottles[1] for carrying Spaw water etc. in, saw them twiging of them for which they have not quite 13d. English per doz. . . .

1717

June 19th. Mr. Wright[2] went with me to some Cole Pitts, we went most of ye way by Bote, they wind up about one Hoggshead and a half of water at a Time with 3 or 4 strong Horses, the Cole Pits are generally very deep, and some of them above 80 Fathom, at one Pit I saw a Place like a Well made of Brick with a Bucket of Fier which hung down in it to prevent ye Damp, and over it there was a Chimney like that of a Glasshous."

[1] Encase bottles in basket work made of willow, a trade still extensively followed in wine-making countries.

[2] Rev. Peter Wright. A secular priest, confessor to the English Canonesses of the Holy Sepulchre at Liège.

He makes no comment on the usefulness or otherwise of these primitive efforts to protect the unfortunate miners.

Nicholas visited the spa again, apparently in hopes of being cured of his ague which greatly interfered with his pleasure while at Liège. There he met Roger Dicconson of Wrightington who was outlawed for having taken part in the Stuart rising.[1] "June 27th. I went on a hired Hors from ye Spaws to Burset where I saw ye Boyling Springs which were so hot it was not possible to put ones hand into them, there came a very great Smoke or Steame from them, they teast like the Sulper Spaw in York Shire but not so strong. Then I went to Eaz[2] where I took a glass of wine with Collonel Bellingham[3] at ye Golden Dragon, I suped and lodged there . . . Eaz is famous for Making Needles. I have bene told that 6000 persons are maintained in that Town by making Needles."

By this time the frenzy of both Jacobites and supporters of the Government had simmered down, and during the summer of 1717 a royal Act of Clemency was passed. Such Jacobite prisoners as had not been executed, died in prison or been transported, were now released, and Nicholas, among many others who had sought refuge from the storm in Flanders, decided to return to his native land.

The two little girls accompanied their parents on their homeward way as far as Calais. When the moment of parting arrived let us hope that Mally and Fanny found some consolation in their new clothes, and their father's unwonted generosity in the matter of pocket money. Thus the Disbursement Book:

"Green Poplin Sute for Mally and Carriage
    to Dunquerk £3 5 7
Linnen Apparrell for my Children, viz.
    Shifts, Heads and Ruffles etc., Lace,
    Ribans, Silk for short Aprons and Huds,
    Stockings and Gloves £10 14 2
Pocket Money for my Children ...   ...   £3 16 9"

[1] Gillow.
[2] Aix.
[3] Colonel in the army of William III in his Irish war. See Burke, Also *Bellingham's Diary*, ed. Hewitson.

When Nicholas and his wife bade farewell to their children at Calais they knew the parting was to be of six years' duration.

V

"July 31st. I got my Goods Searched and leaded and put on bord. My children returned back to Graveling.

Aug. 3rd. We went on Bord Mr Gallaways Vessell ye Betty Yot and sailed out of the Harbour at Callis with a tollerable good Wind to Ramsgate where we Ancored.

Aug. 4th. We sailed to Broad Stairs where we cast Ancor and most of us went on Shoer to ye Bricklayers Armes as I take it, where they dined, but I turned back and went on Bord with Mr Glover who searched the Vessell and seazed on some Brandy. My Wife and I walked to Margarit where we lodged at ye Whit Hart.

Aug. 5th. We went from Margarit by Bote on Bord ye Betty and Sailed with a very brisk wind almost all day; we came to London. My Wife and I lodged at ye Cross Keys in Gratius Street.

Aug. 6th. I went to ye Custom Hous etc. in hopes to get my goods on Shoer but could not . . .

Aug. 7th. I was busy all morning about getting my goods on Shore which at last I did, but could not bring them to my Lodging."

London friends were soon pressed into the returned travellers' service.

"Aug. 9th. Mr Berry went with me and helped me to get home my Trunks . . .

Aug. 10th. Mistress Anne Aldred went with me to help us to buy new Clothes, my Wife bought a Red Satine Sute and I a Dove-colour Sute."

In this finery they proceeded to make the most of their sojourn in the Capital to which they could not expect to return for several years. For nearly a month they met friends, visited theatres and saw sights indefatigably: St. Bartholomew's Fair afforded them much amusement. "There" writes Nicholas "we saw a Farce acted as is called Robin Hudd and Little John . . . A Poppy Play called Patient Grissell, & the Babes in the Wood."

The Diarist explored, as was his wont. He found Kensington Gardens "very large and fine. Two Walks in it with Rows of Elme Trees on each side trimed on ye Top and Sides like Hedges, the Trees are 40 Foot high . . . I saw Marlburgh Hous, tis a pritty little Hous, and some very good pictures drawn by L'Garr[1] . . . thence we went to Buckingham Hous which is really Noble and fine and severall Pictures in it of great Vallew . . . We walked thorrow St. James's Park where we saw some of the Trees as was blowed up by the Roots and some as were snapped off 7 or 8 Foot from ye Ground by ye Great Storme of Wind which happened upon ye 21st. Instant in the Morning and the night precedant, some of ye Trees were about 3 yards in Circumference . . ."

The same circle of co-religionists was frequented as on the occasion of the Diarist's sojourn in London nearly two years previously. One set of friends was visited under distressing circumstances. Robert Scarisbrick, with two other Lancashire men, John Ashton and John Gregson, who had been in hiding, had surrendered themselves when the Act of Clemency was passed. They were committed to Newgate to await trial.

"Aug. 29th . . .I made a visit to Mr. Scarisbrick in Newgate. I drank there with Mr. Blackburne[2] who has been a Prisoner there as I take it above 21 years. Mr Gregson and Mr. Ashton was also with us."

It is almost unbearable to think that when Nicholas calmly penned those lines, Robert Blackburne had still another 30 years of imprisonment to undergo before death released him while he was *still awaiting trial* for supposed complicity in the bogus plot to assassinate William III in 1694. Possibly he was arrested later than the other Lancashire gentlemen tried and

---

[1] Louis Laguerre, died 1791, a French painter who did much work on the ceilings, staircases, etc., of great houses in England.

[2] Son of Richard Blackburne of Thistleton, Lancashire.

acquitted at Manchester, among whom were the Diarist's father and grandfather. The friends who made persistent but fruitless efforts on his behalf, died as the years went on, until at last the prisoner died himself, friendless, after having spent half a century in custody.[1]

The other prisoners mentioned by Nicholas were tried at Lancaster in 1718 and released on bail.

The Blundells sent their luggage home in advance by " ye Waganers," starting from the Castle and Falcon in Aldersgate Street. On September 1st " there was a Bon Fier and Illuminations in St. James's Squair for the Victory obtained by Prince Eugaine over the Turks."

After witnessing this festive scene and holding many farewell gatherings in " Wills Coffy Hous " and elsewhere, the travellers returned to Crosby.

[1] Gillow.

CHAPTER XI

I

HOME AGAIN

1717

NICHOLAS and his wife soon slipped back into the life described in earlier chapters; the blank in it occasioned by the absence of the two little daughters whom they were not to see again as children, must be left to the imagination. Neighbours from all quarters came to bid them welcome home; others sent them presents.

"Mrs. Smith of Aintry sent my Wife a present of some Fowl ... My Lord Molyneux sent me a Present of Part of a Stagg ... Mrs. Edwardson of Liverpool brought my Wife a Present of Indian Sweetmeats ... We dined at Ince with Ailes Tickley. We eat of a very good Chees as was twelve years old."

A pilgrimage to Holywell was undertaken, no doubt in thanksgiving for a safe return from their travels. On this occasion the Diarist relates that on their homeward journey he traversed the dangerous sands and the river Dee alone to find a guide on the opposite shore, and brought him back to escort his wife over the perilous crossing. After the accomplishment of this pious expedition Nicholas applied himself immediately to his wonted occupations.

"I took two Hives of bees ... I was busy most of ye Day booking my Disbursements ... I helped Edward Howerd to bottle off a Rundlet of Aile ... Will Thelwall[1] clensed ye Jack and our little Pendulum ... I took a Swarm of Bees at ye Grannery Stairs it had a Bundance of fine Hunny."

Gardening was resumed with zest; a jobbing gardener was employed to plant and prune " frute trees from London ", to set

[1] A carpenter. Son of Walter Thelwall.

"forrun Tulops" and to sow "flower seeds from Gaunt." A shelter was built along the garden wall for the protection of choicer wall fruit; pear trees were "inocculated" with cuttings of "Parson Wairings best Pares"; "cutings or snips of ye Apple called ye Summer Queening" were procured.

The Diarist's generation had learned to appreciate fruit as a food during the twenty years which had passed since the French traveller Misson[1] recorded that fruit only appeared on the tables of the very rich "and then but seldom."

The Diary does not reveal the result of one curious experiment:

"I grafted the Leomond Apple the highest, Miss Dimple next, and ye Blossom Russet ye Lowest, all between the Wood and Bark on the Hodg-Podg Tree."

The accommodating tree had already received other grafts, or to use the Diarist's word, "imps."

John Gillibrand duly resigned his stewardship of the family purse.

"Oct. 8th. Coz. John Gelibrand and I stated Accounts and he counted and paid me what Money was remaining to ballance Accounts."

John Gillibrand had £341 11s. 4¼d. to account for, "which," states the Disbursement Book "is thus evened:

	£	s.	d.
"By Gold in a bag	215	4	6
"By Silver	100	0	0
"By Thomas Syer's Bill on demand ...	16	0	0
"By Walter Thelwall's Bill on demand	8	10	0
"By Thomas Kerfoot's Bill on demand	7	16	10 "

No wonder highwaymen pursued a lucrative calling in those times, when tenants, merchants and others had to carry large sums about in bags, in pursuit of their business. But as the death penalty awaited the convicted thief, however small the sum he stole, it is possible that such robberies were compara-

[1] *Misson's Memoirs and Observations*, translated by John Ozell, 1719.

tively less frequent then than they would be now were we to be deprived of the convenience of cheque-books.

When the Disbursement Book had been brought up to date, the Squire turned his attention to the task of registering his estate in compliance with the new law. Chambers Slaughter complains to the Commissioners of Forfeited Estates in a letter written from Preston on March 29th, 1717, that papists had petitioned the House for a longer time of grace in which to register their estates, and meanwhile were endeavouring to provide for themselves "by stripping of their Lands of timber, plowing up their green swards etc."[1]

If some landowners, knowing that envious relatives or neighbours intended to sue for possession of their estates, did indeed take steps to realise at least part of their value, they could hardly be blamed. But Nicholas had no relative, even the most distant, who was not a co-religionist, and he lived on the friendliest terms with his non-Catholic neighbours. He seems to have made no effort to evade the law in any way, but summoned Walter Thelwall and John Gillibrand to his assistance.

"Oct. 4th. I began to writ out some Particulars of my Tenants in order to Register.

Oct. 9th. Cozen John Gillibrand and Walter Thelwall were very busy all day helping me to prepare for registering.

Oct. 14th. I went to Wiggan, it being ye first day of ye Sestions.

Oct. 15th. I registered my Reall Estate at the Sestions in the Town Hall. I came home through Ormskirk where I took a Glass with Dr Lancaster at the Talbot."

The Registration was not an expensive affair: Mr. Plumbe's fee, presumably for his advice only, was 3s. 6d., while Walter Thelwall and "ye Clarke for registering" each received 10s.

The annual value of the Crosby and Ditton estates, to which Mrs. Blundell's annuity from her grandmother was honestly added, was registered as £482 12s. 2½d. According to the Register,[2] the Diarist's income was among the best in Lancashire, if the great land-owning families of Molyneux of Crox-

---

[1] *Non-Jurors.*
[2] *Non-Jurors.*

teth, Shirburne of Stoneyhurst and Gerard of Garswood be excepted. A Squire's financial circumstances, however, varied with the weather upon which his own and his tenants' crops depended.

Nicholas now had to husband his resources steadily for his daughters' future establishment in life, which would begin with an expensive journey to fetch them home, and a large outlay on the wardrobes they would require as grown-up young ladies.

The home farm was still let to Thomas Syer who continued to occupy half of Crosby Hall until 1720 when he and his family removed to a new home in Great Crosby. Mr. and Mrs. Blundell now only employed two maids in the house and three men out-of-doors; casual labour was engaged as required. The windfall provided by a wreck must have been doubly welcome at a time when the Squire kept only one cow.

"Dec. 5th. Ellen Rigby brought me word that there was a Ship loaded with Butter as had suffered damage ye last Night. Some of it was brought up to Great Crosby & she bought us three Muggs of it."

Father William Gillibrand resumed his task of keeping Mrs. Blundell's household accounts for she quarrelled with his brother John.

"A grand fawling out over Coz. Gelibrand turning her out of his office," writes the Diarist, alluding to his wife only by the pronoun, his usual note of displeasure.

This year the distribution of Soul Cakes[1] on November 2nd, All Souls' Day, is mentioned in the Diary for the first and last time. In pre-Reformation days a collection of alms for procuring Masses for the Souls in Purgatory had been made from house to house, the cakes being bestowed as a reward to those who undertook this work of charity. The Diarist's spelling in this instance is erratic to a degree unusual even for him; presumably it was dictated by his pronunciation of soul as *sawl*.

"Nov. 2nd. We delt Saw loves to the Poore, it being ye first time any Saw-Loves were given here as I remember; of two

---

[1] See *English Custom and Usage,* Christine Hole.

Bushells of Barley we made 420 Loves, but they were too little, if three had been made into two they would have been pritty well. Althô it was a fine day and the ways very good, yet I believe there was about one third part of ye Saw-Loves left and very few came as were not inhabitants of this Parish."

Mrs. Blundell must have been deprived of the pleasure of choosing new clothes for a considerable time, since she and her husband had apparently laid out the last of their foreign money on new attire before leaving Flanders. Nicholas states in the Disbursement Book that Apparrell of all Sorts for my Wife " and "Apparrell of all Sorts for me," cost £101 11s. 4d. His wife, however, had entered into some degree of emancipation; perhaps she demanded it after having moved in a wider circle than that provided by the Lancashire squires and their dames. She was now allowed the disposal of £20 out of the £100 a year left to her by her grandmother. This was not in the nature of a dress allowance, for the Disbursement Book continues to record outlay on her husband's part even for such minor matters as :

" A Hand Karchaff for my Wife "
" Mending Wives Shoes "
" Outside and Lining for my Wives Cloak and maiking it "
" Altering Mantews etc."

In fact it was a tacitly accepted part of the eighteenth century marriage bargains that husbands should pay for their wives' clothes and keep a tight hold of their money. Nicholas probably considered himself generous in allowing his wife a small share in her own inheritance after fourteen years of wedlock.

In the midst of planting and pruning and transplanting the young trees he had raised from seed so industriously sown in former years, the Squire was confronted by a new preoccupation. The thousands of thorn trees which he had grown from haws now played their part in enclosing fields.

" Nicholas Sumner and two others from Formby bought tenn Hundred of Thornes from me . . . Mr Houghton of Leverpoole sent two men for Thornes. I furnished them with fifteen Hundred . . . . I finished pricking out year-old Thornes. I have pricked out in ye Gardens above 146,000."

Nicholas did not attempt to enforce his own will with regard to enclosures, and these were not carried out with the barbarous indifference to the fate of smallholders and cottagers which characterised them in too many parts of the country. Here they were authorised and supervised by a village jury for the benefit of tenants and yeomen who already occupied the land and had access to " ye waste."

"I met most of my Jury in Woodholme viz: John Sumner, John Jackson, Gabriell Norris, Thomas Radcliffe etc., to adjust between William Gray about enclosing there, but Gray would not comply with what we all thought reasonable. Thomas Syor, James Scarisbrick and I met William Gray, Roger Neal etc. at Mrs Rothwell's in order to reconcile a difference among them but could not do it."

The woods and coppices and the hedges along the lanes and roads crossing his estate still testify to the Diarist's untiring energy in planting bushes and trees. The fields are in general divided by ditches, and those water-courses which caused the only recorded friction between the Diarist and his immediate neighbours. Indeed the friendly relations between the families of Ince Blundell and Little Crosby and their respective tenants had been nearly wrecked by a lawsuit on the subject of water-courses in 1714 during the long minority of Robert Blundell. Each side accused the other of neglect, and only the tactful and able intervention of John Gillibrand saved the situation.

"Coz. John Gelibrand writ fair over the artickleys of Agreement between Ince and me relating to mending ye Watercourses and prevent a Sute . . . The Matter seems now to be Much what concluded."

Ditching was paid for by the rood:

"Rob Marser measured some Ditching in severall Parcells as he had helped to ditch."

A minor improvement brought about by enclosure, and the consequent more intensive cultivation of the land, was the destruction of the swarms of snakes.

"Some of my Servants killed 50 Adders most of them in some old Hay lately put out of ye hayloft and layed behind ye Stables severall of them were of the largest Size."

Moles also troubled fields from which they have now long since disappeared.

" I had five Women spreding Mole Hills."

While her husband was so busy out-of-doors Mrs. Blundell was not idle in the house.

"Feb. 4th. My Wife finished spinning of Strick Hemp, she has had five going wheels on foot at once for some few days last past."

The five spinners were paid in all 2s. 10½d. "besydes Vitualls." Sevenpence per week was the wage paid for spinning flax.

The number of "hands" always available for the most trivial jobs reflects the under-employment rife among young people. Now "8 or 9 Hands" are reported as assisting "my Warrenders as were diging out foxes in ye Sandhills," now some are shown dealing with preparations for making one of the Squire's favourite strong drinks :

" I had five Hands and sometimes more Pilling Leomonds most of ye Afternoone and squeezing 80 Leomonds. I had 3 quarts and one gill of Juce to which I put 6 quarts and two Gills of Brandy. I infused the outward Pill of 5 Score Leomonds about 3 Hours in 6 quarts of Brandy. Thomas Cooper of Kirkby brought me some Burch Water. We boyled some of it with Hunny to make Mead on and the rest we ordered for Burch Wine."

Priests now came and went freely once more in the surrounding district although shadowed by the danger that the Penal Laws might be invoked against them, as Hitchmough and Chambers Slaughter were still in pursuit of money and valuables devoted to "superstitious purposes" in Preston and its neighbourhood.[1]

" Pat. Gillibrand came very late and brought word we might soon expect a sevear Serch for Priests. . . . We expected som unwelcom Gests. I prepaired for them."

Doubtless sacred vessels and vestments were consigned to the "Fals Roof" and Mr. Aldred was once more incarcerated in the Priest's hiding-hole, but nothing untoward happened.

[1] *Non-Jurors.*

II

"April 13th. My Wife writ a letter in my Closet."

This was the second of the two missives from Mrs. Blundell to be copied into the Letter Book.

"To my Sister Middleton from my Wife.

Dear Sister,

Thanks for yours and am glad you design me the favour of so long a Viset but much wonder you will talk of paying for the time that would be extreamely unkind in me especially after your great Civility to my Dear Child so hope you will not think of paying; you may depend of a Hearty welcom from Mr. Blundell as well as from myself but shall not pretend to Treat you like a Stranger, but a Friend with two Dishes and those such as you lick, if you will be so kind as to name what you would have; for Mr Blundell having let his Demesney and part of ye Hous we keep but a few Servants, however we have ye Garden in our own hands and keeps a good Roome or two to lodg a Friend in and if you please accept of this accommodation you shall be truly welcom as any Friend or Relation we have and hope you will be so kind as to let me know some weeks before you come and we'l send one to meet you by which you will oblige

Your ever loving Sister
Frances Blundell."

In view of entertaining guests, the house and its furniture required some attention :

"Mr Crumpton of Leverpool ye Upholsturar dined here. He came to see what work I had for him."

The Disbursement Book reveals that Mr. Crumpton was given an order.

"Curtans and Vallance for ye Windows in ye Gallery & the two best Roomes, and for covering 10 Cushions and one Squab-face etc for Repairing ye Beds in ye Garden and Parlour Chambers and for Workmanship in ye four above-mentioned Roomes   ...   .   £8 1 0."

The Squire's fingers had to be in this pie also.

"Charles Howerd and his Man came to Appolster for me. I was busy most of ye day helping them and puting things into order.

June 17th. I went to ye Sail of Goods at Croxteth,[1] and bought some of Thomas Syer etc.

June 23rd. I fixed the Sedar Chest of Drawers as I bought at Croxteth in my Closet."

The Disbursement Book accounts for other goods bought at the sale:

"Press for hanging in My Wives Cloths	...		1	10	0
A Sedar Chest of Drawers	...	...	1	10	0
An Ovell Table ...	...	...		1	6
A Large Wooden Chaire ...	...	...		5	0
Frame for warming Plates...	...	...		2	6"

Now the inner walls of the house had to be improved.

"To Whit Limers, when all my part of this					
Hous was whit washed, some of them					
had 8d. per day ...	...	...	...	2	6	2
Given ye Whit-Limers to drink ...	...		1	2
Hair & Lime	...	...	...	...	5	9
Pitches for Size					
Paint, whit, Black etc & Oyle." ...	...		2	2

The work of painting and white-washing occupied four men for 3 or 4 weeks.

Decoration of the walls next received attention.

"I was most of ye day scouring and clensing Pictures and putting them up in the Chappell, Gallery and severall other Roomes. Rob. Weedon helped me all day.

Rob. Tompson and Rob. Weedon were with me most of ye day helping me to put up Maps Pictures and Scutchons etc. in the Hall, Staircase and Entryes."

The contents of the pantry had to be brought up-to-date at great expense:

[1] Following the recent death of William, fourth Viscount Molyneux.

"Plates of London Puter at 18s. per Doz. ...	4	10	0
Water Dishes of London Puter at 2s. per Pound	2	17	9
Carreage of ye Box of Puter from London and two other Boxes at 1d. per Pound ...		15	0
Knives & Forks of each one Dozen with Ivory Hafts and Silver Hoops	3	12	0
Guilt Coffy Spoons, six	1	12	0 "

On the tenth of July my Lord Langdale arrived with his widowed daughter Mrs. Middleton and her two servants. Entertaining on this scale was not so easy in the reduced circumstances at Crosby as it had been in former years, but neighbours helped : Mr. Gillibrand of Astley sent " a large Salmon of a present. My Lord Molyneux sent his keeper to me with a side of Venison."

Mrs. Blundell's difficult ways with her domestic staff did not tend to smooth her own path.

" July 8th. Ann Bradley came to be Cook here awhile being we expected my Lord Langdale and Sister Middleton.

" July 9th. Being my Wife thought Ann Bradley would not do well in ye Kitchen, I sent her to Leverpoole."

James Burnes, the new butler, only stayed long enough to be useful during Lord Langdale's visit and no doubt to secure his " vails ". But other temporary help was engaged :

| "Cook while Lord Langdale was here ... | 1 | 10 | 0 |
| Char Women ... ... | | 11 | 0 " |

As his own farm was let, the host had to buy food for the visiting horses as well as for his own.

| " Pasture and Hay for my Lord's Horses ... | 1 | 3 | 11 |
| " Oats for my Lord's Horse ... ... | 1 | 6 | 8 " |

Shooting, coursing, race-meetings and dinner parties kept visitors and hosts fully occupied, and a great deal of punch was consumed. This proved to be the last visit to Crosby of the Diarist's father-in-law : he died a few months later and was succeeded by his son Marmaduke, who was thenceforward no longer alluded to by Nicholas as "my Brother Langdale" but as "My Lord Langdale."

A formidable washing list and bill appear in the Disbursement Book for the first time after the departure of this houseparty. Evidently the reduced staff could not cope with the accumulation of laundry.

"Washing Napkins, Wallets and small
    Linnen being 84 dozen at 4d. per doz. ... 1 8 0
Washing 41 pairs of Sheets at 3d. per pair   10 3
Washing 8 doz. of Shifts at 18d. per doz.   12 0
Washing 9 doz. Table Cloths 9 0
Washing five under Pettycoats   ...   ...   6"

III

Nicholas now caused Mr. Plumbe to draw up a new settlement of his estate upon his daughters, not it may be supposed, without many a sigh for the son who was never born to him, for the property had descended from father to son for 600 years. A minor but engrossing interest was however occupying his mind at the time : he had decided to build a combined house and chapel for his friend Father Aldred, who cannot have been very comfortable in Ned Howerd's small cottage. No architect was consulted, no estimate from a builder was sought : the Squire himself was the architect and he "barganed" with a master brick-maker to produce the bricks from, and on, his own land. The initial start was made early in the year 1719.

"Jan. 16th. After dinner Thomas Syer and I etc., went into ye Ackers to boare for Marle, or rather for Clay for Brick we tryed in four or five places, the farther we went into ye field from the gate, the deeper was the feigh.

Jan. 19th. James Banner should have come to discourse me about making Brick, but he sent his Wife."

Perhaps Mrs. Banner was the ruling spirit for there is no further mention of a discourse about the bargain, and preparatory work began immediately.

o

" Jan. 20th. Thomas Syer and I set out a place in the Ackers where Brick was to be got out.

Jan. 22nd. I began to fey for Brick in the Ackers."

"Feying" was removing the surface mossy sod, or feigh. Several hands were employed upon the job.

" Jan. 26th. I went before and after dinner to my Work Folks in ye Ackers. I took some Aile with me for them.

Jan. 29th. I went to my Work folk in ye Ackers and helped to set my Pump there.

Feb. 16th. James Banner and one other Hand began to cast Clay for Brick in ye Ackers."

No doubt they worked all the hours of daylight and in a fortnight had dug out the amount of clay required, leaving three small ponds to bear witness to their labours in a corner of the field still known as "The Ackers."

The clay was left exposed to the air for six weeks before the next step was taken :

" April 18th. I sent some Clay to the Mugg House and Pipe-Makers to be tried there."[1]

The test was satisfactory but the actual brick-making did not begin for another two months.

" June 15th. James Banner etc. came in the evening in order to begin as soon as they could to make Bricks in the Ackers.

June 16th. I went to ye Brickmen in ye Ackers. They were prepairing against tomorrow.

June 17th. James Banner began to make Brick for me. I fenced the ground with a Rope where the Brick were to lie."

The land was evidently found to be insufficiently drained.

" June 19th. I began to ditch in ye Ground where my Brick are to be made. I was with them most of the after noone.

June 22nd. I had a second Molder of Brick began today to Mold.

---

[1] The pottery industry had been greatly extended in Liverpool during the seventeenth century and in the second half of the eighteenth century fine china and porcelain were made. See H. Boswell Lancaster *Liverpool and her Potters.*

August 12th. I went to my Brick-Men and brought them some Bottles of Aile. I boar'd there in ye Brick-Kill Hole in ye Ackers about five yards and a half deep all in good Marle and found no Bottom of it.

August. 14th. My Brick-men James Banner and Henry Marginson finished Molding Bricks for me.

August 25th. Thomas Syer and I helped James Banner to count the Brick he has made for me.

Aug. 26th. James Banner and his Partner began to make ye first of my two Brick-Kills in ye Ackers. I went to them."

The transport of fuel for the kilns was a simple matter.

" I warned some Boones of this Town to lead Sleck ... I met severall of my Boons at the West Lane Gate when they came from the Cole-Pit with Sleck for my Brick ... Some of my Boons as led Sleck for me today came past ye Hous to shew me their loads. ...

Sept. 1st. My Brick men set the first of my Brick-Kills on Fier in the Ackers. I was with them whilst they were fiering it.

Sept. 7th. James Banner and Henry Marginson, having set my second Brick-Kill on Fier in ye Ackers and now having done working for me, I payed them all I ought."

The Brick Men's labours were concluded by a day's holiday.

" Sept. 8th. My Brick Men and some of this Town went out a-coursing with my Bitch and Thomas Syers Dogg."

The Disbursement Book tells the full story of costs and the small share thereof earned by the two Brick-Men.

" This summer I made two Hundred Thousand Bricks and burned them in two Kills

	£		
Feying for ye Clay at 8d. per day ...	3	4	8
Carting off ye Clay at 2s. per day ...	4	15	0
Leveling ye Ground, Push-plowing it and fensing round ye Brick, clearing ye Water, fiting a Cable for ye use of it and ye use & repair of my Pump ...	1	17	10
Leading Sods & Sand at 2s. per day ...		8	0
Given to ye Workmen in Drink, Money, Tobacco and Hors Grass		10	0

Leading Coles & Sleck with my own Teame and Boones which I reckon at 2s. 6d. per day...	15	2	0
Coales at 7s. 6d. per Work	3	0	0
Sleck at 3s. per Cundit	3	0	0
Turves & leading them		7	8
Geting Sods at 4d. per Cent.		7	0
Lodging paid for ye Work-Men at 5d. per Week for each Person	1	13	4
Casting, Molding and Killing Two Hundred Thousand Stock-Brick at 4s. per Thousand	40	0	0
Allowed my Farmers for ye Loss of the Ground upon all Accounts for making Brick there		15	0 "

In the same column of the Disbursement Book the following entry occurs :

s.

"Given Lord Molineux his Keeper for
bringing a side of a Buck to me ...   5   0 "

The amount of this tip compared with that for the making of a thousand bricks throws a beam of light on the attitude of the day towards labour. It would not do for "my Lord Molineux his keeper" to be dissatisfied, but James Banner and Henry Marginson had to be content with what they could get.

The present of venison was undoubtedly exceptionally welcome on that day when much company was entertained. The Squire had been in person to Formby "to seek after Fowl" for the occasion, Dorothy Blundell came "to prepaire" the day before and "all hands were as busy as possible."

"August 3rd. My Lord and Lady Molineux, My Lady West-moreland,[1] my Lord Belew,[2] the Ladys of Maghull,[3] Mr.

[1] Wife of Thomas Fane, sixth Earl, and widow of Richard Beaumont Esq. of Whitby. She was daughter of Thomas Stringer Esq. of Charleston, Yorks.

[2] John, fourth and last Baron Bellew of Duleek of the Peerage of Ireland, born 1702, died 1770, leaving no heirs. *Burke's Extinct Peerage.*

[3] Probably members of the Molyneux family living at Peel, Maghull.

Trentham and Mr. Turvill etc. dined here; Mrs. Blundell[1] and her Doughters Mrs. Bridget and Margaret made a Viset here. Coz. Gillibrand of Chorley, his Wife, his son John and Doughters Margaret and Jane Lodged here."

Lady Westmoreland was the guest of Lord and Lady Molyneux. Mrs. Blundell had already been " to wate of " her at Woolton, and had subsequently sent " two cheeses of a present, ye one to Lady Westmoreland and an other to my Lady Molineux."

Guests would be popular indeed in these days, could they thus requite any civility shown to them!

When the bricks were ready for use, Nicholas made a first draught of the building which was to be called West Lane House, but as he did not include space for a chapel he had to begin again.

" I drew a second Drought of a Hous for Mr. Aldred, this has a Chappell in it, I went to his Hous and showed him the Drought . . . the Hous being now to stand in another place, I was forced to alter this days drought and draw it over againe . . . Mr. Aldred, James Rigby, William Gray etc. consulted how to build the Hous near ye West Laine Gate."

William Gray was a carpenter, James Rigby a builder. The second draught was evidently found unsatisfactory, for after a further consultation with Mr. Aldred and John Voce, Nicholas " began to make an other Drought for ye West Laine Hous, being ye Chappell is now to be in ye Garret."

At last Mr. Aldred was satisfied and his friend " finished ye Drought of ye whole Building."

The Squire provided stone as well as brick :

" John Mason and Thomas Marser began to work at my Stone Delf for Mr. Aldreds Hous."

Neighbours from the adjoining parish helped in the good work.

"Some of Formby Teames led Slate for Mr. Aldred . . . My Teame and six others led Slate for Mr. Aldred from Ashurst Hill . . . My Teame brought two Bolster Lod of Timber for Mr.

[1] Of Ince Blundell.

Aldred out of my Lord Molyneux his New Park, there were five other Teames.

September 30th.   John Voce began to build the West Laine Hous. I laid the first stone with my Coat of Armes and ye first Letters of my Wives Name and mine engraved of it, it is the Foundation Stone of the most Westerly Corner."

Nicholas, as Squire and architect, kept his eye on the village builders :

" Oct. 1st. James Rigby the Sawer and his Partner David Rushton began to work for Mr. Aldred towards the building of the West Laine Hous." Later : " I went to the West Lain Hous and discourced John Voce about making the Stone Stayres according to my Way.' '

The " Rearing " of the priest's house seems to have been a sober affair in every sense of the word, for there is no mention of the large gathering usually associated with such occasions :

" Nov. 10th. The West Laine Hous was Reared. I was with them most of the while and till they had reared it." The entry however concludes with : " Pat Gelibond and I had a good bowl of Punsh with Mr. Aldred."

Other local and parish interests occupied the Diarist while work continued on the building.

He took the mill, which had been let to Thomas Syer, back into his own hands at the end of September, 1719.

" Oct. 7th. I went the first time to take up Tole Corne since I had the Mill in my own Hands. I discourced the Miller about serving me."

The Miller declined, for a few days later we read :

" Oct. 11th. This being Goosefeast Day, my Wife and I stayed at home & kept the Hous. I sent William Carefoot to see if he could horken me out a Miller but he could not."

The Diarist and his wife seem to have lived on the best of terms with Yeoman Syer and his family in the divided house. The Syers received as paying guests or " tablers ", Mr. and Mrs. Sale and " Old Mrs Sale," recently widowed, of Hopcar in the district of Leigh. Young Mrs. Sale was a daughter of Yeoman Tristram of Ince-Blundell. She gave birth to her first child, Richard, while at Crosby, and a fortnight later the Diary tells us :

"This was Mrs Sales Upsiting Day. They had a deal of Company."

A matter which gave Nicholas and his neighbours much concern about this time was the definition of the boundaries, and consequent titles to fore-shore fishing, on their respective estates.

"Great Crosby Jury and my Jury met Mr. Crisp[2] and me at the Sea-Side where we staked out ye Bounderys between Great Crosby & the Morehouses that each Town might know their Liberty to fish in. . . Mr. Crisp, I, Charles Howerd and Willliam Wignold marked out my part of the Sands where it parts between me and the Grange . . . I went to Crosby Court where I proposed to ye Jury to join with them in prosecuting of those who fished in our Coast but it was not accepted."

The distribution of "Corne to ye poore" required regulating :

"I made Card Tickets ready for most of ye Poore of this Parish again next year. . . . I gave Tickets in ye Morning to most of the Poore of this Parish, they are to receive their Almes by them for the next year. . . . Ellen Harrison not being at home, I served ye Poore."

The value of the corn thus distributed is entered in the Disbursement Book quarterly, the amount varying between £1 and £3.

"Cource Linnen for Shifts for ye Poore" is an occasional item in the accounts, while "Physick for ye Poore" occurs regularly.

Small bequests "for the Poore of this Town" were administered by the Squire in consultation with the Overseers of the Poor.

"I signed ye Towns Accounts they are to be brought tomorrow to ye Sessions. I acquainted ye Overseers of the Poore John Sumner, John Molineux, Richard Ainsworth etc. that I had got a place to put out the Money belonging to ye Poore of this Town.

[1] Agent to Lord Molyneux.

I let Rich. Blevin have some money. Part of my own, part belongs to the Poore of Little Crosby as is expressed on ye Back of ye Bond. He and Richard Boon gave Bond for it. . . .

Humphrey Darwin showed me John Bryansons last will containing five Pounds left to the Poore of the More-houses. John Molineux payed me five Pounds as was left by Lawrence Johnson to the Poore of this Town."

Vagrants were cruelly dealt with by the law of the day.

"There was an impudent disbanded Souldior carried hence by the Cunstable to Leverpoole where the Maior ordered him to be whiped."

Constables were called to account strictly if they did not whip hard enough.[1] The Town Crier of Liverpool received 6d. for every beggar whipped.[2]

Every parish strenuously resisted the establishment within its boundaries of any person or family who might become a burden to it. When Richard Webster, the smith of Little Crosby, was sold up for debt, the village jury and that of the neighbouring village of Thornton hotly contended before the Mayor of Liverpool as to which of them was responsible for keeping the family. The Mayor gave an order that the pauper should be removed to Thornton, but Thornton disputed the decision and the case was heard again before the magistrates.

"May 2nd, 1720. I was at part of the Tryall between Thornton and our town concerning ye Settlement of Richard Webster and his family. There was Mr. Entwistle[3] ye Chancellor, Mr. Rich. Norris, etc. upon ye Bench."

The Mayor's directions were upheld, and Richard Webster and his family were bundled off to Thornton after his goods had been sold, and payments made to his creditors, including one to the Squire for rent of the smithy. Nicholas was resolute in upholding the Law of Settlement, but he assisted vagrants with money. Quarterly entries occur throughout the Disbursement

[1] Parson Woodforde.
[2] Touzeau. *Rise and Progress of Liverpool.*
[3] Recorder of Liverpool.

Book such as: "Given to poore Begars 5s." "Given to Wandarars 1s." "Carity 4s." "Charity to Begars 13s. 6d."

If an aged or sick person who was a genuine inhabitant of "ye Towne" became destitute, a home had to be provided for him or her. A cottage, probably a one-roomed hovel, was built, and after the death of the man or woman in question, the little dwelling was sold by the overseers.

A quotation from the Tenants' Book will serve to illustrate this system.

"Swift, Henry A.D. 1713 bought by my consent a small Cottage which was built at ye Charge of this Township for Martha Tompson for which he payed 30s. to Thomas Marrow then Overseer of ye Poore. But afterwards he being at want of Money and I not thinking it proper to have a Freeholder thô of onely a Cottage, I gave him A.D. 1718 the like Sume of 30s. for ye same Cottage and to enjoy it for 99 years determinable upon three lives, onely doing yearly one day Reaping or paying instead thereof yearly sixpence. When his time is out there might some Rent be pay'd besides the Boone above-mentioned."

When an old Mrs. Aughton returned to Little Crosby as a widow to claim right of domicile there, she first established herself and her few possessions in the parlour of a house in the village probably inhabited by a relative. The arrangement however was only temporary.

"Elizabeth Swift *alias Aughton* and I signed our bargain to each other for a little cottage she has built upon ye Waist."

IV

Nicholas derived considerable satisfaction from defying the Law in the matter of contraband.

"Feb. 3rd, 1721. This Night I had a Cargo of 16 Larg Ones brought to Whit Hall.

Feb. 4th. W.Ca.[1] covered the Cargo very well with Straw."

Charles Howerd, the tailor, and his brothers, were the Diarist's confederates in this matter.

[1] William Carefoot.

" I was at the farther end of Barbary Walk with Thomas Howerd and his brother John, and furnished them with two good Kasks. . . .

Charles Howard brought me a good provision for Acqua Coelestis. I showed him his goods well stored in Whit Hall."

The smugglers did not escape suspicion on the part of authority :

" Mr. Thomas serched the West-Lain-Hous and a deale of the Out-Housing at this Hous for Brandy as he heard was conceiled here."

But Mr. Thomas evidently did not think of looking under the straw in White Hall. Charles Howerd was accustomed to wait upon the gentlemen of the manor houses to receive their orders. "Aug. 25th, 1721. Charles Howard and his two men came to make my Winter Sute with French Buttons."

Perhaps the tailor made it convenient to conceal and convey bottles of brandy or claret in his bales of cloth.

The Squire himself concocted his favourite drinks acqua coelestis and shrub.

" I scoaped 30 Leomonds, ye Juce of them made one Pint, and about the fourth of a Pint. I put to it one Pint of Brandy. I also made some Shrub; the proportion was Brandy 2 qts., Crab Vargious 1½ pts., Leomond 6, Dubble Refined Sugar 1 lb. The Proportion of Mixture for my last Brue of Acqua Coelestis was Brandy 2 qts., Crab Vargeus 1 pt. and 1/5th of a quart, Lime Juce 1/5th of a quart, Lisbon Sugar 1 lb., Leomonds 3 and being the Brandy was very good I put to it 4 qts. and 1 pt. of Water, the water was first bouled,[1] the outward Rine of the Leomonds was infuesed into it, so they were also in the Shrub, but the Brandy and the Leomond Juce had not any Rine infuesed into it."

Cowslip wine was a cheap and useful addition to the vast quantities of home-brewed beer, mead and birch wine. Cowslips do not grow in south west Lancashire but it was worth while to have a quantity sent from the neighbouring county.

[1] Boiled.

1721. "July 15th. I began to make wine of ye Cowslops as came from York.

July 18th. We tunned the Cowslop Wine."

The Diarist was always ready to join in any small enterprise for the benefit of the neighbourhood such as " geting a Rode made over the Key at Leverpoole." He and many of his neighbours subscribed to a little fund for the furtherance of this cause, and convivial meetings took place at the Wool Pack where they met to " discource " upon the subject. He signed " a Petission to ye Parleament to make ye River Wever Navigable ". An Act for the purpose was in fact passed in the following year (1720). He frequently subscribed for a plate to be contended for on the Crosby race-course and once entered a galloway of his own but without success. These small race meetings promoted neighbourly gatherings : the thrilled excitement of the supporters of the rival stables on such an occasion as " the Galloway Race at Great Crosby " can be imagined. " My Lord Molyneux his Brack Rowly and a Mare of Mr Heskeths ran for the Plate. My Lord Molyneux won it."

An account of any serious damage done by storm, or of outbreaks of sickness among men or beasts is added to the short statement concerning the weather at the end of the Diary for each month. That of August, 1719 is thus concluded :

" Never was known so forward a Corne Harvest in these parts, not often so fine an August which made Reapers extreamely scarce & in Cheshire severall gave 2s. per diem to a Reaper, but that was not occationed onely by the Sodanness of Corne growing ripe but also by a great Sickness as was in that County and some others in England, it was not very Mortall, but was a lingering sort of an Aguish Favour. We had something of it in Lancashire but very little within Sefton Parish."

English history of the year 1720-21 describes the country first in a frenzy of excitement from end to end as the South Sea Bubble expanded, and then convulsed when it exploded. But not a ripple from all this commotion is reflected in Blundell's Diary, not the dimmest reverberation from the roar of indignation which echoed through the land when the colossal hoax was exposed, seems to have disturbed the Squire. His money was safe "in a bagg" or cautiously "put out at interest" to a few solid yeomen who invested it in stock which they could see, their bullocks and their field crops, and who paid interest, rents and fines in cash :

"I let Edmund Tristram have four Score Pound for which he and his two sons Richard and Joseph gave me their Bond . . . Thomas Syer paid me £20 for his Rent in Gold."

Chapter XII

GROWN UP DAUGHTERS

I

THERE seems to have been a plan to bring Mally home when she was eighteen, a plan which was not fulfilled owing to the girl's own perversity. It is regrettable that her letters to her father were not preserved, but from his to her it is plain that she asked to be allowed to remain a year longer at the convent school of her choice, and when the arrangement was duly made she not only wrote herself asking that the decision should be reversed, but induced the convent chaplain also to write in support of her petition. Her father's indignant reply to Father Daniel shows how very much he was influenced by the opinion of his friends. The whim of a schoolgirl would hardly seem to warrant such a serious attitude on his part.

> "To Mr Daniell at Gant.
> July 20th, 1722.
>
> Sir,
>   It was no small satisfaction to receive yours of the 15th instant and as great a surprise when I found the contents. I think I love my dearest child as well as any parent can do, yet am not willing to indulge her in what will be no credit nor advantage to her but on the other side a very great reflection on me, first to say I would go to fetch her, then to say I would defer it one year longer upon her desire and yet after all to have her come all of a sodaine is what I can no wayes consent to. Pray Sir consider what will be said upon this sodain Motion, for it is now known not only by all my Relations but by all my Friends and Acquaintance from North to South that I have let her stay one year longer by her own desire for her improvement . . . others will say We formerly looked upon Mr Blund : as one whose word might be

relied on, but what he means by this Jugling in saying and unsaying we cannot conceive; 'tis well if his daughter has carried herself as well as she ought to doe, that he sends for her home so sodainly, and perhaps when anyone treats with him for a Match with her he may also fly off and on in that affaire too. . . . The only way to avoyd the reflections above mentioned is to let it pass (as I writ to Mally May ye 22nd) as if she stayed by her own desire, that will make all sids easy and redound to her credit, for she is much commended for desiring to stay one year longer which she had not done, but on Account of her letter which she says I interpreted rong, but tis now too late to recall it. . . . She says how glad she would have been to have seen us this summer, she may assure herself it would have been no small satisfaction to us to have seen her, but as we have deprived ourselves of that comfort so long for her good it is her duty now to comply to us, both in obedience and for our credit as well as her own. I would not have her valew herself too much as being an heiris, for if eather of my daughters disoblige me it is in my power to clip their wings, not that I have the least thoughts to doe it and hope I never shall have the least Provocation for none can be more deare to me than my dearest children are, and when I have a conveniency I shall not faile to settle them in the world to their satisfaction to the best of my power, but would not have them to think I will settle any of my estate on them as long as I live or at least of several years to come.

To Mally (enclosed in the last).

My dearest dear child,

I am sorry I misunderstood your last letter though hope your stay one year longer will be an advantage to you.

Had we not considered your good more than our own satisfaction, which still we doe, we should never have suffered you to be out of our sight. You are not yet 18 years of aige so cannot think it too long to stay a few months more from this time, and in one month now you may improve more than you did in the first whole yeare. I hope you have still pensioners as will be companions for you, if not you must apply yourself more dilligently to your Improvement, or if it will be any satisfaction

to you I shall let you goe eather to Graveling or Dunkerk or Brussels where you were formerly. . . . I would not my dearest child have you harbour too vain thoughts as being an heiris, for I can dispose of my estate as I see good, but none can be more deare to me than my dear children, and I assure you I have the same true love and affection for you as ever I had, and so has your loving Mother and doubt not but you'l still carry yourself so as to deserve it, which is the Hearty and dayly prayer of
Your ever loving and kind father
Nich. Blund.

Mally seems to have been having a pleasant time among companions of her own age in what would now be described as a " finishing school ".

Six months after the letters quoted were written, preparations for the home-coming of grown-up daughters are announced in the Diary.

" Feb. 5th. 1723. Henry Marser etc. began to cut ye Windows in ye Nursery in order to have them made in an other Form against my Doughters Lodge there.

Feb. 13th. William Thelwall and Arthur Wilson fixed up their Benshes in ye Hall to work the Wainscoting of my Doughters Roome.

Feb. 28th. My Doughters Roome being muchwhat Wainscoted quite Round, they began to draw it into Panels.

March 1st. Mary Fleetwood sent two with Glass for ye Windows in my Doughters Chamber and ye Green Roome.

April 1st. The Appolstaror finished new vamping up the Green Bed in ye Parlour Chamber.

April 3rd. I helped Mr Marsh, Mr Crumpton's Man, to fix up the Blew Bed in my Doughters Roome.

April 4th. My Wife and I lay in ye Nursery which is now fiting up for my Doughters but ye Bed is not quite finished.

May 11th. Thomas Marser cut a Hole at ye End of my Doughters Closet and put a Window Frame into it to look into ye Pump Court."

For weeks beforehand Nicholas was preoccupied with plans for, or in connection with, the coming journey to Flanders.

"Aprill 12th. Being I designe soone to goe to fetch my Doughters home I gave Jackson directions what he was to doe in ye Gardens whilst I was abroad.

Aprill 13th. My Eyes being very ill I was not able to Reade, so I began to lay Ready some things against my Journey to Flanders.

May 21st. I sent my Luggage to ye Carriers in Leverpoole to be carried to London. I gave William Carefoot full directions what to do in my Absence and read my Orders to him."

William Carefoot, or, as the Diarist sometimes spells it Kerfoot, is described in the Disbursement Book as "Hind and Groom." A bailiff was no longer employed.

"May 23rd. We had a good Dish of Beanes and Bacon for dinner . . . Mr Shepherd came to wish me a good journey."

The above is among the very rare passages in which Nicholas refers to food. From this year onwards allusions to where and what he drank are infrequent, in marked contrast to the two earlier volumes of the Diary.

"May 25th. Ned Howard writ pretty much for me both before and after diner. I packed up a Mailes Trunk against my journey tomorrow. Mr Blundell and his Lady etc. came to wish us a good journey."

The young Squire of Ince, now married,[1] was aged 23 and Nicholas had of course known him intimately from his cradle; while a schoolboy he is alluded to as "Mrs Blundell's son," in the Diary, his mother having been in the position of a Squire while he was a minor; but as soon as he reached man's estate Nicholas formerly styled him "Mr. Blundell".

On May 26th the travellers were off.

"Mr Crisp, Thomas Syer etc. came to take leave of us. We went over from Leverp. in Eastern Boat and dined at Hooton with Doctor Low, thence to Chester where we lodged at the Coach and Horses. We found Cozen Thomas Gillibrand and his Doughter Jane there."

[1] Robert Blundell of Ince Blundell married Katherine, daughter of Sir Rowland Stanley of Hooton, Cheshire.

Jane Gillibrand was to be escorted by Mrs. Blundell to school at Ghent, so could only have been in her early teens, but in future allusions to her Nicholas usually respectfully styles her " Mrs Gellib."

It can be imagined that the Squire and his wife immensely enjoyed this journey, travelling to meet their children after the long separation, and entering the world outside Lancashire for the first time in six years with the exception of one short trip into Yorkshire.

Only ten days were spent in London.

" June 2nd. I went with Mrs Gillib. to St. Pauls and walked with her over London Bridge.

June 3rd. My Wife, I, Mrs Gillib. and Mrs Aldred saw Cartooch acted at the New Play-Hous.

June 4th. I made choice of some Cloth at Mr Humph. Traffords for a Sute of Cloths for me.

June 7th. Mrs Hatton went with my Wife and me to look at some Lodgings against my Doughters come to Town. Barton the Taylor brought me a new Sute of Cloths he had made me. I shewed Mr Parks how to make Acqua Coelestis and helped him to make it.

June 9th. I walked with Mrs Gillib. to St James his Park etc. . . I gave my Fair-well at Mr Parks to Humph. Trafford, Captain Knight, my Landlord Hatton etc. . . . .

June 19th. We began our Journey from London towards Calis, we went by Coach from our Lodgings to ye Old Rose in Shade, Themes, where we got a Refreshment. Mr Parks and our Landlady Mrs Hatton came with us to ye old Rose, thence we went by Boat to Greenwich where we went on Bord the Duke of Charas, Captain Knight Master, and sailed thence to Graives End, at Five in ye Evening we weighed Ancor.

June 11th. We went on shore at Margit at night we cast Anckor in the Downs opposit to Daile.

June 12th. We landed at Calis about three of the Clock after Noone and went to Table Royall where we lodged. Captain Knight went with us to Mrs Depues and then I went with him to his Lodgings, the Signe of London, where we drank together.

P

June 13th. From Callis we came in a Convenience to Graveling and lodged at the Signe of ye Angell."

Here they found Fanny, but the Diary contains no comment whatsoever upon the re-union of parents and children. Fanny is mentioned for the first time when, travelling via Dunkirk, Newport and Bruges, they arrived at Ghent a week later.

"June 21st. From Brudges we came by the Boat to Ghent, my Wife and I lodged in ye out quarters,[1] Fanny and Nelly Howard for one Night onely at ye Barkers, and Miss Gellib. went in to be a Pentioner.

June 22nd. I writ down some of my last Disbursements.

June 23rd. I showed my Doughter Frances the Grand Baginage and went with her to severall good Churches in Town. Mally declaired her Mind fully to her Mother."

This is the first allusion to Mally, three days after their arrival in Ghent. It must be conjectured, from her father's letters presently to be quoted, that, after first asking to be allowed to remain at school a year longer, then when her request was granted, begging to be taken home earlier, she now announced a wish to become a nun. It can also be conjectured that such a desire on her part deeply distressed her father who looked upon her as heir to the home and estates which meant so much to him. He states that he promised never to force either of his children to marry against her will or choice, but evidently he insisted upon bringing Mally home and introducing her to "ye worlde" before allowing her to make a final decision. During the next three weeks of travelling from town to town, sight-seeing, visiting various convent "grates", treating nun friends to tea and coffee and priest friends with wine, it is Fanny who appears as her father's companion, Mally only being included impersonally in "my famoly" or "we seaven", or "my Wife and Doughters." It would appear from this that he and his eldest daughter were on uncomfortable terms.

At Brussels "Fanny and I were at the Palace and saw the Appartments which were extreamely Fine and Rich, we saw one

[1] The wing of the convent allotted to the "externe" or unenclosed nuns, and visitors.

Table made of curious inlaid Marble and other Rich Materialls all made in Flowers and other pritty Figures that Table was said to cost Fifty Thousand Patacoones. The Privat Closet was small but most extreamely butifull, the Doars etc were inlayed with Images and Flowers of Silver and the Floor was inlayed with a Map of the World, each Kingdom being distinguished by Plates of Brass of various Colours and there were other Plates of Brass of various Figures inlayed in the Floore . . . . there were severall small Looking-Glasses Fixed in ye Wainscot etc. which made a great addition to the buty; the other Roomes were butifull, most of them finely Painted at ye top and hung with good Tapestry."

On a market day in Ghent the Lancashire Squire was deeply interested in the weighing of butter before it was offered for sale:

"They gave about one Penny for weighing twenty pound and so proportionable, and then each received a stamped paper with ye wight of their Butter and ye Day of ye Month writ on it."

Nicholas also comments at length on the Flemish method of breaking flax which he evidently considered primitive, and "ye Gunn which shoots a Bullet with Wind instead of Powder" intrigued him greatly.

Between the first and second visit of the Diarist to Flanders and the Low Countries, these war-ravaged lands, after passing from Spanish to French domination, had been handed over to the Austrian Empire. The Diary affords no glimpse of the struggles with which the city and provincial governments obstinately opposed infringement of their ancient rights by the Emperor's officers, nor does it refer to the profound unrest among the working classes.[1] War had been so long incidental to the European scene, that its aftermath was taken for granted.

Nicholas and his party embarked at Calais on August 4th, after passing six weeks gregariously on the continent in a mixed but wholly English society composed indiscriminately of lords and ladies, priests and sea captains, the wig-maker, the tailor,

---

[1] H. Pierenne. *Histoire de Belgique.* Vol. V.

the wax chandler. They escorted Mistress Pigot[1] from school home to London.

"Aug. 6th. We landed at London and lodged at Mr Rollins a Perug-Maker at the Signe of ye Golden Lamp in Bow Street. I brought Mistress Pigot to her Fathers.

Aug. 8th. Mr Parks helped me to get my Luggage on Shore and to clear it. I went on Bord and brought my Luggage to the Customs-Hous Warf where it was sirched and some Spirituall Books and Pictures taken from me to be burned. . . . I drank at ye Golden Key and Golden Lyon with Mr Parks and Captain Knight and paid him for our Passage and Mrs. Pigots."

It was a practical custom of the day for the traveller to pay part at least of his fare after he had safely reached the shore of his destination. If the ship foundered his heirs were not at a loss of the money and the shipmaster was no worse off.

Complete new outfits[2] were purchased for the grown-up daughters, costing the generous sum of £177 7s. 7½d. It is disappointing to turn from a perusal of the list of finery to the portraits of Mally and Fanny. "The extraordinary fine Flanders Lace for Heads and Ruffles" which cost £42 15s., the lemon-coloured and red damask ordered especially from Paris, the "Flye Sutes" for which £35 14s. were paid, the Holland and fine cambric for shifts and aprons—these rich stuffs should have clothed such elegant persons as Sir Joshua Reynolds or Sir Peter Lely portrayed. But Mally and Fanny look forth from their frames, a graceless pair of country lasses in spite of their fashionable clothes. However Nicholas knew well that "ye Worlde" would be more interested in their dowries than in their faces. Society would surmise that a man who could afford to turn out his girls so well could also dower them well, but in any case that matter would of course be made quite clear between negotiators before a suitor had an opportunity to form any opinion as to the looks of the bride "proposed to him."

[1] Probably Rebecca, daughter of Nathaniel Pigot of Bockingham, Essex, and the Inner Temple. She returned to Gravelines the following year to become a Poor Clare nun.
[2] Appendix VI.

Young men indeed appear upon the scene immediately the co-heiresses arrive in London.

"Aug. 9th. Mrs Butler and Mrs Ann Scarisbrick made us a visit, so did the two brothers Scarisbrick and severall others.

Aug. 10th. Sir Girvas Cliften's[1] son William and my Doughter Frances stood Gossops to Mr Parks Son William.

Aug. 11th The two Brother Scarisbricks dined with us. The two Brother Traffords made us a visit. My Wife and Doughters went to St. Paules. My Lady Gerard made us a visit after it was dark.

Aug. 13th. We removed our Lodging from Bow-Street to Mr Smiths, Fraim-Maiker at ye Golden Head in Great Duke Street."

The two months spent in London must have been full of thrills for Mally and Fanny, between the enjoyment of young society of both sexes, the buying of fine clothes and the seeing of sights.

"I went with my Wife and Doughters to Mr Alexanders and bought some Silks for them ... Mrs Berry helped my Wife and me to buy Materialls for Habits for my Doughters. She dined with us. I went with my Doughters to St. Bartholomew's Fair. We saw a Droll, a Little Man and a Popit Play." On the following day, Aug. 27th, he visited the renowned fair again. "I was at Bartholomew Fair in Smithfield. I saw the Famous Jugler and a fine Tumbler at one Booth and Patient Grissell at an other. Aug. 29th. I delivered some Boxes to the Leverp. Wagganer. I went with my Wife and Doughters to Sadlers Wells and saw the Diversion there."

A hanging was apparently not considered suitable entertainment for the girls:

"Sept. 9th. My Wife and I saw Humphrey Anger and Joseph Middleton hanged at Tyburn. Mrs Blevin made us a viset."

A hackney coach in which the whole family were coming home from a visit to Lady Westmoreland at Twickenham, was overturned.

---

[1] Sir Gervase Clifton of Clifton, Baronet, was the father of fifteen sons by his wife, Anne, daughter of Dudley Bagnell of Newry Esq. *Non-Jurors.*

" Fanny's Arme and my side was hurt.   Surgeon Gihee let me Blood."

The next day Surgeon Medcalf was called in " to look at Fanny's Ailement and mine." Mally was " let blood " two days later but Fanny was spared that enfeebling process until she was " taken very ill ", when it was immediately resorted to and she was unable to be one of a theatre-party on the following day.

" Sept. 17th. Mr Will. Clifton gave my Doughter Mary and me the Play called Love for Love."

The names of North country neighbours, so familiar in each volume of the Journal, are mentioned on almost every day spent in London; these squires and merchants had their own club.

" I was at ye Lancashire Club in Fleet Street with two Mr Traffords etc. . . . Mr John Culceth[1] made me a visit and told me he was soone for going into ye Country. . . . I was at ye Lancashire Clubb at the Legg with Mr Nick Parker, Mr Fleetwood Leigh etc. . . . I was Chearman at ye Legg Club.   There was Mr Parkes, two Traffords etc. . . ."

Nicholas did not neglect his wife and daughters but led them on divers and almost daily excursions:

" I shewed my Wife and Doughters the Tower, Bedlam and Westminster Abby. . . . I went by Boat with my Wife and Doughters to Hammersmith, we made a viset to the two Miss Webbs and got a Refreshment at Thomas Gorsuches. . . . I went with my Wife and Doughters to the Camp in Hide Park thence to Kensington we walked below in the Hous and looked through the windows into ye Gardens which are extreamely fine but might not goe into them.   Thence we went to Strand on the Green where I saw part of Nicholas Parkers large Nursery. I pay'd all I ought him and he treated us very handsomely.

We took Coach and went to Hanever Square. . . . Mr Medcalf went with us to Summerset Gardens where we took Boat and went towards Foxhall and then went to the New Spring Gardens coming Home we went into ye Chappell at ye Banket-

[1] Of Gray's Inn. Son of John Culcheth of Culcheth by Mary, daughter of Hugh Dicconson of Wrightington. *Non-Jurors.*

ing Hous. . . . We went to see ye Duke of Norfolk's fine Hous in St. James Square. . . . Mr Medcalf went with us four to the Play called Hamlet Prince of Denmark."

Finally, after bidding farewell to Lady Gerard, Lady Webb and members of the Clifton, Scarisbrick, Gorsuch, Culcheth, Blevin, Darnell and other families who were in town, "I and my famoly" writes Nicholas, "began our Journey homewards in Chester Coach in company of one who called herself Jackson. We dined at ye Black Bull in St. Albans. Mr Rob. Scarisbrick and Mr Medcalf met us there and dined with us."

Mr Medcalf may have been son of Surgeon Medcalf, for he does not appear upon the scene until after the Surgeon had "let Blood" for Fanny and Mally, but thereafter he seems to have been most attentive.

The Diarist varied the tedium of the return journey. "Oct. 2nd. I hired a Hors at Coventry and overtook ye Stage Coach at ye Welsh Harpe where I left my Hors."

The party arrived at the Golden Raven, Chester "a very cheap Hous," on October 3rd and were met there by their own horses. "Oct. 4th. We came over in Eastom Boat but there not being Roome in it for my Horses, I left them and my Men in Cheshire. My Wife lodged at Mrs Leckonby's,[1] I and my Doughters Lodg'd at ye Woolpack in Leverpoole.

Oct. 5th. My Horses came over ye Water to Leverpoole and then we all came home. I was busy most of ye Afternoone," adds the ever-practical Diarist "unpacking my Luggage which was come from London."

During the first few days after the family's return the usual stream of callers came to wish them welcome home, some bringing presents of partridges, woodcock and oysters. Nicholas was much occupied with estate business but soon his ruling passion claimed him, inflamed by the arrival of trees, plants and seeds acquired in his travels, as well as by his growing ambition to be a creator of woods.

"Oct. 19th. I was very busy all ye afternoone marking out

[1] Probably wife of Richard Lekonby of Great Eccleston. *Victoria History*. Vol. III.

places in ye Crofts where I intend to set Ackhornes, being resolved to make that part into a wood and shall hereafter call it the Vistow Wood.[1] I planted some London Trees, viz Goosberry, Apples on Paradice and Stocks and Pear Stocks. . . . I set my Roots of Anemonys, Renunculas and Tulops which I brought out of Flanders."

Meanwhile Mrs Blundell had placed herself under a new Doctor.

"Doctor Broomfield[2] was here. I payed him off for coming to dress my Wives Legg. . . . Dr Broomfield made a viset here, he Lanced my Wives Gumbs."

Mally is reported as taking numerous "doces of Pills." Possibly both girls' complexions gave trouble for their father writes that "Mrs Blundell[3] brought something for my Doughters to take inwardly and also for an outward Application." The patients must have suffered weakness as a result of the bleeding so frequently resorted to. They had not been long at home before Richard Cartwright's skill was invoked on their behalf, but in vain.

"Jan. 18th 1724. Rich. Cartwright came to let my Doughters Blood but could not neather in the Arme nor Foot."

If the girls had anaemic countenances the fact did not deter interest in their fortunes on the part of eligible young men and their friends. The first approach was made on behalf of Mr. Strickland of Sizergh by the Reverend Thomas Roydon, a secular priest who ministered now in one place, now in another in Westmorland. Thomas Strickland was aged twenty-three; he had succeeded to an impoverished estate owing to the adherence of his family to the Stuarts, but he was in full possession of his inheritance including the beautiful ancestral home of Sizergh Castle. In Blundell's view he was most desirable as a son-in-law. It was unfortunate that Mally, far from being pleased and flattered at the idea of making such an important marriage, refused even to consider it. Her father's reply to a letter from

---

[1] It is still known by that name.
[2] Dr. Broomfield was a chief promoter of the building of the Liverpol Infirmary, the city's first important hospital.
[3] Of Ince-Blundell.

Mr. Roydon reveals that he had opened negotiations before ascertaining her views.

"To Mr Roydon   Jan. 10th 1724.

" Sir

. . . .The caracture you give of Mr Strickland is very good and I question not but he deserves it, and as to his estate and what I should have settled on my daughter, I question not but we could have adjusted matters so as to make all things easy and both sides and the young Cupple Happy. I did not think proper to acquaint my daughter with what I was about until I was resolved where to fix, but upon my arrivall home I told her, haveing severall in choyce (without nameing the person,) that I hoped I had heard of a gentleman with whom she might be happy, his caracture being without exception. But she told me she was not the least disposed to marry as yet, so beged I would not urge her to it, which I was really sorry for. I should have been truly glad of an Allyance to so worthy a Famoly and so deserving a Gentleman and do sincerely wish him well settled to his Content and Satisfaction. You may be assured that I shall never mention anything that this affaire was ever in agitation, neather shall I ever forget your readiness in endeavouring to procure me a good husband for my daughter. Your letter was extreamely particular to all Poynts and very obleging."

Father Joseph Blundell was the next to put forward a candidate for marriage with one of his nieces, but the aspirant's identity is not disclosed.

"To Brother Joseph.   May 16th, 1724.

Dear Brother

Yours of April 21st I received not till the 2nd inst. . . . I do not find my doughters are desirous to marry nor I to settle any of my estates upon them whilst there is the least prospect of a son, all I shall do is to settle conditionally and, in case I have a son, then such a portion certain, but as for a present fortune and the estate at last, 'tis what no one can reasonably expect. I have had severall proposed but will not fix of any only such as I am pretty well assured my doughters may live comfortably with, for I assure you they are deserving of good husbands and when I think I can light of such a one I shall not slip ye opportunity. But to tell me he is a Barronet's son and will have £1500 per annum will not tempt me, I have already refused a Barronet of a better estate. I vallew the persun, parts and humours of the man (for that must make a woman happy) more than quallity. When I know who the Barronet's son is, and have enquired sufficiently of his Person, Parts and Humour, I shall think of fixing upon Preliminaries if I find his caracture be to my licking, so have writ to Mr Busby to know who the person is, and have sent it enclosed that you may see what I write. This I suppose is sufficient for a Blinkered as now is

Your affectionate brother

Nicholas Blundell.

Three months later Nicholas wrote in his Diary:

" August 20th. Mr Eckleston[1] sent his Servant with a letter of Grand Apportance but to no Purpose."

His answer to this missive duly found a place in his Letter Book.

"To Mr Eccleston in answer to his sent to me by his servant.

Sir

When I last had the favour of your company I told you what my Resolutions were, that I was not in haist to match my daughters till I had severall proposalls made, and then I would endeavour to choose the best" . . . He stated the financial arrangements which he was prepared to make, and continued: " I have had some Persons of good familys and others of good

---

[1] The Reverend Thomas Eccleston, S.J., the last of the old Lancashire recusant family of Eccleston of Eccleston, near Prescot, was distantly connected with the Diarist through his mother who was Eleanor, daughter of Robert Blundell of Ince Blundell. Remorse for having allowed himself to be drawn into a duel in which he killed his adversary, caused him to enter the Society of Jesus in order to devote the remainder of his life to the priesthood. His estates were forfeited in 1716 but he had settled them on his cousin John Gorsuch of Gorsuch Hall who succeeded in obtaining possession of them. Father Eccleston was chaplain to Lord Petre at Ingatestone Hall, Essex. From the chilly reception of his suggestion it may perhaps be inferred that he had proposed an impecunious younger son for the heiress.

estates proposed, but none so well qualified in all respects as to think deserving of my daughters for I will do the part of a good and kind father as far as in me lyes to settle where I think they may be truly happy. But to give you a positive answer at so short a warning is what I hope you don't expect. I have so good an opinion of you that I will not give you now an absolute denyall, but in a few weeks you shall heare againe from

Sir

Your affectionate kinsman and humble servant

Ni. Blu.

During the following winter the Squire and Fanny were both ill.

"Dec. 4th. Fanny and I went to Wigan to be under Doctor Francis Worthington, my health being very bad, the Coach was overturned and when we came neare Wigan it was laid fast, ye Rode being so deep, so we left it in ye Laine all Night, and we went with our Horses to Wigan where we lodg'd at Kendalls, the Leggs of Man.

Dec. 5th. I sent the Horses home but kept the Coach in Wigan. We dined at oure Inn and then Fanny and I went to Doctor Francis Worthington. We suped at Mr Goldings where we are to Bord, Fanny Lodges there and I lodge at Mrs Heskeths."

Doctor Worthington's treatment consisted mainly in the administration of purges and vomits. The Squire on one occasion "took by mistake two Doces of Pills instead of one" but without ill effects.

The usual stream of visitors, and servants sent to enquire, followed. Gillibrands, Molyneuxes, Standishes, Dicconsons— they had all heard that their friend and his daughter were at Wigan for their health, and called or sent "of a how-doe-you." Mr. Aldred, Mally, and Robert Weedon also came from Little Crosby. Poor Fanny's illness was prolonged throughout the winter, causing great anxiety to her family. Nicholas soon got tired of the pills, potions and inactivity of his sojourn at Wigan, and went home, but Fanny remained there for five weeks and seems to have returned to Crosby in worse plight than she left it. She was next sent to Liverpool to be under the care of Doctor Broomfield for a fortnight but was worse than ever when she came back. The unfortunate girl must have been bled almost to death by this time. It has been seen that Rich. Cartwright could produce nothing from either her hand or her foot. Two days after her return from Liverpool "Doctor Broomfield called and cooped[1] Fanny between the Shoulders."

Strangely enough the patient was better for a week; her father records that he took her out riding and that she accompanied her mother and sister on a visit to Ince. But on February 11th the scene changes.

"Fanny was so ill I sent in ye Night for Doctor Dickings.[2] He Lodg'd here.

Feb. 12th. Mrs Cottom[3] came to see Fanny so did Mrs Blundell, Fanny being extreamely ill Mrs Blundell came againe to see her and stay'd till near Midnight.

Feb. 13th. Fanny was so ill of ye Convultion Fits that Mr Aldred gave her the Holy Oyles. Doctor Fernihough[4] of Chester met Mr Dickins here, they had a Consult and lodg'd here.

Feb. 14th. Dr Dickens went hence. Coz. Scarisbrick sent to see Fanny and stay'd till Night. Pothecary Livesley[5] came this morning before day. He dressed some of Fanny's Blisters and lay'd on more Blistering Plaisters."

This entry suggests that the result of the doctors' "consult" had been torturing indeed for the patient. Pothecary Livesey dressed the blisters again a few days later, and supervised the

---

[1] Cupped.

[2] Dr. Dickens of Liverpool married at about this time the daughter of the prominent merchant Richard Houghton. He was a trustee of the Blue Coat Hospital.

[3] Probably the wife of the cloth merchant in Liverpool with whom Nicholas was on friendliest terms. A yeoman family of the name with branches at Garstang and Preston is mentioned in *Catholic Non-Jurors.*

[4] In the *Rolls of the Freemen of Chester* for the year 1724-5 Philip Fernihough is described as "in medicin doctor."

[5] Edmund Livesey, surgeon, son of Gilbert Livesey, merchant of Liverpool.

administration of "vomits." In another month the case was less interesting:

"March 11th. Apothecary Livesleley sent his Brother to see Fanny."

On March 21st Doctor Lancaster, Doctor Dickens and Apothecary Livesey "made a visit" and at last, after all the unconscious ill-treatment by her physicians, comes the statement on March 29th: "Fanny took the Aire in ye Charriot 'tis ye first time she has been out of her Roome for severall Weeks." A passing relapse is reported a few weeks later.

"June 6th. Fanny had one of her Violent Convúltion Fits, such as she had not had of Severall Weeks, it was Occasion'd by seeing a Mous in her Roome."

By the end of June the patient had sufficiently recovered from the effects of her illness and its treatment and the shock of seeing a mouse, to be able to "ride double" behind her father. Finally on July 8th:

"I rode out with Fanny it is the first time she has Rode out single this 8 Months as I think."

The Disbursement Book reveals how very costly that trying year had been. From the time when, in 1717, John Gillibrand handed over the accounts which he had kept for his cousin while he was abroad, Nicholas entered his expenses quarterly without mentioning monthly dates. At the end of the third quarter of the year 1725 headed:

"From Mid-Summer Exclusive to Michaelmas Inclusive," he writes:

"Being Fanny is but just recovered of her Distemper which seased her about this time Twelve Month and ye Apothecary's Bill still increasing, I have yet booked none of ye expenses Occastioned eather by her Sickness or my own which began about the same time as hers and lasted me halfe a year, what next followeth are our Expences occationed by oure long Sickness, but Physic and Doctors Phees for me are booked long since.

Expenses by Men and Horses when we went to Wigen, when Servants etc came to see us and whilst Fanny was at Leverpoole:

	£	s.	d.
		5	9	5

Meat, Drink, Lodging Fire and Vailes for
us two and a Maid 5 3 0
Washing and Candles for us three ... 11 3
Wine, Biskets, Sugar Candy and such
things for Fanny 2 10 8
Coffy, Tea, and Sugar 15 5
Doctors' Phees 19 2 6
Phisick for Fanny 13 4 6
Messinger to fetch Doctor Fernihough
from Chester ... ... 10 6"

The Diarist does not sum up the depressing total of
£47 7s. 3d. but proceeds immediately to his financial history of
the next quarter which opens with the line "Wives Allowance
for Michalmas £10 0s. 0d." Mrs. Blundell did not receive a
quarterly allowance of her own money as the entry might
suggest. "Wives Allowance" and "Doughters Allowance"
were paid alternate half-years, the girls receiving £7 each.

All this time the Squire was far from being unconcerned
with Mally's matrimonial future. Her perversity when Mr.
Royden renewed his approaches on behalf of the well-endowed
Mr. Strickland, must have been hard for an eighteenth century
parent to bear. Again the identity of another suitor alluded to
in the following letter is not disclosed in the Diary.

"To Mr Roydon

April the 6th, 1725
Sir
I am glad to find by yours of the 4th Ult my two got safe to
hand and am beholding to my friends for the good caracture
they are pleased to give my daughters . . . I do not find my
daughter any more inclineable to marry than she was, yet am
entirely of opinion that she is not so averse to it that an
accomplished gentleman with whom she may be happy may
obtain her favour. However I thought it would be rude to let
any one come to court her, and then for her to declair she would
not marry. That would look like an imposition upon a Gentle-

man and he might really take it as an affront put upon him. But if Mr Strickland or any other deserving gentleman think it worth while to try if he can gain her affections I am not against his coming. . . . I perceive there has been another gentleman proposed to my Doughter but she returned the same answer that she was not as yet disposed to marry. I long since told her I would not compel her to marry, much less to marry one she could not love and so to make her miserable as long as she lives, so leave her entirely to pleas herself, all I require is that he be a Gentleman of a cumpotent Estate, one of a good caracture, and a Catholick. I have never ceriously proposed marriage to Frances, my second doughter, so cannot tell how she stands affected, but my opinion is Mr Strickland would not dislike eather her person, parts or humour. But self praise is no praise so excuse me for giving a good Caracture of my own dear Child, which would seem much better of another hand. Though she has been long ill I hope she will in time recover for I can by no means say she is unhealthful."

The intermediary was evidently instructed to arrive at definite information as to the heiress's fortune, before pressing the suit any further.

"To Mr Roydon   April 30th.

. . . You are pleased to say I have a Full Purs, but if I can stretch so far as to pay £1000 in hand tis the utmost I can reach to, and £1000 more at my death if I have a Son (which tis 20 to 1 I have not), and if no son then £400 per annum and a very good Hous; this I hope, with a good wife, may make Mr Strickland or anyone elce happy who is not hard-pushed for Money; but as I have said before tis my cheif aime to settle my daughters to lickeing and that they may make choyce of a man they can love, and I'll doe my endeavours to propose such to them whose Sarcomsteenses may make them happy, which is the reason I gave consent for Mr Strickland to come to Crosby to try if he could gain my daughter's affections, and since then, another being proposed, I also gave my consent for him to come to see which my daughter licked the better, and this I was the more willing to do because I heard Mr Strickland was married to the daughter of Mr Higgens the Goldsmith, which, by yours I find is a Story. If my daughter approve of the Gentleman who makes his Addresses to her and that he is content with what I am at present able to do as for Jointure and provition for the younger children etc. those things may easily be settled. So think tis not necessary to give Mr Strickland the trouble of my company at Sizargh, however returne him thanks for his kind invitation and his Civility, to conduct me to his Hous, and Heartily wish Matters may be Adjusted to the Satisfaction of him, to the comfort of my Daughter and according to the real desire of

Sir

Your Humble Servant

Nicholas Blundell."

The more emphatically the Squire wished to make plain his financial plans, the wilder became the vagaries of his spelling! However Mr Strickland was sufficiently impressed by Mr Blundell's financial offer, to wish to try his luck personally with the indifferent Mally, and after another month of bargaining, Nicholas thought a meeting between the persons principally concerned might be authorised by himself.

"To Mr Strickland   June 29th, 1725.

Sir

Finding by yours of June 17th that you are desirous of an Alliance, I shall endeavour to give you the opportunity of an Intervieu which I hope may be don without troble or much notice being taken. Tuesday and Wednesday the thirteenth and fourteenth of next Month there will be Hors-Raises at Ormschurch. The first day is likely to be the best diversion, and then my Doughter will be on the ground if it be a fit day to stir abroad on; if you find she answers your expectation we may adjourn to Crosby or elce where as may be then Agreed upon, to discource the Affair; and though I have already profered more than I can without inconvenience comply to, yet perhaps I may make you a further Proposall. If I can be assured you'l be on the Ground I shall most certainly be there, let the Weather be what it will."

The pre-view evidently proved satisfactory although at this

juncture in his family affairs, the Diarist commits little of interest to paper.

" July 14th. My Wife, Doughters and I went to Ormschurch Race. There were three that ran and the Bolton Mare won. Mr Plumb and his Son and Mr Cotton were there. Mr Strickland of Sizergh and Coz. Gelibrond of Astley were there. They came home with me and Lodg'd here."

Mally is not specifically mentioned during the few days in which her would-be suitor was in the house. He took part in various bowling matches. He was introduced to "the famoly of Ince" and to Mr Aldred. "He" (Mr. Aldred) "gave ye Ladies Coffy and we Men had a Bowl of Punsh."

It appears from the Squire's next letter that Thomas Gillibrand of Astley was interested in another candidate on whose behalf he had put out feelers. This was the son of Ralph Standish[1] and his wife Lady Phillipa, daughter of the sixth Duke of Norfolk.

" July 29th. Coz. Gillibrand sent an Express with a letter from Lady Phillipa.

Aug. 3rd. Young Mr Standish and Coz. Gillibrand dined and lodged here."

The young man only stayed two days on this occasion but soon returned.

"Aug. 16th. Mr Standish made his second visit to Mally he lodg'd here.

Aug. 17th. We heard my Sister Middleton etc designed soone to come hither so Mr Standish went hence to Wooton."

Mr Standish made no more favourable impression upon Mally than Mr Strickland had done, and Nicholas determined not to lose sight of the first, and from his point of view, the most desirable candidate.

---

[1] Ralph Standish, senior, of Jacobite fame, escaped arrest in 1694 and consequently was not tried with the other Lancashire gentlemen at Manchester. Over two centuries later documents were discovered in a hiding-place in the coppice wall at Standish Hall which revealed that he had indeed been engaged in activities on behalf of the exiled Stuarts. See Lancashire and Cheshire Antiquarian Society Vol. 50.

R

" To Mr Strickland   Aug. 10th

Sir

Yours of July 24th I received and delivered the enclosed to my Wife. They were both very obliging and I shall be so favourable as to think they were also sincere. When Mr Standish heard you were gon, he was desirous to pay his Addresses to my Daughter provided you were not lickly to Suckseed, which Favour I could not handsomely refuse, but first tryed to see how her Pulce bet; she gave me the same answer as usual, that she was not as yet inclined to marry, however I let him, or at least his friend, know that he was welcome to come, for I am well assured that eather he or you would make her happy.

" To Mr. Strickland   Aug. 22nd, 1725.

Sir

On Monday my daughter and I received a Letter from you which I answered the same day and had intended to have sent it to you the day following but for some reason (which you shall know when next I see you) I defer'd writing till now. As to what you mention of the Match being concluded by Mr Standish and me, I answer you that report is entirely falce, no other proposalls being made or further Agreement concluded upon than the same which passed between you and me : viz. to know what I would give with my Daughter, but I do not find she has settled her Affections on eather of you, and she still seems to be Adverce to Marriage.

I hope you cannot say but that I have don the Honourable part in leting you make the first address to her, you being the first I ever treated with upon that Subject. I shall continew in the same opinion to leave her entirely to her own choyce, and wish she were well settled. I am dayly expecting some company to stay with us some time which will fill my Hous, but when they are gon I shall acquaint you and make you as welcome as eaver, by which I hope you will eather have the good Fortune to obtaine your desire or be convinced from my Daughter's own mouth that I am no Obstruction to it, but that I am

Your sincere Friend and Humble Servant

N. Blu :

"To the Same   Aug. 31.

Sir

If you received mine of the 22nd Instant I hope it would convince you there was no Conclusion made between Mr Standish and me and that my Doughter is entirely left to her own choyce so need say no more as to that Point. I also told you I expected a Housefull of Company, which indeed I have had, but not my Sister Middleton etc which was that Company I then expected, but Mr Standish and his Son etc have been here. I do not find my Doughter has settled her affections upon him nor do I find her so desirous to Marry as I could wish. I have pushed home so far as I thought proper in order to have her think of Marrying you or some one elce whom she could love; but she still answered she was not in haist to settle in the World, but had positively resolved not to marry you, for she thought she could never sincerly love you (I wish she may make a better choyce) so you see there is no hopes; however being I promised when we parted that you might come againe I am not against it, but I fancy you shall lose your labour, but shall ever find me to be

Your sincere friend and humble servant

N. B."

During the next two months young Mr Standish had the field all to himself and seems to have wooed as ardently as custom would permit.

" Aug. 25th. My Wife, Mally and I went to Ormschurch Race where my Lord Molineux his Roan Hors beat Lord Darbys Gray Mare. Mr Standish, his lady, two Sons and Coz. Gelibond of Astley came home with us and lodg'd here.

Aug. 26th. Mr Standish and I etc went to see three of my Lord Molyneux Horses[1] sweat upon Crosby Marsh. Lord Molyneux and Mr Clifton[2] came before the horses had don Sweating. Lord Frederick Howard[3] dined and lodg'd here.

---

[1] Lord Molyneux' horses were trained upon the Crosby racecourse.

[2] Thomas Clifton of Lytham Hall.

[3] Sixth son of Henry, sixth Duke of Norfolk, by his second wife Jane, daughter of Robert Bickerton.

Aug. 27th. My Wife, Mally and I went with our Guests to make a viset to Ince.

Aug. 28th. Lord Frederick and my Standish Guests went hence.

Sept. 1st. Young Mr Standish came hither whilst we were at Dinner. He went to Wooton.

Sept. 2nd. My Wife and I and Mally dined at Wooton with Lord Frederick, Lady Phillipa Standish etc. We took Fanny with us and left her at Leverpoole; coming back we called at Leverpoole and took Fanny and Mrs Williamson to see the Commody acted called the Busy Boddy, we came home and left Fanny to Lodge at Mrs Williamsons.

Sept. 6th. Young Mr Standish made his fifth Viset to Mally.

Sept. 14th. . . . My Doughters came home from More Hall. Young Mr Standish came with them."

The wooer again stayed for several days; the whole country-side must have been watching the courtship with deep interest and there was much coming and going of neighbours.

"Sept. 22nd. . . . This being Mally's bearthday Tatlock played here and we dansed till Morning.

Sept. 25th. It being Fanny's Bearthday Tatlock played here. We dansed both before and after Supper. Mr Henry Blundell suped here. We played with him at Chaiseing ye Whistle. A Strowling Fiddler played here and his Doughter dansed.

Sept. 26th. Mrs. Blundell and her two Sisters-in-Law Mrs Margaret and Mary made a Viset here. Mr Standish went hence."

But the next race meeting gave him an excuse to come back again.

"Oct. 2nd. . . . Mr Standish lodged here.

Oct. 4th. I was at the Race in Crosby Marsh where four Horses ran for a Saddle. . . . I also saw the Foot Race, five Lads ran for a Hat, a Servant of my Lord Molineux's Keeper wan it. When the Race was over I went to Hesketh's and drank with Parson Acton, Parson Wairing, Rob. Bootle etc. My Wife and Doughters went in the Coach to Mrs Parrs and were driven by Mr Standish part of the way."

They were all in fact having a merry time and Mr Standish seems to have been hopeful of success in winning Mally's hand.

" Oct. 6th. Being matters are now likely to goe forward, Coz. Gelibond and I began to consider what proposals were proper to be made to Mr Standish."

Meanwhile young Mr Standish remained at Crosby for the merry-making connected with Crosby Goose Feast. Next Nicholas stayed at Astley for a few days in order to get down to business under the guidance of his cousin.

" Oct. 20th. Coz. Gillibrand and I dined at Standish . . . old Mr Standish, I etc. discoursed of Proposalls for my Doughter Mary's Settlement. . . .

Oct. 22nd. I came home. Coz. Gillibrand came with me part of ye Way and then went to Standish Hall.

Oct. 23rd. Coz. Gillibrand sent an Express with an Account of yesterday's Proceedings at Standish.

Oct. 27th. Coz. Gillibrand and I din'd at ye Queen's Head in Ormschurch with Mr Standish we considered of some Heads to be drawn into Forme for a Marriage between his Son Ralf and my Doughter Mary."

At the end of the month Ralph was back again and remained in close attendance upon the ladies of Crosby. In fact Mally allowed matters to go very far indeed before she made up her mind, and the elders evidently thought that all was going well.

" Nov. 15th. Mr Standish and I went to Ormschurch to meet his Father and Cozen Gelibond of Astley."

But presumably when the suitor was empowered by his parents to make his formal proposal, Mally decided that she could not love him after all.

' 'Nov. 20th. Yester Night and tonight my Wife took a Doce of Pills. Mr Standish went hence," and squeezed in between the lines is the statement evidently added at a later date : " This was his last Viset."

" To Mr Gellibond of Astley.   Nov. 24th, 1725.

" Dear Coz.

Thanks for yours of the 23rd. As soone as you were gon Mally was in a flood of tears and so continued upon account that matters were going so forward, as I was told; for she imparts not her Mind freely to me, elce would not have told a Confidant that she was desirous to have the Treaty brock off; this was told me, but whether by Mally's orders or noe I know not. My Answer was that I expected to heare it from her own Mouth, and if she would tell me herself she was desirous to be Religious, or that she thought she could not be happy with Mr Standish, I would by no meanes oblige her to Marry him, to which she answered, as I was told, that I knew her mind and she would not speak to me any more about that affaire.

I know she has often told me, as you have heard me own to her, that she had a mind to go beyond the seas, but that was generally in Transitu, not that she was ever so free as seriously to advise with me. I suppose the young Spark can give the best account what hopes he has; tis my desire things should go forward, but not entirely against the Graine.

I can hardly for shame (you having had so many journies upon this Account) desire you personally to give me Account of tomorrow's transactions, but if you did you might better informe yourself how her pulce beats and so proceed accordingly.

A Happy Conclusion to the Affaire is heartily wished by
Your affectionate Kinsman and humble Servant
Nich. Blundell."

The next day Mally recovered sufficient good sense to explain herself to her father.

"Nov. 25th. Mally discoursed seriously and told me her mind."

Letters arrived by messenger from both Standish and Astley but Mr Gillibrand did not come himself. No doubt he was highly indignant at the unexpected turn of events at the end of the three months courtship which he had so industriously promoted.

"To the same   Nov. 26th. 1725.
(Mr Gillibrand)

Dear Coz.

By mine of the 24th you'd find how uneasy Mally was, and that she desired to have the Treaty brock off as I was told; however not hearing it from her own mouth my words in the same letter were tis my Desire things should go forward *but not entirely against the Graine* thus far as to my last, since which she has seriously imparted her Mind to me, and says she thinks she cannot be happy with Mr Standish if he be of that suspicious Gellous Humour she takes him to be and if ever it be her fate to marry him, as she hopes it never will, 'twill be entirely by your persuasion and becaus she finds I desire it, but not in the least according to her own desire or inclination. If this really be her Thought (which I as well as yourself have but too much reason to believe) tis full time to put a Stop to proceedings for you know 'twas always my promis to her that I would not oblige her to marry against her Will, and 'tis much better to break off than to proceed and make not only the young Cupple unhappy, but the whole family with which they were to live, so hope you'l acquaint Mr Standish herewith, for I find twill be to noe purpose for the young gentleman to come againe, 'tis but to entangle him more and more and I hope he will light of one who will have a greater love for him than I feare my Daughter ever will, and question not but one with a much greater fortune, in the present at least, which I heartily wish he may.

'Tis but reason Mally should be entirely left to her own Choyce, and if I be reflected upon for not compelling her, I would rather be taxed with that than give any occasion of being esteemed a harsh or unkind Parent, but let the Matter be as it will I shall ever have a true Vallew for the Famoly I was in hopes to have been Allyed to, and must always return sincere and cordiall thanks for the paines you have taken to bring Matters about, which I am well assured you would not have done but that you thought it would be to my Daughter's content and Happiness. I think I have said enough upon this disagreable subject so must conclude with my service to the worthy Famoly of Standish and subscribe myself.

Your affectionate Kinsman and Humble Servant
N.B.

My dear Fanny has been these two days troubled with the Collick and is yet no better. She has a Cold and her Face is much swelled."

As Mally apparently did not discourage Ralf Standish's court-ship until she discovered him to be of a "suspicious Gellous Humour," and as she eventually married another man, it is obvious that she had not a genuine vocation to the religious life. She was evidently a high-spirited girl, determined to a degree unusual in her day, to manage her own life for herself.

Ralph Standish was scarcely banished from the Crosby scene before Mr Royden tried to re-open negotiations on behalf of Mr Strickland.

"To Mr Strickland   Jan. 15th, 1726.

Sir

Yours of the 30th ultimo to me and my Daughter came in due time, but you must give me leave to tell you eather Mr Roydon has in one point (in part at least) misunderstood me or you do not entirely take it Right from him, but when 'tis my good for-tune to see you alone, I can easily convince you of the Mistake.

My Daughter still says she is not yet disposed to Marry, how-ever if you think it worth while to make another attempt I assure you both my wife and I will use our utmost endeavour to serve you and you may be assured of a sincere and cordiall Welcom at Crosby. If you can gaine my Daughter's Affections all other things will I hope be easily adjusted. . . ."

So Mr Strickland now resumed his interrupted wooing during a fortnight's visit to Crosby. The Diary during the period is mainly concerned with gardening memoranda and estate matters. But when the suitor departed Nicholas reported once more to his cousin Gillibrand.

Feb. 22nd, 1726.

"Deare Cozen

Mr Strickland went hence the 15th but with what hopes I cannot say, but at least not in Despaire as he did the time before, so hope in time he may Suckseed, for my daughter has no aver-tion to him as formerly, I question not but he'll make a kind husband, and though he profers not *Cart Blanch* yet hope he'l comply to anything as shall be thought reasonable, but more of that when I see you at Crosby. . . ."

Mr Strickland seems to have been waiting at Sizergh to hear

how the land lay and in due course a discouraging letter was addressed to him.

"To Mr Strickland   March 12th, 1726.

Sir

As you have not wanted Freends to speak in your behalf to my Daughter, though in some Respect there is no great Occation for it, for I hope the former avertion she had to your Person has worne off, and as to your Estate, I and all other Friends are convinced tis what you say. After you went I thought it proper for some time not to urge her too much for I know she does not love to be teased. However the other day I attacked her with all my Returick and logick, and layd the case positively home to her, and told her what the effect would be if she would not Marry; she spoke indeed nothing of you but what was handsom and becoming, but her answer still was she could not think of being Happy in a Married State and that I could not compell her to say the words of Matrimony.

I wish I could send you more agreable News, but being I could not I still deferred answering yours of the 23rd Ult. However you may be assured not only of my Wive's endeavours and mine, but of severall good Friends to bring Matters about if possible, and I doe really believe (though you seem to feare the contrary) that you have noe enemies at work to lessen your Estate, caracture etc; that would be malice only without prospect of Suckcess, for 'tis impossible to set Mr Standish treaty on foot again, 'twill meet with more opposition than they are awair of."

Thus discouraged, Mr Strickland went to London, but he had not given up hope and Mr Royden again appeared at Crosby.

"To the Same at London.   May 5th, 1726.

Sir

I suppose Mr Roydon has Acquainted you of his having been here lately and that he found no great encouragement from my Daughter to hope Suckcess. I wish I could send you better Newes.

My wife received one from you which she answered about a Week since.

I think now and then a Letter to my Daughter would not be

amiss, and if I see the least Hopes, I shall give you the trouble of a Viset. But without Business calls me I care not to stir from home, however I returne you thanks for your kind invitation and shall not despaire of seeing Sizergh before I die, but should be glad of a good Occation to draw me thither which I would gladly hope time and patience may bring about. For that generall excuse I will not Marry is not often very lasting; however at present I can give no encouragement for another visit, and am truly sorry you spent so much Money the last time to so little Purpose, but this I must tell you, you have universally got the good opinion of all who have seen you, and where you had one Friend the first time I think I may safely say you now have Forty, but none more firme than

Your truly faithfull and humble servant
N.B."

The end of the long-drawn out story is abrupt. Nicholas was much occupied at the time with the entertainment of his cousin, Richard Butler,[1] who was staying with him.

"May 26th. Coz. Butler and I dined at Scarisbrick but went soone home being Mr Strickland was come, but he stayed not long after we came home being he had received a positive Denighall."

That must have been a day of agitation at Little Crosby, the suitor arriving unexpectedly, a messenger galloping to fetch the Squire back from his dinner-party, the heiress deciding her own fate before he could intervene. The Diary however offers no comment whatsoever. Nicholas had recently bought four black horses for his coach and for the moment seems to have been more interested in these than in his daughter's waywardness. However good manners necessitated a formal winding up of the disconcerting affair.

"To the same   June 7th.

Sir

I was truely concerned at our last parting and have but too much reason to think I shall never see you againe at Crosby

---

[1] His first cousin, the second son of Richard, fifth Viscount Mountgarrett by his wife Emelia, daughter of William Blundell the Cavalier.

upon the like Occasion, for my Daughter still continews in her Resolution not to Marry. However as nothing has been don on eather side dishonourably, I hope we shall always meet Friends. . . . My Daughter gave me some days since the Letters sealed up which she received from you, and I do verily believe she never showed them to anybody unless the two first which I read, and I really think they contained a great deale of truth, though do not now remember one expression in them. I must beg your Pardon for keeping them so long. I thought they would be too many to send by Post and was unwilling to send them by Tom Long the Carrier, but there is a Hors-Race at Ormschurch upon the 13th and 14th Instant where I think I shall be both days, and if anybody asks me for any thing for you I shall deliver them, but if I heare nothing from you ere the 20th Instant I'll send them by post . . . the Rest of your Friends are much your servants but none more than

Sir
Your Sincere and Humble Servant
Nicholas Blundell.

Neither of Mally's suitors broke their hearts. Thomas Strickland married Mary Dorothy, the eldest daughter of Simon Scrope, Esq. of Danby, in 1728. Ralph Standish chose an Irish bride, Mary, daughter of George Butler Esq. of Ballyraggat.

Curiously enough the inheritances of these two young men became the united property of their descendants through the marriage in 1762 between Thomas Strickland's grandson Charles and Ralph Standish's granddaughter Cecilia.

CHAPTER XIII

THE END OF THE DIARY

NICHOLAS may more insistently have urged Mally to marry than he would have done had not his main hope of leaving descendants behind him rested in her. For Fanny was constantly and seriously ill. The frequent administrations of " vomits " had succeeded bleeding; various doctors and Apothecary Livesley were never long absent from the house. On one occasion the Diarist records that his Jesuit cousin Father Thomas Gorsuch[1] came on a visit " to help Fanny," as though he despaired of her ultimate recovery and relied on the priest to prepare her for death. But his daughters were of his own tough stock; infants of earlier generations had survived birth in a filthy prison of the day and nurture in open fields,[2] and Fanny triumphed over " convulsive fitts," " quartan ague," laimeness of the hip and thigh," having " a wart cut off her breast" and the effects of all the ghastly treatments administered by doctor and apothecary. The first improvement in the girl's health seems indeed to have ensued after her father once more took matters into his own hands :

" April 26th. Fanny having had a quartidian ague ever since ye 5th. of March without the least Alteration, and finding no good by anything she has taken, I rode out with her to try if Aire and Exercise would do her any good."

Thereafter less is recorded of poor Fanny's ailments and she is more frequently mentioned as her father's companion.

" I rode out with Fanny to take ye Aire in the Coach, twas ye first time I went out with my Blacks. . . . I rode out with Fanny, we Rode past Ince Greene, they were bowling."

The Squire, having given up his efforts to settle his eldest

[1] *Vere* Eccleston. Foley, Vol. V.
[2] *Crosby Records.*

daughter in a prudently opulent marriage, proceeded with his work of planting orchards, experimenting with roots and bulbs, growing thousands of thorn bushes, and raising forest trees from seed.

" I sowed in ye first Bed in the Nursery in ye Vistow Wood Alder Berrys, on ye Second Bed I sowed Black Cherrys which had been steeped in Brandy. . . . I planted the Border in ye Old Hasley Walk with Hasles which came from Large Nuts sow'd. . . . I examined the Holes or place in the Vistow Wood where I set Achornes in Spring AD 1704 and pulled up severall of them, some becaus they grew too thick, and others becaus they were not likely to be good trees. . . . I garded most of the Elme Trees which are set on two sides of ye Little Moss Hey, by making a good Hedge behind them and seting some Briar Roots."

Hundreds of currant and gooseberry bushes were raised from cuttings; experiments with " imps " or grafts on apple and pear trees and with the treatment of seeds were continued.

" March 23rd. John Lunt whip-Grafted seaven Paradice Stocke with seaven different sorts of Apples in ye Close Hedge-Garden; he layed the Yew Tree in the Stone-Garden to get Suckers from it.

Oct. 30th. I set my best Tulops in ye four Hearts in ye Flower Garden and in ye New Flower Pots at the Side of ye Kanall.

Nov. 4th. I set eight Hundred and half of Tulops on three beds in ye Kill Garden, they were all Seedlings of different Aiges."

The Canal, often alluded to in the Diary, was a water-course bounding the gardens, which has since been diverted, its bed remaining as a dry sunk fence between the garden and the park.

Formal flower beds, ornamental flower pots and trim hedges emerge into view through such lines as those last quoted, but glass-houses with all their possibilities for the ardent horti-culturist, were as yet only within the reach of the very rich. The hot bed however was worked hard :

" . . . . I made a Plaine Hot bed for Cowcumbers all on the

Terras and sowed Cowcumber Seed which had been Steeped six Hours in New Milk."

The question of Enclosures now occasionally claimed the Diarist's attention.

"Mr Write of Cronton showed me his Proposall for getting an Act of Parlement for enclosing the Commons of Ditton[1] . . . I drank a Bowl of Punch at Thomas Syors with Parson Wairing, Mr Thomas Whittle and Mr Jackson of Leverpoole; we agreed Matters amongst us as far as we could concerning Inclosing Crosby Marsh."[2]

Meanwhile the social life of the countryside afforded plenty of company:

"My Wife, I etc. dined at Eccleston . . . as we went one of the Wheele Horses slipped off ye Plot and fell into ye Gutter. We lodged at Prescot . . . I had a Merry Night. We dansed in ye Dining-Roome viz Mr Fazackerley, young Mr Hollywell, Mr Heskaine etc. . . . The Country People dansed in ye Hall. My Musick was Anderton and Marsh."

So young men were not wanting to enliven this tranquil period for Mally and Fanny. During the summer of this year (1727) they spent some weeks with their widowed "Aunt Middleton" at York; they travelled on horseback, their father escorting them to their destination; he started on his return journey the very day after he had left his daughters with his sister-in-law, and was "discoursing" Mr Plumbe on business in Liverpool two days later.

The Diary proceeds with its chronicle, now casually mentioning a misfortune to Mrs Blundell: "My Wife fell into ye Hors Poole"; now showing the Squire busy in his "Closet": "I put the Leaves of Whit Lillys into ye two Glass-Bottles, they are to make Oyle on for a Burn or Scald."

---

[1] This was not effected until 1797.

[2] Crosby Marsh was not finally enclosed until the year 1815 when William Blundell, the Squire of the day, made the following note in the *Great Hodge-Podge*: "Great Crosby Marsh was enclosed and divided and let by divisions of the same to different tenants having first fenced and ditched the same and I cut a deep drain through the old Moss to communicate with the new drain."

Roger Dicconson, outlawed in 1715 reappears upon the scene:

"Mr Rodger Dicconson and Apothecary Gerard[1] etc were at prayers at Mr Aldreds. . . . I warned Boones to goe to ye Slate Delf for me and then went to Crosby Greene where I found Mr Rodger Dicconson, Parson Acton[2] etc."

The deaths of several neighbours are recorded during this summer and autumn, among others that of Mrs Ann, the Crosby inn-keeper on whose premises so many gatherings had taken place to witness cock-fights. The Squire was ever ready to help where he could.

"August 15th. Mrs Ann being ill I took Account as well as I could what she ought and what was owing to her.

August 11th. Charles Howard, the Overseer of ye Poore, and I took Account of Mrs Ann what Money was owing to her, she being in Danger of Death."

Mrs Ann, however, lived on for another five weeks.

"Sept. 22nd. Mrs Ann being dead William Harrison and Edward Rothwell advised with me about her burial."

During this same autumn Fanny had one of her recurring bouts of illness, her father suffered constantly from ague and Mr Aldred was seriously ill for many weeks. Nicholas seems to have been genuinely alarmed when his wife developed some unusual malady.

"Sept. 17th. Doctor Lancaster came to see my Wife.

Sept. 18th. My Wife being extreamely ill of the Rash or some such Distemper, I sent againe for Dr Lancaster he came and gave her a Vomit. Lord Molineux sent me a Hansh of Venison.

Sept. 19th. Doctor Lancaster came a third time to see my Wife and now aprehends her to have something like ye Small-Pox . . There was a Purs run for on Crosby Marsh . . . my Wife I and Doughters were none of us there."

During the next few days Mrs Blundell was ordered first a purge and then "to be bluddied," which operation was carried out by John Pendlebury "Cozen Butler's servant." On the second day of the race-meeting the Blundell family were still absent,

[1] Of Wigan. *Non-Jurors.*
[2] Thomas Acton, curate of Sephton, buried there 2nd December, 1727.

but on the third "my Doughters were at the Race," writes their father. John Pendlebury's skill with the bleeding knife was exercised on both girls, and meanwhile illness and death were widespread in the countryside.

"Oct. 20th. Cecily Roscow[1] having been ill a great while, went to Warrington in hopes to be cured. I went part of the way with the Corps of Thomas Bootle. I was entertained at Henry Williamsons with Robert Bootle, Parson Wairing etc. . . .

I sent of a How-doe-you to Scarisbrick ye famoly most of them being ill. . . . Mr Blundell not being well, I went to see him. . . . Fanny went to see Pat Gorsuch, being he is not well."

At the end of the year the Diarist added to his usual summary of the weather and harvests, the following account of the current malady:

"Never so sickly a time known in Lancashire as from May till the end of this Year, abundance died but generally those above 50 years old, the Distemper was an uncommon sort of a Fever which eather took them off or ended in a violent Ague which often lasted severall Months and was scarce possible to be cured and most who had these fits had them after different Mannors so that they scarce knew when to expect them, being sometimes Quartan, tersion etc., and som had an easy Fitt and as soon as that was gon off had a most violent Fitt; in som other parts of England their fair'd not much better and beyond ye Seas it was a very sickly time. When the Distemper began to a-bait the Horses in severall Plaises were ill, being seas'd with a running at ye Nose and a Cough of which som few dyed."

In general however no gloom pervades the Diary during this last year of its course. A few quotations will show its writer obviously enjoying his busy, gregarious life amid his family and neighbourly circle, occasionally as much occupied with an unimportant small task as with urgent estate business.

"I was very busy drawing a Patron for a worked Pincushion. I lay'd my Munkey[2] in ye Cart Hous Pit . . . I went to John Blansherd's Rearing and drove a Pin. There was Mr Molineux of the Grange and I think" (the writer seems to have returned

---

[1] Maid at Crosby Hall.
[2] A receptacle for liquor. Contraband liquor is here alluded to.

somewhat hazy from the feast) "William Blancherd and Nicholas Plumb. Mr Crisp pay'd me some Interest Money. I pay'd him a Customary Rent of 4d per Annum due to Lord Molineux . . . We were very Merry about Thomas Fleetwood's Wiggs. Nathaniall Buck came to see if I would subscribe to his Proposalls for Publishing the Perspective Vews of some old Abbies, Castles etc in Lancashire, Cheshire and Darbyshire."

As the Disbursement Book offers no information on the subject it must be inferred that the cautious Squire declined Mr Buck's invitation.

The Diarist still confidently administered remedies to sufferers:

"I took a Blistering Plaister off Mary as I lay'd on yesternight. I applyed Plaisters of Venus Turpentine to William Carefoot's Rists against ye Ague Fits."

Mary Wogdon was the Cook to whom Apothecary Livesley had administered a vomit two days earlier when she was "extreamely ill." She does not seem to have been overwhelmed with gratitude for these ministrations for not long afterwards the Diary announces: "Mary Wogdon left her service abruptly and without any occasion and took no leave."

In February, 1728, Nicholas, who was at the time "very ill of his eyes," sustained a grievous loss.

"Feb. 23rd. Mr Aldred dyed. I helped to lay him out and took charg of his best things.

Feb. 24th. Pat. Hardesty[1] prayed for Mr Aldred in his Chappell, there was a pritty large Congregaison. I sent my Cart to Leverpoole for Meat and Drink for Mr Aldreds Funerall and went to his Hous to see part of it carefully taken care of.

Feb. 25th. Mr Aldred was Buried in the Harkirk there was at his Buriall or at least in the Hous the Famoly of Ince, Parson Wairing, Mr Cottom, John Rose, Rob. Bootle, John Blansherd etc."

During March, Nicholas continued to suffer much from his

---

[1] Rev. John Hardesty, S.J., vere Tempest, fourth son of Thomas Tempest of Broughton Hall, Yorks., by his wife Anne, daughter and heiress of Henry Scroop of Danby, Yorks. Father Hardesty was at that time serving in Liverpool.

S

eyes; he still faithfully took Dr Cawood's remedies at such times, but now decided to consult one Mr Chisleton.

"March 19th. Cozen Butler sent an Express to let me know when Mr Chisleton would be at Chester."

A consultation followed in Chester.

"March 23rd. Mr Chisleton, Dr Fernihough etc. came to my Lodging I advised with him about Mally's Eyes and mine and about Fanny's laimness. Dr Broomfield dined with us. Coz. Butler and I made a Viset to Sir Henry Bunbury,[1] we drank there with Mr Senior Chulmondeley[2] etc.. Coz Butler and Mally suped at Sir Henry Bunbury's."

It does not appear that the Diarist's medical advisers counselled abstention from strong drink which perhaps would have brought about an alleviation of his eye-trouble. For the next two years the Disbursement Book often sets forth the hitherto rare items:

"Doctors Phees for me
Physic for me."

Such expenditure is usually accounted for in the following order, only the amounts in each category varying:

"Dr Phees and Phisick for my Wife ...	2	1	4
"Dr Phees and Phisick for me		18	4
"Dr Phees and Phisick for my Daughter ...	2	3	2
"Phisick for ye Servants		2	6"

Usually "Phisick for ye Poore" is added, and occasionally "Phisick for ye Horses."

In fact at the age of fifty-nine, the Squire's hitherto robust health was evidently declining. The last few days in which he wrote his Diary show him to have been occupied with his

[1] Lord of the ancient manors of Stanney and Bunbury, M.P. for Chester 1700-1727. He is thus described in Omerod's *Cheshire*: "Sir Henry Bunbury, gay, good-humoured and lively, was an intimate friend of Farquhar, the comic writer who drew from him the character of Sir Harry Wildair."

[2] Charles Cholmondeley of Vale Royal, Member of Parliament for the County of Cheshire.

usual interests, although a few lines are much blotted and corrected.

"April 1st. I began to uncover my Asparagus and fork over the Beds.

April 2nd. Mr Moss sent his Servant to know what Mr Fazackerley ought me. I set it down upon ye back of a Subpena and Signed it. Mr Sadlor brought me a Silver Tobacco Box on which he had engraived my Crest.

April 3rd. Ellen Easton came to be Maid here.
April 4th. Fanny rode out behind me. I enquired of Richard Renold etc for Seed Oats. I set som Kidney Beanes in ye Hot-Bed in Order to rais them early."

There the long, tranquil, intimate chronicle abruptly ends.

The Disbursement Book contains no record of a serious illness that year. The Squire's advisers at Chester may have ordered him to write less, but the long columns of the Disbursement Book show only his hand-writing for a further eight years. A possible explanation of the sudden close of the Diary in the middle of a week may be the loss, or accidental destruction, of an accumulation of the Small Diurnals before he had been able to transcribe them owing to pain in his eyes. The last of the three volumes of his Great Diurnal contains many blank pages at the end, and the narrow columns prepared at the beginning for his own peculiar "Tables," were made ready for the year 1728 but were not filled in.

Chapter XIV

FROM FATHER TO DAUGHTER

NEARLY two years after the last recorded lines were written in the Diary, the now sparsely furnished Letter Book introduces John Coppinger, the young Irishman who at last won Mally's heart. The letter, dated Jan. 27th, 1730, is addressed to "Mr Nailor, Superior of the Benedictens" and is couched in indignant terms. It accuses Father Walmesley, a Benedictine monk, of having let fall some remark disparaging to John Coppinger at the dinner table. The words complained of are not cited but Nicholas demands a written apology, adding:

" Mr Coppinger's Credit and good Caracture is at present most deare and valuable to me, being he is now making his Addresses to my eldest Daughter and I hope she will in a short time be more happy in him than she could have been in any other yet proposed to her, he being of an incomparable good temper and unblemished Caracture and coms of an ancient and worthy and good Famoly and is not only the Heir to a plentiful Estate but has a kind and indulgent father who has settled in present upon him not only what is extreamely handsome but even more than I could have hoped or desired, which makes me the more to resent what is said against him which I take as a Reflection upon me."

Stephen Coppinger of Balyvalone[1] and Barriscourt, Co. Cork, the kind and indulgent father alluded to, had in fact sent his heir to England in charge of his Protestant friend and patron, James Barry, 4th Earl of Barrymore, who had benevolently undertaken to find a well-dowered bride for the young man. Lord Barrymore's second wife, Lady Elizabeth Savage, had inherited the estate of Rock Savage in Cheshire from her father Lord Rivers. Upon her death he took as a third wife Lady Anne

[1] Information concerning the Coppinger Family, and quotations from their letters are taken from W. A. Coppinger's *History of the Coppinger's,* published 1884.

Chichester,[1] and with her occupied Rock Savage. Thither he brought John Coppinger, in 1729. Lord Barrymore, an adherent of the Stuarts, had many friends among English Jacobites. The Coppinger family had suffered much as recusants, and had been almost ruined in the cause of James II. Stephen had followed the exiled King into France, and had there married Joan Goolde, the daughter of another Irish fugitive, in 1700. When the couple returned to Ireland, they found themselves hampered on every side by debts. It was plain to them that the only way to save the family inheritance was by the marriage of its heir to an heiress. Hardly was young John established at Rock Savage than he received a letter from his father urging him not to marry in haste for immediately after his departure from Ireland the brilliant prospects of an Irish girl had been brought to his parents' notice.

".... There is Mr Harrold's daughter he engage if you stay two years longer she'll be about 13 years of age he'll give £6000 and if he dies without more children, as in all likelihood he will, ye girl would be worth at ye least £20000 in cash besides anything else. And you know," adds the candid parent, "father and grandfather and all the world covet nothing more."

Probably John Coppinger had already met Mally Blundell, for his father seems apprehensive lest the dazzling financial prospects of a child bride might be ignored by him.

"I only say all this," proceeds the letter, "that ye may be easy and not so impatient as to go headlong to work. The longer you stay unmarried the better your fortune will be. There is no greater noise in Cork than that my Lord got ye a fortune of £10,000. Several asked me whether I had any account of it. I gave them ye ear and said my Lord may do with ye as he pleased."

John was indifferent to Mr. Harrold's offer and proceeded with his successful courtship of Mally, Lord Barrymore's candidate. His father settled his estate of Ballyvalone upon him, and managed to meet the bride's future portion of £400 a year with an allowance of £500 a year to his son. Altogether it was a most

---

[1] Daughter of Arthur, third Earl of Chichester, whose grandson, the fifth Earl, was created first Marquis of Donegal.

satisfactory match. The wedding took place in the summer of 1730. but only tantalising glimpses of the festivities appear through a page of the Disbursement Book. There was evidently a goodly gathering of friends and neighbours for the event; two extra cooks were engaged, 15s. was paid to the fiddlers, and the gloves "given at my Doughter Coppingers Marriage besides what my Son and Doughter gave" cost £2 5s. 3d.

Presumably Nicholas would not entrust the Marriage Deeds to the Post, for Thomas Syer undertook a journey to Ireland on his behalf. In addition to the "Gratuety to Syer for his care £1-14," and the present of "Canell Work sent to Barriscourt £1-2-6," Syer's expenses amounted to £10 8s. 0d.

Mally was given £50 for her trousseau and £10 were paid for Fanny's "Cloths for ye Weding."

In the following autumn Fanny visited her sister in Ireland and during her absence her father made tentative advances on her behalf to a possible suitor whom she had never seen.

"To Mr Fleetwood Butler,   Oct. 11th, 1730

Mr. Webb was in Lancashire very lately, I was in his company, but he never in the least mentioned my Daughter; I wish he had, for he seems to be a very sober good-tempered Man, and I could have liked him very well. If I thought it were to any purpose, should be glad it were proposed to him; I fancy if he had seen my Daughter he would not have disliked her, only not having a present fortune would probably have been a great Objection. However if he be in the Sercumstance as I heare he is and were really in love with her, that would be no great impediment for I have reserved for her the £1000 of land which I intended to leave her at my death, and have power to charge the other part of my Estate with £2000 besydes what I may be able to leave her when I die; so that I think she may well be said to be worth better than £3000. But I have already said too much on this Subject unless there were a better prospect than I know of, however should be glad to know your Sentiment in this affaire, being willing so far as in me lies to give what I am able to my Daughter to see her well settled during my Life."

Perhaps Mr. Webb was looking out for a more financially valuable bride, or perhaps Fanny was not to be tempted home from Ireland to be offered in wedlock to a gentleman who might " not have disliked her." For nothing more is to be discovered about Mr. Webb, and in the following spring Mrs. Blundell dealt summarily with another aspirant to her younger daughter's hand.

" To Mr Merry[1] from my Wife.   April 25th, 1731.

Sir

I received the favour of yours. As to my Daughter coming over I know not when it shall be for Mr Blundell does not go for her of some time, and perhaps she may come before, he thinks his telling you that his Daughter could not think of marrying you was a sufficient reason for you to have no thoughts of it, and she also told her Father that she had given you a positive Deniall and desired you would settle your affections elce where, which makes me surprised you should stay on, but whose fortune it may be to marry her I know not, but do entirely leav it to her to make her owne Choyce."

Fanny, as far as can be gleaned from the Disbursement Book, now enjoyed quite a luxurious life at Crosby. There are no more evidences of economy. Valuable horses are bought freely; the household staff is augmented by a " chamber maid " as well as " wives' maid "; Fanny has a maid for herself, Ellen Chantrell, who receives 10/- per quarter. When Fanny and her father visited the Coppingers at Barriscourt in the spring of 1732 no expense was spared.

" Vailes at Barris-court by me Ni. Blundell £3 13 0
Vailes by my Doughter ...   . 5 2 6"

That autumn Fanny was sent to Buxton, no doubt for her health. Her father of course escorted her to Buxton and fetched her home again.

" Going twice to Buxton and coming back,
      in all ye Travelling expenses £7 18 2
Fanny's Expenses at Buxton in all   ... 11 2 10 '

[1] Probably of Kniveton, Derbyshire. See *Non-Jurors*.

In 1733 Fanny married Henry Peppard, a member of an old Irish family established in trade in Liverpool.

The Squire had kept his word and had not forced either of his daughters into an advantageous marriage against her will. While he was highly pleased with the Coppinger alliance, it is not unlikely that he considered Mr Peppard inadequately equipped financially to enable him to make a suitable "bargan" in the marriage settlements. No outlay is recorded for Fanny's clothes for the wedding but she was given a dictionary which cost 17/6. There were heavy bills for her mother's clothes at the time, however, including lace and holland from Dunkirk and ten pounds' worth of lace from Ghent, so perhaps Mrs. Blundell found means to meet her daughter's immediate requirements. The marriage took place in the summer. Extra help was engaged in the kitchen but "musick at ye Weding" only cost 7/6 showing that but half the number of minstrels who played at Mally's wedding had been engaged on this lesser occasion, while the value of gloves bestowed on retainers amounted merely to 5/6 which looks as though Mr. Peppard's family employed a very modest staff.

On turning the page of the Disbursement Book it is pleasing to discover that after all Fanny received some handsome presents which were paid for in the following quarter.

> "Coffipot given to my Doughter Peppard ... £9 12 0
> Hand Bord of Silver to my Doughter
>   Peppard 2 10 0
> Chinea to my Doughter Peppard 1 8 0

So Doughter Peppard went off to live in Liverpool and the Squire now had to ride alone to watch, with failing eye-sight, the doings of wheat-shearers, turf-getters and moss-burners.

In 1734 befell what must have been the greatest sorrow of the Diarist's life. Mally died while on a visit to Crosby. The Disbursement Book tells little but reveals that the illness was short since the bill for "physick for Doughter Coppinger" amounted only to 4/4. A messenger was sent for Doctor Worthington but no "phee" is mentioned; possibly John Coppinger paid him. Offerings for Masses are mentioned thus :

"Lord Bishop etc for Doughter 1 17 6
  Ditto Pat. Tootell[1] 5 6
and there is the pathetic entry:
  "Rosemary for ye Buriall ...   .   3 9"

Two years after Mally's death the widower married the
daughter of Michael Moore of Drogheda. Mally's only child,
Stephen, died in 1745, so it was Mariana, John Coppinger's
daughter by his second wife, who succeeded to the Ballyvalone
estate.

Meanwhile Fanny's little boy Christopher was much at Crosby
during the last two years of his grandfather's life. We find
that "Kitts Red Coat" cost 18/- and "Fushton for Littoll Kit"
1/7. The following year the child evidently began his first
lessons for the item "School Wages 1-0" is inscribed.

The Diarist's own writing becomes smaller and smaller, and
the lines in the Disbursement Book more steeply sloping until,
in the midst of the accounts "From Lady Day to Midsummer
Inclusive" 1736, they begin to be inscribed in another hand.

The column is headed "Disbursed by me Nicholas Blundell"
and begins as usual with details of outlay on attire for his wife:

"Silk ferreting for my wife 7 0
  Dimaty for my wife 3 4
  Wives Shoos and Cloggs ...   .   2 5 3"

There follows a list of heterogeneous expenses such as

"Flannen for me 3 9½
  Mending Harnish 6 0
  for London Mops ...   .   5 1"

And finally the very last entry
  "For Little Master Kit   ...   .   14 0"

This concludes the quarter "From Christmas exclusive to
Lady Day March 25th inclusive" 1737.

[1] Rev. Christopher Tootell, *alias* Charles Dodd, was then chaplain
to the Throgmorton Family at Harvington Hall, Worcestershire, where
he completed his *Church History of England*. He was member of a
Lancashire family and may have been visiting his native county in
1734.

The following month, on April 21st, 1737, Nicholas Blundell died. He was buried in the Blundell Chapel of Sephton Church where his ancestors had been laid, even during the days of active persecution of Catholics.

During the years covered by the Diary, its author many times recorded having made his last Will. The very last was dated May 8th, 1736, less than a year before his death.[1] Mindful of the amount of money he had laid out on the occasion of his father's funeral—money which later in life he probably concluded could have been put to better use—Nicholas ordained that his own funeral was to be conducted with " as little pomp as decency will permit." No bread or beer was to be distributed, but instead threepence per head was to be given to the poor. He left to his " loving wife" household linen, "any horse she chooses with best saddle and pillion," his mother's diamond ring and (characteristically of the age) *her own* diamond ring and other trinkets. All brood mares and colts under five years old were bequeathed "to my son Peppard," personally. The Crosby and Ditton estates had already been settled upon his surviving daughter Fanny should Mally leave no heir. It only remained to stipulate in the Will that pictures " such as are of my relations be kept and continued at the Hall ", and that one of his grandsons should take the name of Blundell.

Fanny, her husband and their younger children were known by the surnames of both families, as Peppard-Blundell. But after Henry Peppard's death in 1771, their eldest surviving son Nicholas took the name and arms of Blundell of Crosby.

[1] The will is included in Vol. 66, published by the Lancashire and Cheshire Historic Society.

APPENDICES

APPENDIX I

Note that if I dine abroad from my hous, where I am a Gest or my viset be made etc. to that Famoly, 'tis then to be found in ye Table or Index as if it happened at my own house, and severall other things I have set down which do not altogether agree exactly with ye Tickle,[1] being unwilling to make more tickles; but those that anithing can best be brought under, I apply it to, and severall things I put under 2 or 3 heads so if I look under any of those Proper Heads I can find it; and where a thing is somthing doubtful under what Head it should be put, I put it under every Head or Chapter as it can anywayes be applyed to.

This work of mine may seem to some to be very useless. I confess severall things that are set down are of no consequence, yet consider-ing ye uncertainty both of ye things I shall afterwards have a desire to know, or ye day of ye Month which may be necessary for me to give account of, it is not improper to be something particular, seeing

[1] Title.

ye troble is so small; and the advantage that I Nicholas Blundell have already found by it has been very great and has abundantly over ballanced my Trouble.

[At the end of volume I]

The Index or Table at the Begining of this Book being so very larg, I have made ye Following one in ye same Forme, only abundantly shorter, having onely set down in it those things which I think I shall have hereafter most occation to look for or to desire to know, it containing not I think one third part of what was in ye first.

[There follows a slightly shorter version, but as it is in much the same form it is not as " abundantly clear " to the reader as it evidently was to the writer.]

APPENDIX II

Eccles Wakes

It is unlikely that the forms of entertainment provided at Lancashire country wakes altered appreciably between the early eighteenth and the early nineteenth centuries. The programme for Eccles Wakes in 1819[1] is therefore reproduced. here to illustrate the type of fun enjoyed by the Blundell children and their companions on these outings.

Eccles Wakes

Monday and Tuesday, 30th and 31st Aug. and Sept. 1st and 2nd, 1819.

Programme.

On Monday the Ancient Sport of Bull-Baiting may be seen in its various evolutions.

A Dandy race for a purse of silver—the best of heats, the second to be entitled to 5/-.

A foot race for a hat by lads not exceeding 16 years of age.

Tuesday.

A Jackass race for a purse of gold value £50—the best of heats : each to carry a feather—the racers to be shown in the bull ring at 12 and to start at 2. Nothing to be paid for entrance but bringers of each steed to have a good dinner gratis, and a quart of strong ale to moisten his clay.

Same Day.

An apple dumpling eating by ladies and gentlemen of all ages. The person who finishes repast first to have 5/- the second 2/- the third 1/-.

[1] Anon, *Bygone Lancashire*, p. 174.

Wednesday.

A pony race for tits not to exceed 12 hands high, for a cup value £50—the best of heats.

Same Day.

A foot race for a hat value 10/6 by men of every discription.

Same Day.

A race for a good Holland smock by ladies of all ages—the second best to have a handsome satin riband.

Thursday.
A game at Prison Bars.
also

A grinning match through a collar for a piece of fat bacon—no crabs to be used on this occasion.

Same Day.

A young pig will be turned out with its ears and tail well soaped. The first person catching and holding him by either will be entitled to same.

APPENDIX III

The following is an Abstract of an Act for the further Preventing the Growth of Popery (11 and 12 William III c. 4 1700).

WHEREAS there has been of late a much greater Resort into this Kingdom than formerly of Popish Bishops, Priests and Jesuits and they do very openly and in insolent Manner affront the Laws and daily endeavour to pervert His Majesty's natural born Subjects which has been occasioned by neglect of the due Execution of the Laws already in Force: For preventing the further Growth of Popery and all such treasonable and execrable designs and conspiracies against His Majesty's Person and Government and the established Religion as have lately as well as frequently heretofore been brought to light and fully defeated by the wonderful Providence of God; be it enacted that from and after the five and twentieth day of March, One thousand and Seven hundred [1701 new style] all and every Person and Persons who shall Apprehend and Take one or more Popish Bishop, Priest or Jesuit and prescribe him or them so apprehended and taken until he or they be Convicted of saying Mass or of Exercising any other Part of the Office or Function of a Popish Bishop or Priest within these Realms shall have and receive from the Sheriff or Sheriffs of the County where such Conviction shall be made (without paying any Fee for the same) for every such Offender so Convicted the sum of One Hundred Pounds within Four Months after such Conviction and Demand.........

And for a further Remedy against the Growth of Popery over and beyond the good Laws already made be it further enacted.........that if any Popish Bishop, Priest or Jesuit whatsoever shall say Mass or Exercise any other Part of the Office or Function of a Popish Bishop or Priest within these Realms or the Dominions thereunto belonging or any Papist or Person making Profession of the Popish Religion shall keep School or take upon themselves the Education or Government or boarding of Youth in any place within this Realm or the Dominions thereunto belonging such Person or Persons being thereof Lawfully Convicted that then every such Person shall on such Conviction be committed to perpetual Imprisonment.........

And be it also further enacted.........that from and after the nine and twentieth day of September which shall be in the Year of Our Lord Seventeen Hundred if any Person Educated in the Papist Religion or Profession the same shall not within Six Months after he or she shall attain the age of Eighteen Years take the Oaths of Allegiance and Supremacy and also Subscribe the Declaration set down and expressed in an Act of Parliament made in the Thirtieth Year of the Reign of the Late King Charles II to be by him or her made repeated and subscribed in the Courts of Chancery or Kings Bench or Quarter Sessions of the County where such Person shall Reside every such Person shall in respect of him or herself only be Disabled and made Incapable to Inherit or Take up the descent Devise or Limitation in Possession Reversion or Remainder any Lands Tenements or Hereditaments within the Kingdom of England, Dominion of Wales or the Town of Berwick upon Tweed and that during the Life of such Person or until he or she do take the said Oaths and Make Repeat and Subscribe the said Declaration in manner as aforesaid the next of his or her Kindred which shall be a Protestant shall Have and Enjoy the said Lands Tenements and Hereditament without being Accountable for the Profits by him or her received during such enjoyment.........And that from and after the tenth day of April which shall be in the Year of Our Lord Seventeen Hundred every Papist or Person making Profession of the Papist Religion shall be Disabled and is hereby made Incapable to Purchase either in his or her own Name or in the Name of any other Person or Persons to his or her Use or in Trust for him or her any Manors Lands Profits out of Lands Tenements Leases Terms or Hereditaments with the Kingdom of England Dominion of Wales and Town of Berwick upon Tweed.........

And whereas by an Act made in the Third Year of King James I Whoever shall be Convicted of Sending or Causing to be Sent any Child or any other Person under their Government into Parts beyond the Seas out of the King's Obedience to the Intent that such Child or Person so sent should be Educated in the Romish Religion contrary to the said Act to Forfeit One Hundred Pounds Half to the King's Majesty the other Half to him that shall Sue for same: for the greater Encouragement

and Reward of those who shall Discover such Offenders be it enacted
that the said Sum of One Hundred Pounds shall be Paid to the Sole
Use and Benefit of him or her who shall Discover and Convict any
Person so Offending...............

APPENDIX IV

Apparell for my Daughters.

	£	s.	d.
Flye Sutes,[1] two, outside and all other Materialls and Markings	35	14	0
Leomond Damask 23¾ yds. Red Damask 21¼ yds. Prime Cost at Paris, bringing to Calis & Duty at Calis, in all	18	15	0
The Damask comes to about 8s. 4d. p. yard besides what I gave for Bringing it safe to England which is elcewhere mentioned and comes to 1s. 2d. per yard.			
Night Gowns and Petty Coats, Linings with all Materialls and maiking them	8	14	7
Cherry Derry outside for Mantew and Petty-Coat ...	1	6	4
Quilted Petty-Coats	3	19	2
Altering Mantews and Pettycots and for Materialls of all sorts to enlarge them or make them up with	2	5	0
Scouring and Dying Silks		7	0
Stays two Pair	4	8	0
Hoop Petty Coats	1	11	0
Riding Habets, Outside and Marking	4	17	0
Riding Hoop-Petty-Coats two		17	0
Linnen for Riding in	2	14	6
Whips, two	0	6	6
Silk for Aprons, Maiking and for Fringe	1	4	10
Barmoodas Hats and Hat Bands	1	17	0
Silk and lining the Hats		8	3
Fanns	2	4	0
Flanders Lace for Heads & Rufs...	42	15	0
Lace and Edging bought at London	3	17	2
Holland for Shifts & Aprons and Cambrick for Carchaffs	14	8	0

[1] Probably fashionable travelling suits. Stage coaches were known as
flys long before the word was used to denote a one-horse hackney
carriage.

	£	s.	d.
Cambrick, Muslin and Holland for Heads, Ruffles, Aprons & Carchaffs and for Maiking them	8	19	0
Starching and maiking up Heads and Ruffles, maiking new ones and altering some	1	0	0½
Ribans, Girdles, Scullkaps, Wiers, Pinns, Rowls, Powder, etc.	1	6	0
Girdle Buckles		19	0
Black Silk Hoods		10	6
Bobbin, Silk Lases		4	0
Diomond Eare Rings, drops and Gold Eare Rings ...	4	9	0
Setting a Pair of Diomond Ear Rings and for Drops and Gold Eare Rings	1	18	0
Gloves and for Washing Gloves	3	12	8
Stockings		10	6
Shoes, Clogs and for mending	2	5	10
Bushs of Whealbone		2	8

Apparall for my Doughters £177 7s. 7½d.

APPENDIX V

Weight of Beasts Slaughtered at Crosby in the XVII Century

22 Dec. 1651 — Beef 843 lbs⎫ an ox fattened for
Suet etc. 142 ,, ⎭ 11 months.

1654 — One flitch of a very large sow, "when dry and long hanged" weighed 105 lbs.

1660 — An ox bought lean for £5-19/ , fed for 8 months, had 18 bushels of oats (summer grass), forequarters weighed 154 lbs, hind quarter 140 lbs.
A cow weighed 473 lbs in all, without the hide.
"She was a cow of a middle size."

1663 — The oxen were six to nine years old when killed, having been used for the plough. They were sometimes fattened for a long time. "April 1663 I killed an ox which was fed about 22 months. He was judged before he was killed to be well worth £11-10/. He was six years old. His quarters weighed 746 lbs, his chine 171 lbs so that all the beef weighed 877 lbs. The whole weight including the hide 1143½ lbs. Its yoke fellow's complete weight was lbs 1205. Both were six years old and had been worked for two years before fattening.
One side of a small heifer weighed 109 lbs.

T

1665   " A Passing large Hogg " " reasonable well fed yet too young for killing to ye best advantage. The body weighed 337 lbs, the fat 14 lbs and a little more."

1669   A cow calf 9 or ten weeks old, forequarter 29 lbs, hind quarter 35 lbs. " it was exceeding fat and well raised."

1685   Total weight of an ox judged to be of enormous size, hide etc included, 2205 lbs.

APPENDIX VI

PEDIGREE OF BLUNDELL, OF CROSBY.

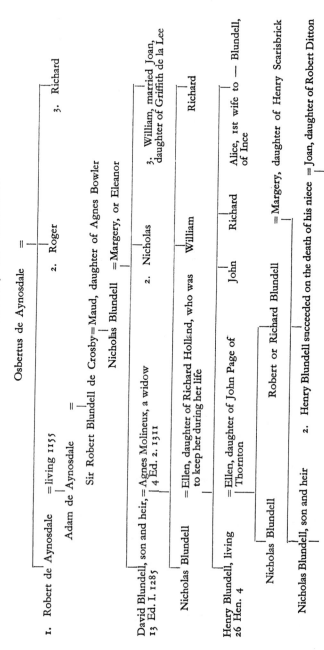

Osbertus de Aynosdale =

1. Robert de Aynosdale = living 1155   2. Roger   3. Richard

Adam de Aynosdale =

Sir Robert Blundell de Crosby = Maud, daughter of Agnes Bowler

Nicholas Blundell = Margery, or Eleanor

David Blundell, son and heir, = Agnes Molineux, a widow   2. Nicholas   3. William, married Joan,
13 Ed. I. 1285   4 Ed. 2. 1311   daughter of Griffith de la Lee

Nicholas Blundell = Ellen, daughter of Richard Holland, who was   William   Richard
                   to keep her during her life

Henry Blundell, living = Ellen, daughter of John Page of   John   Richard   Alice, 1st wife to — Blundell,
26 Hen. 4   Thornton   of Ince

Nicholas Blundell   Robert or Richard Blundell   = Margery, daughter of Henry Scarisbrick

Nicholas Blundell, son and heir   2. Henry Blundell succeeded on the death of his niece = Joan, daughter of Robert Ditton

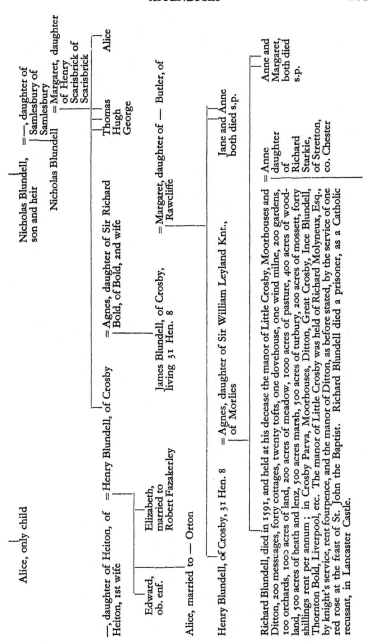

Alice, only child

—, daughter of Heiton, of Heiton, 1st wife = Henry Blundell, of Crosby

Edward, ob. enf.

Elizabeth, married to Robert Fazakerley

Alice, married to — Orton

Nicholas Blundell, son and heir

Nicholas Blundell

=—, daughter of Samlesbury of Samlesbury

=Margaret, daughter of Henry Scarisbrick of Scarisbrick

Alice

Thomas
Hugh
George

=Agnes, daughter of Sir Richard Bold, of Bold, 2nd wife

James Blundell, of Crosby, living 31 Hen. 8

=Margaret, daughter of — Butler, of

=Margaret, daughter of — Rawcliffe

Henry Blundell, of Crosby, 31 Hen. 8

=Agnes, daughter of Sir William Leyland Knt., of Morlies

Jane and Anne both died s.p.

Anne and Margaret, both died s.p.

=Anne daughter of Richard Starkie, of Stretton, co. Chester

Richard Blundell, died in 1591, and held at his decease the manor of Little Crosby, Moorhouses and Ditton, 200 messuages, forty cottages, twenty tofts, one dovehouse, one wind milne, 200 gardens, 100 orchards, 1000 acres of land, 200 acres of meadow, 1000 acres of pasture, 400 acres of wood-land, 500 acres of heath and lenz, 500 acres marsh, 500 acres of turbury, 200 acres of mossett, forty shillings rent per annum ; in Crosby Parva, Moorhouses, Ditton, Great Crosby, Ince Blundell, Thornton Bold, Liverpool, etc. The manor of Little Crosby was held of Richard Molyneux, Esq., by knight's service, rent fourpence, and the manor of Ditton, as before stated, by the service of one red rose at the feast of St. John the Baptist. Richard Blundell died a prisoner, as a Catholic recusant, in Lancaster Castle.

William Blundell, of Crosby, born 1560, was imprisoned five years for recusancy, ob. 1638. = Amelia, daughter of Edward, son of Sir William Norreys, of Speke, ob. 1631

Richard
James

Jane, wife of — Maddison

Nicholas Blundell, Esq., of Crosby, died in 1631 = Jane, daughter of Sir Roger Bradshaw, of Haigh

Anna, wife of — Gillebrand

Margaret, died s.p.

William Blundell, of Crosby, son and heir. On the first day of his service in the civil war, before he had mustered the 100 dragoons which he was commissioned to raise, he had his thigh broken at the siege of Latom House; following upon this, his goods were plundered, his lands sequestered for ten years, when they were sold, and bought by his friends, but with his money. He was four times made a prisoner, and paid his ransom twice. = Anna, daughter of Sir Thomas Haggerston, 1st Baronet, of Haggerston, by Alice, his wife, only daughter of Henry Banaster, of Bank

Richard
died s.p.

Emilia,
Dorothy,
Margaret,
Annie,
Winifred,
Francisca

2. Amelia, wife of Richard Butler, son of Edmund Viscount Mountgarret

Jane,
Margaret,
Alice,
Francisca

Mary,
Clare,
Francisca,
Anne,
Bridget

2. William, died in 1702 = Mary, daughter of Rowland Eyre, of Hassop, Co. Derby

Nicholas Blundell, son and heir. died s.p.
3. Thomas Blundell

NICHOLAS BLUNDELL, of Crosby, son and heir, died in 1737, and was succeeded by his daughter = Frances, daughter Marmaduke, 2nd Lord Langdale

Richard,
Joseph

Mary,
Anne

Margaret
Winnifred

Mary Blundell, eldest daughter and co-heiress = John Coppinger, Esq., of Ballyvolane, Co. Cork

Frances, younger daughter, and eventually sole-heiress to her father's estates, ob. 17 April, 1773 = Henry, grandson of Thomas Peppard (who was M.P. for Drogheda, 1640). He died 23 November, 1771, aged 79

an only son, ob. enf, 1745

Nicholas Peppard, succeeded to Crosby, and in 1772 assumed the surname and arms of Blundell only, and died 6 Jan., 1795, aged 55 = 2 Clementina, 3rd daughter of Stephen Walter Tempest, of Broughton, Co. York. She died 21 July, 1821

- Christopher, died s.p., 1771
- William
- Frances
- Mary, wife of Richard Lacon, Esq., of Linley, and had issue

William Blundell, Esq., J.P. and D.L. of Crosby, J.P. and D.L. He died 11 July, 1854 = Catherine, daughter of Sir Thomas Stanley-Massey-Stanley, Bart., of Hooton, in Cheshire. She died 12 Jan., 1862

- Frances, married, 1808, to Sir Edward Mostyn, Bart., of Talacre, Co. Flint, and died 27 January, 1825, leaving issue
- Clementina, died unmarried, 1820

Nicholas Blundell, Esq, of Crosby, Co. Lancaster, J.P. and D.L., Major in Duke of Lancaster's Own Rifle Militia, Lieut.-Colonel Commandant, 1872, married November, 1847 = Agnes Mary, 3rd daughter of Sir Edward Smythe, Bart., of Acton Burnell

- William Charles, married Louisa de Usovics, and had issue
- John, married Catherine, daughter of Peter Middleton, and had issue
- Thomas
- Clementina, Catherine, Frances, Mary Emily Anna Maria

- William, b. 1851, died s.p., 1909
- Francis, b. 1853, 1884, died = Mary, daughter of Michael James Sweetman, of Lamberton Park, Leix, Eire
- Osbert
- Mary Agnes, Clementina Mary, Josephine Mary Catherine, Fermina Mary

Francis Nicholas, b. 1880, died 1936 = Teresa, daughter of Wilfrid Ward, second son of William George Ward, Esq. of Northwood Park and Weston Manor, Isle of Wight.

- Margaret
- Agnes

- Nicholas, b. 1925, died s.p., 1949
- Hester Mary, b. 1928 = Brian Whitlock, Esq.
- Richard, b. 1930, died 1936

Mark Francis, b. December, 15th, 1950

INDEX